FINAL SCORE!

Sports Devotions

Volume Five

Dan Farr

Final Score! Sports Devotions Vol. V

Copyright © 2023 by Dan Farr. All rights reserved.

Published by Yawn Publishing LLC
2555 Marietta Hwy, Ste 103
Canton, Georgia 30114
1-678-880-1922 | www.yawnspublishing.com

ISBN: 978-1-954617-65-0

Dedication

Final Score! Sports Devotions Volume Five is dedicated

in loving memory of number 5, Robbie Roper.

#LL5

Live Like Five

Love Like Jesus

Table of Contents

1
Five-Star Heart

Be anxious for nothing, but in everything by prayer and supplication, with thanksgiving, let your requests be made known to God; and the peace of God, which surpasses all understanding, *will guard your hearts* and minds through Christ Jesus.

Philippians 4:6-7

Football players from the Naval Academy launched a character initiative called Five-Star Heart. Their idea originated in Notre Dame's visiting locker room after Navy upset the Fighting Irish in 2009. *They may have five-star recruits, but we have five-star hearts.* What does it mean to have a five-star heart?

Coaches love having five-star talent but really appreciate the athletes with the five-star hearts that keep playing hard regardless of the score. In the game of life, a five-star heart is a selfless heart, a heart that helps you battle through adversity and is at peace with God.

Achieving and maintaining a five-star heart helps to create a balanced life in these five areas: emotional, mental, moral, physical, and spiritual. Picture the points of a star numbered 1 through 5. Here are some thoughts regarding each area.

1.   Emotional – You're going to have ups and downs. How do you bounce back? There are things that we can't control, but we can control our mind. Who is your go-to person when you become overwhelmed? Make sure that you have people in your life who will allow you to get things off your chest. Openly expressing your feelings provides stress relief. You can speak with a

spouse, a parent, fellow coach, pastor or close friend with sound judgment.

2.   Mental – Be all that you can be by putting the right things into your mind. Ensure that you are renewing your mind each day with positive thoughts. Coaches mold their teams to keep improving week by week. Sharpen your mind by continuing to grow in your professional field. Be careful not to get sucked up in the negative vortex of social media that can be overwhelming.

3.   Moral – You are familiar with having a good moral compass, which means that you are consistently pointed in the right direction. May we be a model of integrity, honesty, caring, loyalty and trust that builds up others.

4.   Physical – Maintaining your physical condition is a stress reliever. It also matters what you put in your body. Try to go on a walk or run each day, get in a workout to strengthen your body, and enjoy a healthy diet.

5.   Spiritual – My friend Tony was a chaplain at Clemson University. He coined the term "Spiritual Two A Days" just like football teams work out twice a day. He had his players start the day with a daily devotion followed by a prayer, and in the evening, they read scripture and closed their day with a prayer. Meeting with God first thing in the morning and the last thing at night is a terrific way to bookend each day! The proper emphasis on spirituality helps you make good choices in the other four areas and prepares us to live a life filled with Christian love, empathy and compassion for others.

If you have let one of these areas slide, the good news is that it's not game over. Take an inventory and assess how you are doing physically, mentally, emotionally, morally, and spiritually. Pick one area for improvement, create a game plan, and execute the game plan. Start with a fresh perspective and be well on the way to your five-star heart!

2

Who's Got Game?

"For when the One Great Scorer comes to mark against your name,
He writes, not that you won or lost, but how you played the game."
Grantland Rice

On Masters Sunday 2021 our three-year-old grandson Will played
with his plastic golf balls and his plastic golf club. Instead of hitting
the ball in his backyard, he placed a ball on the deck, whacked it as
fast as he could, and just cackled as his mother Allison and AJ (Aunt
Jillian) scrambled to keep the ball from going through the deck rails
into the shrubs below. After he hit his last golf ball into the shrubs,
Will shouted, "I won the game!"

My friend Quentin shared about his initial meeting with a close
friend. He described how quickly they recognized their common bond
in Christ. As Quentin said, "Game recognizes game."

Paul George and LeBron James slapped hands following Paul's
dunk over LeBron and LeBron's answer of a thirty-foot trey. The
players recognized that their games were special. In the heat of competition, game recognized game.

NFL players on opposing teams swap jerseys after games. One
player seeks out another player that he respects, and running backs,
quarterbacks, wide receivers and cornerbacks recognize each other's
games via the jersey swaps.

Consider recognition from a spiritual standpoint. Think of someone whose "spiritual game" you admire. Conversely, who admires
your spiritual game and would seek you out to swap "spiritual jerseys"?

My father, Coach Lester Farr, wrote a message for the sports section of the high school yearbook. He shared this quote from Grantland

Rice, a legendary American sportswriter from the 1920s to the 1950s. *"For when the One Great Scorer comes to mark against your name, He writes, not that you won or lost, but how you played the game."*

My mother, Allene Farr, kept score of my father's basketball games. Before each game she carefully printed the name of each player in the scorebook. During the game she recorded field goals, free throws and fouls, which reflected how each player played the game.

Revelation 20:12 reveals that the name of each believer is recorded in that great scorebook in heaven called the Book of Life. Please ensure that you have "won the game" that places your name in the Book of Life by confessing your sin and receiving Jesus Christ into your life. Revelation 3:5 assures that no name entered in the Book of Life will ever be removed. Your deeds are "marked against your name" according to how you live your life in Christ. Strive to live a life that is holy and set apart (1 Peter 3:15) and guided by the Holy Spirit (Romans 8:26). Others will recognize that you've got spiritual game!

3

Hit the Pause Button for Damar Hamlin

The earnest prayer of a righteous person has great power and produces wonderful results.

James 5:16 TLB

Football fans across the country watched with disbelief as the situation with Damar Hamlin developed on Monday night. After it was disclosed that CPR had been administered to resuscitate him, I remembered the late Chuck Hughes, the only player in one hundred years of NFL football to pass away on the field of play in the Lions-Bears game in 1971. It was determined that he had a pre-existing condition with a blocked artery.

When it became evident that Damar's life hung in the balance, tweets and texts calling for prayer flew across the country and in many of the 181 countries where NFL Team Pass is available. People "hit the pause button" wherever they were and prayed for Damar.

Heroes came to Damar's side. Numerous medical personnel saved his life by administering oxygen and restarting his heart on the field. His collapse was eerily similar to that of Christian Eriksen, the Danish national team soccer player who collapsed in the 2020 Euro Cup and "was gone" before he was resuscitated, according to the team doctor.

As Christian's teammates did on that late afternoon, Damar's Buffalo teammates formed a human shield to give their fallen teammate privacy. It was so moving and heartbreaking to see so many of Damar's teammates in shock and in tears. No one will soon forget the riveting photo of the entire Bills team huddled in prayer.

The on-air coverage and insight provided by the ESPN broadcast team and ESPN commentators was compelling. Ryan Clark, a former

Steelers safety, gave particularly passionate and unique insight from a player's perspective regarding the emotional proceedings.

It is possible for much good to come out of dire situations. Almost 190,000 donations totaling an incredible $6 million was given to Damar's GoFundMe for toys. The GoFundMe goal was $2,500. Six million against a $2500 goal is a miraculous modern-day example of the parable of the five loaves and two fishes that Jesus used to feed an estimated twenty thousand people. Many donors were Bills fans who call themselves the "Bills Mafia." About one hundred Bengal and Bills fans held a prayer vigil outside the University of Cincinnati Medical Center. Putting aside personal agendas and disagreements in a moment that occurs much too infrequently, millions of people came together to pray as one for Damar.

Hit the pause button where you are. Close your eyes and ask God to reveal who in your family, your community or across the world needs prayer. God's gift of prayer, his way of communicating with us, was never designed to be used just in emergency situations. After Eriksen went down, Coach Andy Trevers wrote that his prayer is that we would make prayer our first response, not our last resort. Rev. Dennis Kinlaw wrote, "The most sacred and creative thing, the greatest work that any person can ever do, is to thank God, to praise him, and to pray."

Perhaps there were people who prayed to God for the first time or for the first time in a long time. Maybe those same people thought, *If God can save Damar Hamlin, maybe he will help me in my predicament,* and they began to know God personally through the stirring of the Holy Spirit.

Before you start your day or any time of day, hit the pause button, thank God for your blessings, and pray specifically for the people and situations that God places on your heart. James 5:16 (TLB) reminds us, "The earnest prayer of a righteous person has great power and produces wonderful results." You will be doing the work of a saint!

I asked people to please pray specifically for Damar Hamlin to have a clearly functioning brain, organs that work, and that he will be able to breathe without a ventilator. Nine days later Hamlin left the hospital in Buffalo! Pray for his full recovery, his mother and father, his extended family and for the good citizens of Buffalo who endured such personal tragedy in 2022.

4

Answer!

"But seek first the kingdom of God and his righteousness, and all these things shall be added to you."

Matthew 6:33

Americans were inundated by daily polling results this fall. Usually in the fall it is the weekly football polls that capture the attention of fans as they follow their favorite high school and college teams.

If you were polled for the top ten focal points of your life, what would they be? The majority of people would name family members, careers, relationships, and various personal interests. But where would God be in that poll, week in and week out? God should be atop that poll, but when we take our eyes off him, God drops down in the poll, just like our favorite team after a loss. If God is well down in our poll instead of occupying the number one spot, we will eventually struggle.

How can God help us through our struggles? When the opponent scores a touchdown, there is a plea that goes up and down your sideline. Players and coaches shout, "Let's get it back! Let's answer (their touchdown). Answer!" God is our answer, but he needs our full commitment. If God is not first in some aspect of your life, elevate him as soon as possible and experience the rejuvenation of the Holy Spirit. Depending on the problem, it may take days, weeks, or months to place God in his rightful place. Just as a football team starts with the first play of the drive to answer the opponent's score, take your first step now to move God toward first place in your life.

The Bible provides instruction on the proper order. Exodus 20:3 tells us, "You shall have no other gods before me." Matthew 6:33 reminds us, "But seek first the kingdom of God and his righteousness, and all these things shall be added to you." When God is properly positioned in your life, his grace flows down freely on your family, your career, your relationships and your interests.

How do you keep him in first place? Communicate often with God. When we frequently communicate with him, we receive answers to our questions and help with our problems. Psalm 121:1-2 offers this assurance, "I lift my eyes unto the hills, where does my help come from? My help comes from the Lord, maker of heaven and earth." Let's answer!

5

The Fifth Quarter

"My thoughts are nothing like your thoughts," says the Lord. "And my ways are far beyond anything you could imagine. For just as the heavens are higher than the earth, so my ways are higher than your ways, and my thoughts higher than your thoughts."

Isaiah 55:8-9 NLT

Hornet Nation and the Roswell community grieved the tragic loss of star QB Robbie Roper, who passed away on December 22, 2021. This devotion is dedicated to the loving memory of Number 5, Robbie Roper.

Robbie, Shaun Spence, his close friend and favorite target, and I sat under the pavilion at Ray Manus Stadium on a sweltering July morning, waiting for photographer Maura Roberts to do the senior photo shoot for the FCA program ad. I asked Robbie about his expectations for the upcoming season. Robbie was quite confident about the first three games. I deposited a 3 and 0 start in my mental bank!

Robbie improved his skills during the 2021 offseason by working hard every day, working out, throwing, and perfecting his footwork. His improvement showed immediately during the first four games when he threw for nineteen TDs and received attention statewide.

My favorite throw by Robbie came in game four against Campbell. Near midfield Robbie escaped the rush, rolled right, and waved his receiver deep. He unleashed a tight spiral with a perfect arc that came down over the inside shoulder of the closely covered receiver and just inside the pylon on the goal line. The play came directly toward me. Patrick Mahomes could not have done it any better!

Robbie was injured in game five, and he missed game six. After returning to action, he took his ability to run and improvise to the next level against region competition. I commended Coach Patrick Carlisle, the Hornet Offensive Coordinator, for his work with Robbie and said, "I saw Malik Willis in 2016. Robbie is that good, maybe even a little better."

Game nine was against Alpharetta on a cold, rainy, and windy night. Robbie scrambled for a first down on fourth and seven to keep a late fourth-quarter drive alive. Then he hit Ethan Nation with a perfect screen pass for a comeback win that secured a first-round home playoff game. After an easy first-round win, the Hornets faced a second-round playoff game against nationally ranked North Cobb. That game secured Robbie's legacy at Roswell High.

Against North Cobb's strong defense, Robbie demonstrated his incredible dual-threat skills, engineering five long TD drives. But the Hornets trailed 43-34 with 1:12 remaining in the game, and North Cobb had the ball on their twelve-yard-line. However, the Roswell defense recovered a fumble! Robbie ran twelve yards for a touchdown, which cut the deficit to three.

The Hornets recovered the onside kick! Robbie quickly led his team down the field but faced fourth and goal on the seven with four seconds remaining. Robbie rolled right, reversed his field, and scampered into the end zone for a walk-off touchdown and a 46-43 win! He raced toward the far end zone in a blaze of glory as his teammates deliriously chased him!

Following the game, Roswell Head Coach Chris Prewett told the AJC, "He may not have the recruiting and stuff like that, but I'd follow that dude anywhere. He's doing so well. Somebody's going to be lucky to have him, whether that's a lower level or a higher level. They're going to be so lucky to have him because that dude is a gamer."

Robbie passed for over 3,000 yards and 37 TDs and rushed for almost five hundred yards, leading the Hornets to a top-10 finish in 7A. He was named Player of the Year by the coaches in Region Five, which was replete with big-name talent. Robbie drew recruiting attention from Florida and Ole Miss.

After Robbie passed, Coach Prewett told CBS46 Atlanta that Roper was a "model citizen" with exemplary character on and off the field. "Robbie did everything in life with a contagious, positive and energetic attitude that will be missed by all who knew him." Prewett said, "Robbie fought and battled until the very end like he did everything in life."

Teammate Zeke Moore told CBS46 that, "Obviously everyone knew what he could do on the field, but once he got in the building and started to talk, people who don't know how football works - they know Robbie. He was truly someone everyone knew and looked up to in a lot of ways. He cared about everyone else." Moore added, "He always had a good balance in life, whether it's having fun, working hard, or winning."

Players, coaches, parents and friends gathered at Ray Manus Stadium on the evening of Robbie's passing. Coach Prewett and Roswell Principal Dr. Robert Shaw offered encouragement, and several teammates shared remembrances of Robbie. As Pastor Lyndsay Slocum offered a closing prayer, many people lifted five fingers heavenward to symbolize Robbie's number 5 and held smartphones with glowing flashlights. It was an emotional gathering that honored a young man whose legacy is already making a positive impact through the Robbie Roper Memorial Fund.

God occasionally allows one of his children to come home early in the midst of a blaze of glory while impacting many lives. When a child of God is so young, perhaps that is the most difficult instance for loved ones to understand. The prophet Isaiah 55:8-9 provides a glimpse into God's heart. "My thoughts are nothing like your thoughts," says the Lord. "And my ways are far beyond anything you could imagine. For just as the heavens are higher than the earth, so my ways are higher than your ways, and my thoughts higher than your thoughts" (Isaiah 55:8-9).

Your earthly life is finite and can be divided into four quarters. If you live to be eighty, that would be four quarters of twenty years each. I believe that Jesus welcomed Robbie home after what would normally be the end of someone's first quarter.

Your afterlife, which is your "fifth quarter," is eternal. *Amazing Grace* reveals that the number of days in your fifth quarter in heaven are never-ending.

When we've been there ten thousand years,
bright shining as the sun,
we've no less days to sing God's praise,

than when we first begun.

The lyrics from *For the Good* by Riley Clemmons are based on Romans 8:28, which reads, "And we know that in all things God works for the good of those who love him, who have been called according to his purpose."

> *For the good, For the good, You work all things together,*
> *For the good, For the good, Your promise stands forever,*
> *You alone are my greatest hope, I trust You on the broken road,*
> *You work all things together, like only You could.*

The chorus assures us of God's goodness, faithfulness, and the eternal hope that is found in Christ Jesus, who is here for you no matter what. May the legacy of Robbie Roper bear much fruit for God's kingdom purposes. Live like five! #LL5

6

Mix It Up!

But the Helper, the Holy Spirit, whom the Father will send in My name, He will teach you all things, and bring to your remembrance all things that I said to you.

John 14:26

I received a video featuring our grandson Will holding his left palm up while sweeping his right index finger and hand in a circular motion. He was "mixing it up" just like Ronald Acuna, Dansby Swanson, and the other Atlanta Braves following a big play! Will was proud of himself, almost as proud as his GrandDan watching the video! I have watched young athletes in the past mix it up by locking arms and praying at open gym, praying together after FCA football summer camp scrimmages, and greeting each other in handshake lines.

A common theme of mixing it up is interaction. After Jesus rose from the grave, he interacted with others for fifty days before he joined his Father in heaven. His interactions were crucial because they provided irrefutable historical proof that Jesus was the Son of God who defeated death when he rose from the grave.

Christ's recorded appearances are as follow: At sunrise Jesus appeared to Mary Magdalene after she discovered his tomb was empty. That afternoon Jesus walked with two disciples on the Road to Emmaus who failed to recognize him, and one later said, "Did not our heart burn within us?" That evening he appeared in the Upper Room to ten disciples (minus Thomas).

A week later he appeared to the eleven disciples. Jesus said, "Thomas, because you have seen Me, you have believed. Blessed are those who have not seen and yet have believed." Thomas declared, "My Lord and My God!" Over five hundred men saw Jesus, and he cooked breakfast on the shore for the disciples after they fished all night and caught nothing. Then Jesus said, "Throw the net over here," and they pulled in one hundred fifty-three keepers.

Before his death and resurrection, Jesus promised the disciples that a Helper would be introduced into the mix. Jesus proclaimed in John 14:26, "But the Helper, the Holy Spirit, whom the Father will send in My name, He will teach you all things, and bring to your remembrance all things that I said to you." Moments before Jesus ascended to heaven, he gave these instructions that are captured in Acts Chapter 1:4-5, 8-9 (NKJV).

"And being assembled together with them, He commanded them not to depart from Jerusalem, but to wait for the Promise of the Father, 'which,' He said, 'you have heard from Me; for John truly baptized with water, but you shall be baptized with the Holy Spirit not many days from now'....'But you shall receive power when the Holy Spirit has come upon you; and you shall be witnesses to Me in Jerusalem, and in all Judea and Samaria, and to the end of the earth.'"

Now when He had spoken these things, while they watched, He was taken up, and a cloud received Him out of their sight. Shortly after Jesus's ascension, the Holy Spirit really mixed it up at Pentecost, the birth of the universal church, by anointing the disciples of Christ!

Have you ever felt that you were not part of the mix in God's kingdom? Take heart because the same Holy Spirit that came upon the disciples at Pentecost is the same Holy Spirit that resides in you! You have the same power that the early disciples had when you make your whole heart available to Christ. Let God use you whenever and however he wishes, just as a player eager for action would say, "Just put me in Coach!"

Football coaches are familiar with the run pass option, which is better known as RPO. Stay ready to be used by God by committing yourself to the following RPO: R - Read the Bible daily; P - Pray for others often; O - Obey. Ask God for a fresh filling of the Holy Spirit that will energize you to perform "...the work assigned you by the Lord Jesus, the work of telling others the Good News about God's mighty kindness and love (Acts 20:24 TLB)!"

7

Tiny Bubbles of Hope

"God has chosen to make known among the Gentiles the glorious riches of this mystery, which is Christ in you, the hope of glory."

Colossians 1:27

On October 11, 2020, the NBA concluded a three-hundred-eighty-day season, the longest in pro sports history. Training camp opened on September 27, 2019, and four months later LA Laker and NBA legend Kobe Bryant, his daughter Gianna, and seven other souls perished in a helicopter crash. Six weeks later on March 11, a Jazz player tested positive for COVID-19, and live sports came to an unprecedented halt. In June, the NBA announced plans to complete the season in a bubble in Orlando. The season was halted again in late August when the Milwaukee Bucks protested the Jacob Blake shooting, triggering displays of solidarity for justice and equality within the bubble and across every major sport. The Lakers won their 17th NBA championship and dedicated the season to Kobe and Gianna. LeBron James became the first player to win three NBA championships and three Finals MVP awards with three different teams.

Perhaps the most incredible statistic was that the NBA reported no positive COVID-19 results among the hundreds who were confined to the bubble. The players and coaches in the NBA bubble renewed hope for millions by demonstrating compassion, resilience, solidarity for human rights, and collaboration while enduring the hardships of separation from their loved ones.

High school football teams in Georgia moved forward without the benefit of a big bubble. In-person school was postponed in March and spring practice was cancelled. After extensive planning, small groups under strict protocol returned in June for voluntary workouts. Larger voluntary workout groups were permitted in July, and full-team practice began in August. The regular season was delayed and ended November 20, and state champions were crowned the weekend before Christmas.

The uncertainty for high school athletes increased when more schools moved back to a daily in-person schedule. However, the hope that was generated by programs in the midst of daily uncertainty was powerful for athletes, coaches, their families and supporters. Unlike the NBA's big bubble, high school programs were enabled by their ability to create and maintain individual bubbles, tiny bubbles of protection, for each player, coach, and family member. Those fall sports teams did a remarkable job!

In Romans 5:3-5 from the Amplified Bible, the apostle Paul explained the sequence that sustains hope in our hearts. "And not only this, but [with joy] let us exult in our sufferings and rejoice in our hardships, knowing that hardship (distress, pressure, trouble) produces patient endurance; and endurance, proven character (spiritual maturity); and proven character, hope and confident assurance [of eternal salvation]. Such hope [in God's promises] never disappoints us, because God's love has been abundantly poured out within our hearts through the Holy Spirit who was given to us." Rejoicing in our hardships produces patient endurance, leading to proven character which generates hope because God abundantly pours his love into us through the Holy Spirit!

Roger Lipe, FCA Representative at Southern Illinois University, shared about the importance of maintaining a good attitude in the midst of difficult times and how character affects these situations. "The character of a person, the true nature of his or her heart, is a continual source of either hope or despair. Hope is a confident expectation of good, based on the promises of God. Hope comes from a changed character of someone who has persevered through suffering a difficult circumstance or event. Character teaches us to be confident and to have proper expectations for when the next bad thing happens."

Lipe concluded, "As coaches and athletes, we are expected to attribute good characteristics of hope and confidence through every loss, defeat, or physical setback. Paul says that character produces hope, and that hope doesn't fail because God has put an everyday reminder of his love in our hearts. The Spirit of God is alive in us to remind us of His love and promises. That's what real hope looks like. As you may be affected by tragic or difficult events in the world today, God calls us to have hope in him and his love. Today, remember to let hope arise from your character and prepare you for a great day of competition."

8

Let's Empty Our Pockets

As he was speaking, the Jewish leaders and Pharisees brought a woman caught in adultery and placed her out in front of the staring crowd. "Teacher," they said to Jesus, "this woman was caught in the very act of adultery. Moses' law says to kill her. What about it?" They were trying to trap him into saying something they could use against him, but Jesus stooped down and wrote in the dust with his finger. They kept demanding an answer, so he stood up again and said, "All right, hurl the stones at her until she dies. But _only he who never sinned may throw the first_!" Then he stooped down again and wrote some more in the dust. And the Jewish leaders slipped away one by one, beginning with the eldest, until only Jesus was left in front of the crowd with the woman. Then Jesus stood up again and said to her, "Where are your accusers? Didn't even one of them condemn you?" "No, sir," she said. And Jesus said, "Neither do I. Go and sin no more."

John 8:3-11

In this familiar parable, the Jewish leaders and Pharisees rendered judgment that the adulteress should die. They were driven by their head knowledge of the law of Moses. Just like a young boy drawing a pass pattern at the sandlot, Jesus drew a play in the dirt and called out the following instructions: "You who are without sin cast the first stone."

Jesus introduced heart knowledge into the chaotic scene. Beginning with the oldest man, each man dropped his stone (or stones). The men realized in their hearts that only Jesus was capable of judging this woman. A pastor wrote, "I wish I could have heard the first stone being dropped." How silently those men must have slipped away in their collective shame as they left behind a pile of stones.

When I was a boy on the school playground, I often heard the following saying: "Sticks and stones may break my bones, but words will never hurt me." But the constant intake of various forms of media can place "verbal stones" in our pockets, and we prepare our minds to fling them at differing points of view. We side with other stone carriers and begin to sound like that group of judgmental Pharisees. Even if we never throw the verbal stones, we carry them in our minds and hearts. Eventually they weigh us down and bring us down if we do not act.

There is a better way. Be guided by the teaching and examples of Jesus for how we should passionately support our causes. Why keep stones of bitterness, divisiveness, resentment and unrighteous anger in our pockets that we are not meant to carry, much less hurl? Let's be enthusiastic about our causes, but first and foremost love our neighbors as Jesus loves them, listen to them and learn from them, and follow through with empathy and compassion. "Blessed are the peacemakers, for they shall be called sons of God (Matthew 5:9)." Let's empty our pockets!

9

Let's Do Our Homework!

The earnest prayer of a righteous man has great power and wonderful results.

James 5:16 TLB

I remind high school athletes about the importance of completing their homework. It requires discipline and commitment to make a consistently good effort. If you turn in your homework every day, it can lead to higher letter grades and a better understanding of the material. When you don't make the effort, it's reflected in your final grades.

The discipline and commitment to pray is similar to homework. When you are inundated with demands for your time and family commitments, it's easy for your prayer life to become "Thank you Lord!" before collapsing in bed after another long day. But when you believe with all of your heart that commitment to prayer matters, you will see the positive results in your life and the lives of those you prayed for, and those results should be a motivating factor.

God doesn't give out letter grades for prayer, but he is grateful for our intentional prayers "behind the scenes" that don't draw attention. Matthew 6:6 (ERV) tells us, "But when you pray, you should go into your room and close the door. Then pray to your Father. He is there in that private place. He can see what is done in private, and he will reward you." The rewards can be heavenly, or they can be expressions of gratitude from those for whom we pray.

James wrote about the importance of prayer in James 5:16, "The earnest prayer of a righteous man has great power and wonderful results (TLB)." When we pray earnestly and are in right standing with God, positive results happen more often because our prayers connect with the power source of the Trinity. Our trust-filled prayers connect our Father God with the Holy Spirit, who is God in us (John 14:26), and Jesus, who is God with us (Isaiah 9:6). Both Jesus (1 John 2:1) and the Holy Spirit (Romans 8:26) intercede to God on our behalf.

Let's do our prayer homework by praying boldly and consistently. When your team executes good reps Monday through Thursday, Fridays become paydays. Paydays in prayer are the wonderful results, some of which we will never know about until we get to heaven. Ask a fellow coach, "How can I pray for you this week?"

Here are some prayer bullets for your athletes, coaches, and family members.

- May my God supply all your need according to his riches in glory by Christ Jesus (Philippians 4:19).
- Salvation and sanctification.
- Health and well-being.
- Ask the Holy Spirit to "fit the gaps" by communicating any omissions in our prayers.
- Workable learning and teaching situations and excellence in the classroom.
- Remain optimistic during this unpredictable period.

10

Your Body of Work

Blessed is the man who remains steadfast under trial, for when he has stood the test he will receive the crown of life, which God has promised to those who love him.

James 1:12 ESV

I have followed Matthew Stafford's career closely since he signed with UGA after leading Highland Park HS in Dallas, Texas to a state championship in 2005. Stafford played quarterback for UGA for three years, leading the Bulldogs to a No. 2 AP ranking in 2007 and a No. 1 preseason ranking in 2008. You may remember the Sports Illustrated cover featuring UGA's Dannell Ellerbe, Stafford, and Knowshon Moreno. But the Bulldogs suffered three losses in 2008, and Stafford left for the NFL without an SEC championship ring.

Stafford was the number one overall pick in the 2009 NFL Draft, going to the Detroit Lions, who were 0-16 in 2008. Prior to his trade to the Los Angeles Rams in 2021, Stafford's body of work on the field with the Lions consisted of twelve seasons, over 41,000 passing yards and over 250 TDs, one losing playoff game, several significant injuries, and an overall 74-103 record.

Off the field, Matthew became involved in the Detroit community early in his career. In 2015 Stafford married his college sweetheart Kelly, and they are the parents of four precious daughters under the age of five. In 2019 Kelly made a miraculous recovery after a twelve-hour surgery to remove a brain tumor. In the summer of 2020, the couple pledged $1.5M to UGA for various initiatives, including $350,000 in seed money for a diversity, inclusion, equity and social-justice initiative and two Georgia Commitment Scholarships for students who need financial help. Motivated by his teammates support during Kelly's recovery period and hearing their personal stories of anguish at a team meeting after the Jacob Blake shooting, Matthew authored an essay that expressed his plea for human rights. Stafford wrote, "We can't just stick to football...Listen."

I have been pleased to see Stafford grow as a man, husband, father, and contributor to society. When he completes his career, he and his cannon of an arm will have thrown for a gazillion yards and led dozens of fourth-quarter comebacks. However, statistics do not produce championship rings, and his odds of making the Pro Football Hall of Fame could be long. But his body of work off the field could become his enduring legacy. Surely the love and support that Stafford gave his wife and daughters during her challenging time, and the empathy and leverage that he demonstrated in penning the essay will be some of Matthew's finest hours.

For those of us who are believers in Christ, there will be unique rewards in heaven for each body of work. As stated in 2 Corinthians 5:10..."so that each one may receive what is due for what he has done in the body." Hank Hanegraaff, the Bible Answer Man, was asked, "Are there greater rewards in heaven?" Hanegraaff replied, "No question about it! Lay up for yourselves treasures in heaven, where neither moths nor rust destroy...(Matthew 6:20)." Each believer will be rewarded for the selfless acts of love, kindness, caring and compassion that were built on the foundation that was laid by the Lord Jesus.

The apostle Paul explained to the new church in Corinth how the body of work is tested. He wrote in 1 Corinthians 3:10-15 (ESV), "By the grace God has given me, I laid a foundation as a wise builder, and someone else is building on it. But each one should build with care. For no one can lay any foundation other than the one already laid, which is Jesus Christ. If anyone builds on this foundation using gold, silver, costly stones, wood, hay or straw, their work will be shown for what it is, because the Day (of Judgment—2 Corinthians 5:10) will bring it to light. It will be revealed with fire, and the fire will test the quality of each person's work. If what has been built survives, the builder will receive a reward. If it is burned up, the builder will suffer loss but yet will be saved—even though only as one escaping through the flames."

A good work that is achieved by following God's will and his purpose for our life can inspire other believers to add to their bodies of work. John Wesley, the founder of the Methodist denomination, is often credited with the following quote, "Do all the good you can, by all the means you can, in all the ways you can, in all the places you can, at all the times you can, to all the people you can, as long as ever you can."

Too much emphasis is placed on measuring coaches by their number of championships. Coaches and their programs are often unfairly judged by their won-loss records. A coach who is rebuilding a football program said, " (Going) 5-5 is a state championship for us this season." Coaches should instead be remembered for the complete body of work, which includes the countless examples of pouring into the lives of students and student-athletes to give them bright futures with hope. May the lessons that your players learn and then apply during their high school, young adult, and adult years inspire you to keep adding to your body of work that will last for eternity. Today is a great day to lay up another treasure in heaven!

11

Break Up Your Fallow Ground

Sow for yourselves righteousness; reap steadfast love; **break up your fallow ground**, for it is the time to seek the LORD, that he may come and rain righteousness upon you.

Hosea 10:12

In 2020 a pastor friend reflected that "God has eliminated the cliques in the (universal) church, and we will have real koinonia (fellowship) when we go back." Many church buildings remained fallow (undisturbed) on Sunday mornings, and others were partially full. Some local public school buildings were fallow because students were absent.

After hearing the pastor's statement, I mulled over the word "fallow." What exactly is fallowing? According to gardening.knowhow .com, fallow ground, or fallow soil, is simply ground or soil which has been left unplanted to rest and regenerate. Fallowing soil is a method of sustainable land management that has been used for centuries in the Mediterranean, North Africa, and Asia. Fallowing allows minerals to replenish, improves moisture-holding capacity, and increases beneficial microorganisms in the soil. Studies have shown that a field that lies fallow for one year produces a higher crop yield when it is planted.

Will Christians produce a higher disciple yield after we gather in person? Perhaps we will invite a friend to join a Bible study more often. The Great Commission urges us to make disciples in all the nations. Will that include local neighborhoods? How will our spirit attract others to join us in fellowship?

When we live out Christ in our lives, we reflect his light to a lost world, and others are attracted to the light. The traditional ways of meeting fellow Christians in person have been fallow during this season. However, if you have consistently lived out Christ through a steady prayer life, study of the scripture, and giving your time, treasures and talents to spiritual and humanitarian causes, you are prepared to be a leader in the post-pandemic revival!

A brother in Christ wondered aloud if the less fortunate who have been through the church's food lines will feel welcome to come back for worship. Will we go back and invite them? The apostle Paul expressed his thoughts about helping others in Romans 15:1-6 (MSG). "Those of us who are strong and able in the faith need to step in and lend a hand to those who falter, and not just do what is most convenient for us. Strength is for service, not status. Each one of us needs to look after the good of the people around us, asking ourselves, 'How can I help?' That's exactly what Jesus did. He didn't make it easy for himself by avoiding people's troubles but waded right in and helped out. 'I took on the troubles of the troubled,' is the way Scripture puts it. Even if it was written in Scripture long ago, you can be sure it's written for us. God wants the combination of his steady, constant calling and warm, personal counsel in Scripture to come to characterize us, keeping us alert for whatever he will do next. May our dependably steady and warmly personal God develop maturity in you so that you get along with each other as well as Jesus gets along with us all. Then we'll be a choir—not our voices only, but our very lives singing in harmony in a stunning anthem to the God and Father of our Master Jesus!"

How well have you taken on "good trouble," the troubles of the troubled, and served others during the pandemic? Has God gently tilled the soil of your heart that yielded a crop (Matthew 13:8), or does God need to "break up your fallow ground" (Hosea 10:12)? The degree to which each disciple has spent time with God in Bible study and prayer, and loving, listening, learning, lamenting and leveraging, will help determine the fruit that the universal church produces during the "reboot" season. Let's all prepare our hearts.

12

A Glimmer of Hope

What else is the kingdom of God like? What earthly thing can we compare it to? The kingdom of God is like a mustard seed, the tiniest seed you can sow. But after that seed is planted, it grows into the largest plant in the garden, a plant so big that birds can build their nests in the shade of its branches.

Mark 4:30-32 (The Voice)

When my daughter Allison was a little girl in 1996, she and I stood in the upper deck as our favorite college football team drove inside the opponent's twenty-yard line looking to score the winning touchdown. However, with less than thirty seconds remaining in the game, our quarterback threw an interception. In utter despair I turned to Allison and said, "Get your stuff. Let's go."

We quickly gathered our raingear. As we turned to leave our seats, I looked back at the field through a sea of umbrellas and bodies. Through the smallest of windows I spotted a glimmer of hope, a yellow mustard-colored piece of cloth about a hundred yards away as the crow flies. The back judge had flagged the defense for pass interference! Our team scored on the next play to win the game, and the glimmer of hope turned into a memorable victory.

Our lesson is about another type of mustard. Jesus shared stories called parables with his followers about everyday topics that they understood, particularly the parables about farming. He told them a parable about the mustard seed, the smallest of all seeds, the size of a pinhead and one to two millimeters in diameter.

In Luke 13:18-19, Jesus compared the mustard seed to the kingdom of God. "So He was saying, 'What is the kingdom of God like, and to what shall I compare it? It is like a mustard seed, which a man took and threw into his own garden; and it grew and became a tree, and the birds of the air nested in its branches.'" The people understood that mustard varieties could be used for food, spices and medicine. The smallest of seeds could become a garden plant or a shrub with a minimal amount of water. When the seed received sufficient water, it became a tree large enough for birds to build nests. A mustard tree can grow to be up to twenty-five feet tall.

Amy-Jill Levine, a professor of New Testament and Jewish Studies at Vanderbilt University, opened my eyes to the application of the mustard seed parable in modern times. She stated that an effective parable activates our imagination, and that any interpretations we have are good as long as they are used for good.

I thought about the elementary school age girls in 2020 who made bracelets and collectively raised hundreds of thousands of dollars to save a zoo, supply protective equipment for health care workers, and promote social justice. Their mustard seeds were the tiny strands of thread that became bracelets, motivating others to give and spawning similar acts of kindness across our country.

We can sow mustard seeds such as a timely text, a caring phone call, an encouraging note, sharing an inspirational book or podcast, or having an empathetic conversation. Our job as a receiver of kindness is to never give up hope and keep our faith, even when it seems to be the size of a mustard seed. When we humbly receive encouragement from others, our faith is invigorated. As a giver of kindness, we need to keep our hearts pliable so that we pray for others and follow through with our own texts, phone calls, notes, encouraging words, and acts of kindness, especially for those who are despondent. Because we are each uniquely made, our acts of love and compassion will be different, and that is perfectly fine!

Let's allow the Holy Spirit to work through us and send glimmers of hope to both young and old. While many acts are seemingly inconsequential, sometimes they can help a friend filled with despair to develop a faith that can move mountains. Matthew 17:20 reminds us, "…if you have faith the size of a mustard seed, you will say to this mountain, 'Move from here to there,' and it will move; and nothing will be impossible to you."

To whom will you offer a glimmer of hope today?

13

From 2, 22, and 122A to 1-10-22!

…He makes everything work out according to His plan.

Ephesians 1:11(b)

Stetson Bennett IV dreamed of playing quarterback for UGA since he was three years old. I hope you saw the really cute picture of him as a child on the Georgia-Michigan telecast. Stetson was a five foot eleven inch two-star rated quarterback from Pierce County HS in Blackshear, Georgia. He received his two stars by competing at numerous Elite 11 quarterback camps as a rising high school senior. Bennett wore a U.S. Postal Service cap at those camps to "have something that people would remember me by." That's when he received his nickname, "The Mailman."

When Bennett reported to UGA as a walk-on, he was assigned locker number 122A, which he shared with another walk-on, who was assigned 122B. That's a really high number for a locker! The equipment manager gave him a number 22 practice jersey. That's a really high number for a QB! Maybe that equipment manager knew what he was doing since Doug Flutie, the 1984 Heisman winner and five foot nine inch Boston College quarterback, wore 22.

Bennett remarked that he felt better about the scout team when he could wear a jersey with the number of that week's opposing quarterback because it was a real quarterback number. He drew rave reviews from his coaches and teammates in 2017 when he mimicked Oklahoma quarterback Baker Mayfield so well during Rose Bowl practices.

Stetson left UGA to play QB for Jones Community College (MS) because Georgia had five-stars Jake Fromm and Justin Fields even after five-star Jacob Eason transferred to Washington. After

Fields announced his transfer to Ohio State, Bennett accepted a scholarship offer from UGA Head Coach Kirby Smart to return to Athens.

Stetson appeared briefly in four games in 2019 and played in eight games in 2020, but he lost his starting position to five-star JT Daniels, the five-star USC transfer and preseason Heisman candidate. In 2021 Daniels was injured, and Bennett started ten games and played in every game.

Despite leading the Dawgs to a 12-0 record, many Georgia fans clamored to replace the former walk-on following the SEC Championship loss to Alabama. But Stetson bounced back with arguably the best game of his career in the College Football Playoff semifinal win over Michigan!

Prior to the Michigan game, Georgia Offensive Coordinator Todd Monken told Mark Weiszer of the Athens Banner-Herald, "If you look at the plays he's made, he's made national championship plays," Monken said. "He has. You turn on the film and look at some of the throws he makes, the decisions he makes, the things he does with his feet. There's no doubt in my mind we can win the national championship. There's no doubt in my mind we can win it with Stetson Bennett. There's no question."

Sometimes fans don't appreciate what they have. The average yards per pass attempt (Y/A) is a key quarterback efficiency metric. I compiled the college Y/A average for top QBs from Georgia and Alabama, Baker Mayfield, Joe Burrow and Trevor Lawrence. Bennett is in the top five and the only two-star who made the list. His Y/A is comparable to five-star Bryce Young, the Heisman Trophy winner and opposing quarterback in the 2022 national championship game. Perhaps only Stetson, his high school coach, and his family genuinely believed that he would start at UGA. From two-star, number 22 and locker 122A to 1-10-22, the date of the 2022 "natty", Bennett has the opportunity to lead UGA to a national championship!

In a devotional from the FCA EVERY Reading Plan, Mark Jones wrote, "If you ever feel bad because you are not playing as much as you want, remember that you are on the team because the coach wants you there...Before you set foot in any gym, arena, field or another area of play, remember that '...he makes everything work out according to his plan'" (Ephesians 1:11(b)). Stetson is a splendid example of an athlete who kept dreaming, believing, repping, and working to achieve his team's goals while maintaining a can-do, never-give-up attitude!

Sometimes we feel like we're number 122A chasing our dreams that seem as far away as Jones CC is from UGA. Most people are content to remain two-stars, but God created each of us to be five-stars! Greatness in God's kingdom is possible when we stay true to God's plan for our lives.

Stetson's rise from obscurity to stardom reminds me of these verses that encourage us to keep striving. Post these verses in a visible place and keep believing and achieving! God can help you accomplish the improbable and the impossible!

- God can do anything, you know—far more than you could ever imagine or guess or request in your wildest dreams! He does it not by pushing us around but by working within us, his Spirit deeply and gently within us (Ephesians 3:20 MSG).
- You made all the delicate, inner parts of my body and knit them together in my mother's womb. Thank you for making me so wonderfully complex! It is amazing to think about. Your workmanship is marvelous—and how well I know it (Psalm 139:13-14 TLB).
- "For I know the plans I have for you," declares the Lord, "plans to prosper you and not to harm you, plans to give you hope and a future" (Jeremiah 29:11).
- "And we know that all that happens to us is working for our good if we love God and are fitting into his plans" (Romans 8:28).
- (Jesus) said to them, "…For truly, I say to you, if you have faith like a grain of mustard seed, you will say to this mountain, 'Move from here to there,' and it will move, and nothing will be impossible for you'" (Matthew 17:20 ESV).

14

Pray for Others and Follow Through

...pray all the time; thank God no matter what happens. This is the
way God wants you who belong to Christ Jesus to live.

1 Thessalonians 5:17-18 The Message

When I was a boy, we would get the Macon Telegraph and News
Sunday edition, which had comics in color and a supplement called
Parade Magazine. The magazine annually featured the Parade All-
American High School Football Team long before MaxPreps and Ri-
vals. Parade Magazine also offered a quiz that measured your
knowledge of current events and people in the news.

In that context, I quizzed my huddles this week to evaluate their
awareness of these newsmakers. I used the list as an icebreaker, then
realized it was also a prayer list. Jacob Blake, a 29-year-old father of
six, was shot seven times in the back by a police officer and was para-
lyzed from the waist down. This horrific incident triggered protests in
his hometown of Kenosha, WI and prompted the Milwaukee Bucks to
boycott their playoff game. Overnight Hurricane Laura, a Category 4
hurricane, pummeled the Louisiana coast and the city of Lake Charles,
forcing tens of thousands to evacuate and leaving hundreds of thousands without power during the COVID-19 pandemic. Two thousand
miles to the west, weary firefighters bravely battled fires in the LNU
and CZU Lightning Complexes in California as thousands of homes
were lost.

The news can be overwhelming on many days. Where do we turn
for comfort and reassurance? We can turn to God by praying for others
and receive hope as we intercede. I read a quote that "the most sacred
and creative thing, the greatest work that any person can ever do, is to

thank God, to praise him, and to pray. There is power in thankfulness and prayer."

I have found that organizing my prayer list helps me pray more effectively. I believe in the power of prayer. James 5:16 assures that the prayer of a righteous man has great power and wonderful results. Do you believe in the power of prayer enough to take some time to get organized? It's approaching crunch time as many of you get ready for your first football game. But a simple spreadsheet or the back of an envelope is all it takes! You can also peruse a portion of your phone contacts.

Praying daily for others and their dire situations is a fantastic way to demonstrate empathy and compassion. Empathy is placing yourself in someone else's shoes, and compassion is empathy plus acting or following through. Compassion occurs when we follow through with a text, an email, a phone call, or display other forms of Christian love for someone who is carrying a heavy weight on his or her shoulders.

I watched a YouTube episode of former NFL player Emmanuel Acho's "Uncomfortable Conversations with a Black Man." Acho said that because the Good Samaritan was more concerned about the half-dead man than he was about himself, he took the time to follow through in compassionate ways. In his conversation with Acho, Hillside NYC Pastor Carl Hentz encouraged listeners to avoid selling short their efforts of compassion. Hentz said, "Don't be intimidated and don't minimize what you have (to offer)."

A small action of kindness can go a long way for someone who is struggling. In what ways can you demonstrate compassion this week to your spouse, children, students, athletes or fellow coaches who are hurting? May God reveal your follow-through when you take time to pray.

15

Who Makes Up Your Circle?

Encourage one another as brothers and build each other up.

1 Thessalonians 5:11

After the Ivy League, Mountain West, and Mid-American Conferences announced that they would not play in 2020, the Big Ten and PAC-12 Conferences confirmed on August 11 that they would follow suit. These decisions impacted the careers of hundreds of fourth year and fifth year college seniors who dreamed of their final shot to compete for a championship.

ESPN Analyst Kirk Herbstreit was asked what these seniors should do after receiving the devastating news. He replied, "Find your circle!" Find your circle of people that you trust and confide in, who have supported you every step of the way and are there to help you through disappointment.

At my football huddles I encouraged the athletes to write down the members of their support circle in the form of the defensive chart below. Who are the people in your life that you count on? Who are the people in whom you have a deep trust? Who are the people that will listen to you and take action to help you? They named parents, grandparents, siblings, trusted friends and teammates, coaches, and spiritual leaders.

Then I asked them where Jesus fits into their lineup. Most often the defensive captain is the middle linebacker or inside linebacker. Would you put Jesus at Mike LB as the captain of your support team? Perhaps he only made first team or second team, or maybe Jesus is having difficulty making your travel squad lately. Remember that the

Father sent His Son to earth so that he could experience every type of hurt that you have felt, including the fear of season cancellations.

Let's put our trust each day in God, who holds our future. We can turn to prayer and scripture for comfort and encouragement. 1 Thessalonians 5:11 says, "Encourage one another as brothers and build each other up." Perhaps you can be on the support team of an athlete or coach who is struggling. Hebrews 10:24 reads, "And let us consider how we may spur one another on toward love and good deeds, not giving up meeting together…but encouraging each other." Romans 15:5 tells us, "May the God who gives endurance and encouragement give you the same attitude of mind toward each other that Christ Jesus had." Let's choose Jesus, who gave his life for us, as our captain and follow Him regardless of the circumstances in this new decade and forever.

16

Living a Life Centered on Christ

My dear friends, you always obeyed what you were taught. Just as you obeyed when I was with you, it is even more important for you to obey now that I am not there. So you must continue to live in a way that gives meaning to your salvation. Do this with fear and respect for God. Yes, it is God who is working in you. He helps you want to do what pleases him, and he gives you the power to do it. Do everything without complaining or arguing so that you will be blameless and pure, children of God without any fault. But you are living with evil people all around you, who have lost their sense of what is right. Among those people you shine like lights in a dark world, and you offer them the teaching that gives life. So I can be proud of you when Christ comes again. You will show that my work was not wasted—that I ran in the race and won.

Philippians 2:12-16 (ERV)

Consider some of the football teams that have won state championships, national championships, and Super Bowls. One characteristic that you will find is that they were consistently strong up the middle. The previous devotion, Who Makes Up Your Circle?, is about naming your support team and determining the role that Christ plays on your team. I hope that Jesus is your captain and is smack dab in the center of your life. But how do you keep him there?

A Christ-centered life is a life lived as Christ would live it. However, forces in this world create chaos, uncertainty and confusion that pull us away from a life that is centered on Christ. News cycles constantly report the opposing views of the left and the right. If your focus stays on one of those two viewpoints, it is extremely difficult to remain Christ-centered. The longer you focus on one view, the more convinced you become that the other view is wrong, which can lead to frustration, resentment, dismay, divisive behavior, and even hatred.

As believers we must ensure that our focus remains on the ideals and teachings of Christ. Only through a Christlike view can we love unconditionally, give mercy abundantly, receive grace freely, forgive others readily, and demonstrate compassion as Jesus did, Jesus does and Jesus will do. Hebrews 13:8 assures us that Jesus Christ is the same yesterday and today and forever!

As Jesus hung on the cross, he was physically tormented by two opposing forces, which were the two ropes that were tied to his left arm and his right arm. Both of his shoulders were likely dislocated by the strain caused by the tight ropes and the weight of his body. Because of his immeasurable love for us, Jesus withstood the pain and agony for six hours. Yet his body remained centered on the cross, and his mind remained centered on his Father's will. God raised him from the grave three days later, and the empty grave is the hope that every person has for eternity. Out of sheer gratitude for his sacrifice for our sins, followers of Jesus should be compelled to live a life daily that is centered on Christ.

Here are some Christ-centered verses from the ESV translation that we can stand on.

- But seek first the kingdom of God and his righteousness, and all these things will be added to you (Matthew 6:33).
- Trust in the Lord with all your heart, and do not lean on your own understanding. In all your ways acknowledge him, and he will make straight your paths (Proverbs 3:5-6).
- Do not be conformed to this world, but be transformed by the renewal of your mind, that by testing you may discern what is the will of God, what is good and acceptable and perfect (Romans 12:2).
- The Lord is my strength and my shield; in him my heart trusts, and I am helped; my heart exults, and with my song I give thanks to him (Psalm 28:7).
- Be imitators of me, as I am of Christ (1 Corinthians 11:1).
- I have been crucified with Christ. It is no longer I who live, but Christ who lives in me (Galatians 2:20).
- I can do all things through him who strengthens me (Philippians 4:13).

17

In Loving Memory of
Natajay "AJ" Banks

Therefore, go and make disciples...

Matthew 28:19

Our Open Gym ministry at Mt. Zion UMC in Marietta, Georgia lost a beloved young brother when Natajay "AJ" Banks tragically lost his life on August 2, 2020. On the evening of August 3, fifteen athletes and coaches from the ministry gathered on Zoom to remember AJ, celebrate his life, and pray for his family.

AJ attended Open Gym for four years and was a graduate of Pope High School. Numerous young men from Pope commented how AJ reached out to them when they first started playing at Open Gym. All of us recalled how super competitive he was, but how he played with enthusiasm and good sportsmanship. Several commented on how hard he would work with a Kobe Bryant like drive to reach goals that he set. Often, I asked AJ to close our devotion time in prayer, and he had great insight into the nightly topic and personal advice for his teammates from lessons learned in his life.

AJ was also a peacemaker. When the competition became overheated, I would walk over to AJ and say, "Go get so and so for me" or " Go over and calm him down," and he would help get us back on track. He was small in stature, about five foot eight and one hundred forty pounds, but there was no one who played with more tenacity or toughness. He was a tough competitor, yet he maintained a Christlike competitive spirit.

Just as Jesus had a trusted inner circle, AJ was a member of the Open Gym inner circle for me and Coach Trey Stevenson, who had a tremendous impact on AJ's faith walk during his first year at Open Gym. AJ became a disciple making disciples as evidenced by the number of young men who recounted his positive influence and advice. AJ made a lasting impact on our Open Gym family, and he will be deeply missed.

As we closed the Zoom call, Coach Trey and I invited everyone to commit or recommit their lives to Christ, because that's what AJ would have wanted his brothers to have. Please pray for his family and his best friends, DJ and Alec. I vividly remember the three of them walking into our gym together for the first time four years ago.

Rest in peace, brother!

18

Let's Win the Day!

God is strong, and he wants you strong. So take everything the Master
has set out for you, well-made weapons of the best materials. And put
them to use so you will be able to stand up to everything the Devil
throws your way. This is no afternoon athletic contest that we'll walk
away from and forget about in a couple of hours. This is for keeps, a
life-or-death fight to the finish against the Devil and all his angels. Be
prepared. You're up against far more than you can handle on your
own. Take all the help you can get, every weapon God has issued, so
that when it's all over but the shouting you'll still be on your feet.
Truth, righteousness, peace, faith, and salvation are more than words.
Learn how to apply them. You'll need them throughout your life.
God's Word is an *indispensable* weapon. In the same way, prayer is
essential in this ongoing warfare. Pray hard and long. Pray for your
brothers and sisters. Keep your eyes open. Keep each other's spirits up
so that no one falls behind or drops out.

Ephesians 6:10-18 (MSG)

War Games was a movie that starred a young Matthew Broderick,
who played a computer whiz kid who hacks into a top secret supercomputer which had complete control over the U.S. nuclear arsenal.
The supercomputer challenges him to play a "war game" between the
United States and Russia. Before he realizes what he has done, he ac-
cidentally starts a countdown to World War III. The tension mounts
within the command center as the general escalates the situation to
Defcon 1. The general and his team scramble to determine if the mis-
sile attacks on the projection screens are real or simulated. At the last
minute, the general follows the sound reasoning from the inventor of
the war game and calls off the counterstrike. A worldwide disaster is

averted, and a greatly relieved general announces, "Move us back to Defcon 5!"

There is a different type of war game that occurs daily for each of us. The devil and his demons relentlessly scheme against us in the spiritual realm. We must be able to manage the thoughts in our heads and discern what is real and what is placed there by the enemy. Each person's spiritual battle is different, and the battles seem more intense during these incredibly uncertain times with so many mixed messages. It is easy for our flesh to react and to raise our worry and anxiety "Defcon" level. Therefore, we must protect our minds through solid reasoning that is based upon facts and the truth of God. Just as an out-manned, desperate opponent resorts to talking trash, Satan tries to trash talk us by playing mind games. Satan and his demons are our adversaries who relentlessly stalk us, as described in 1 Peter 5:8, "Be sober, be vigilant; because your adversary the devil walks about like a roaring lion, seeking whom he may devour."

The spiritual battle started when Satan (a.k.a. Lucifer) rebelled in heaven against God's authority. Ezekiel described Satan's initial state: "Thus says the Lord GOD: 'You were the signet of perfection, full of wisdom and perfect in beauty....You were in Eden, the garden of God...You were perfect in your ways from the day you were created, till iniquity was found in you (Ezekiel 28:12-13, 15)'". Satan sought God's power and glory for himself, the sin of pride eventually filled his heart, and he and a third of the angels were cast out of heaven and out of the presence of God. These angels are now known as demons. The spiritual war began in heaven, but earth became the battleground. Satan will scratch and claw daily to pry your allegiance away from God, and his favorite ploy is to dominate your thoughts.

We must rely on God's strength and presence to help us win our spiritual battles. Satan tempted Jesus three times, but Jesus withstood each test and did not sin. Remember that merely experiencing temptation is not a sin. The apostle Paul taught, "No test or temptation that comes your way is beyond the course of what others have had to face. All you need to remember is that God will never let you down; he'll never let you be pushed past your limit; he'll always be there to help you come through it (1 Corinthians 10:13 MSG)."

How do we protect our minds daily? Just as our bodies need healthy food, we must feed our minds healthy thoughts through scripture and positive resources. There is great wisdom that we can take from Ephesians, Chapter 6:10-13, "Finally, my brethren, be strong in the Lord and in the power of His might. Put on the whole armor of God, that you may be able to stand against the wiles of the devil. For we do not wrestle against flesh and blood, but against principalities, against powers, against the rulers of the darkness of this age, against spiritual hosts of wickedness in the heavenly places. Therefore take up the whole armor of God, that you may be able to withstand in the evil day, and having done all, to stand."

Because Satan uses bully tactics, we must man up and fight from the position of strength that we have through our relationship with Jesus Christ! There will never be a break from spiritual warfare and no sympathy from the devil. At the University of West Georgia FCA camp in 2019, over one thousand high school athletes stood and sang in unison, "This is how I fight my battles. It may look like I'm surrounded but I'm surrounded by You (*Surrounded*, Michael W. Smith)." We must depend upon God to fight our battles for us. Romans 12:2 reminds us, "Do not be conformed to this world, but be transformed by the renewing of your mind, so that you may prove what is that good and acceptable and perfect will of God." Allow your mind to be transformed using daily scripture reading, prayer, the power of God, and the perfect love of Christ. Let's win the day!

19

How Often Do You Weep?

Jesus wept.

John 11:35

I read a quote that described empathy as "seeing with the eyes of another, listening with the ears of another, and feeling with the heart of another." Empathy is one of the best gifts that we can give others and receive from others. Developing a keen sense of empathy helps shape our hearts and enables us to respond like Jesus would.

Dennis Kinlaw in *This Way with the Master* shared the following story. A missionary and his pregnant wife traveled thousands of miles to live in a remote village. The missionary owned three doctorate degrees. He was a medical doctor and earned two degrees in theology, so he was certainly well-prepared educationally! The couple lived in a modest home, and a church was built on the outskirts of the community. His wife soon gave birth to a baby boy. They held a worship service every Sunday for four years, but there was just one problem. No villagers ever came.

Then tragedy struck the young family. Their young son became terribly ill and died suddenly. His father built a crude coffin and began to dig a grave to bury his son. While he was digging, he was overcome with grief and fell face down in the wet dirt, sobbing uncontrollably for the loss of his son.

One man from the village was watching him dig the grave. The man grabbed the missionary's hair, lifted his face out of the dirt, and looked into his eyes. He carefully returned his face to the dirt and ran to the village, shouting, "He cries like we cry!" Because the villager saw his broken heart, heard his cry of anguish, and felt his deep hurt, a lasting relationship was formed. The following Sunday morning the little church was packed in support of the missionary and his wife.

How can we cultivate empathy in our hearts? First, we all know people who need empathy for the hurts they have relived during the past few weeks due to events that occurred years or even decades ago. Let's educate ourselves on the issues and examples of racial injustice and oppression.

Second, study the life of Jesus and *his entire body of work.* It is easy to base our view of Jesus on several key miracles or acts of kindness that Jesus performed. But note the story when Jesus angrily overturned the tables of the money changers and drove them out of the temple. Note the time when Jesus grieved about the loss of his brother Lazarus. When Jesus saw the tomb where Lazarus lay, "Jesus wept (John 11:35)." Note the time that Jesus sweated great drops of blood in the Garden of Gethsemane before he took the past, present and future sins of the entire world to the cross as proof of his perfect love for us. Read how Jesus advocated for persons who were treated unfairly, including women, the poor, and the oppressed.

Third, let's strive to live a life that emulates all of the teachings of Jesus and his heart. When we learn to put all of his teachings into action, our hearts become more like his heart. To live out only a portion of Jesus's lessons is to reduce his power and grace in our understanding and responses.

Grooming an empathetic heart will help you reach out and love others who don't look like you or think like you. You will reflect the love of Christ to a world that desperately needs what only his love can satisfy. Hillsong United's song *Hosanna* features the following lyrics: *Show me how to love like you have loved me, break my heart for what breaks yours.* Jesus said, "Let me give you a new command: Love one another. In the same way I loved you, you love one another. This is how everyone will recognize that you are my disciples—when they see the love you have for each other" (John 13:34-35 The Message). May you find yourself moved to tears more often and moved to respond with empathy when you encounter the sins of racism, injustice, and oppression.

20

Moved to Tears

Jesus wept.

John 11:35

The first two rounds of March Madness in 2021 led to moments of exhilaration, demonstrated by 15-seed Oral Roberts' joyous celebration, and moments of despair when Iowa All-American and Player of the Year Luka Garza wept as he came to the bench, realizing that his illustrious four-year college career was ending.

In 1993 NC State Coach Jim Valvano blessed the sports world with his famous ESPY speech, "Don't Ever Give Up." He said that each day a person should do the following three things: think, laugh and cry. "If you do those three things, that's a heckuva day," Coach V remarked. Regarding crying, Valvano described it as being "moved to tears."

What situations move us to tears? The world tries to convince us that real men don't cry. In *A League of Their Own*, Jimmy Dugan uttered the famous line, "There's no crying in baseball!" Yet we've experienced the teary emotion of high school seniors when the last few minutes of their sports careers are ticking away. Each season those tears are expected after hundreds of hours devoted to lifting weights, workouts, practices and games. But when else should we cry?

Jesus gives us an example when he weeps after seeing his friend Mary and her friends crying after the passing of Lazarus, Mary's brother. After learning about the death of Lazarus in the nearby village of Bethany, Jesus delayed his trip from Jerusalem for two days to bring glory to God. The Message translation of John 11:32-35 says that a deep anger welled up inside Jesus as he experienced their sorrow first-hand. "Mary came to where Jesus was waiting and fell at his feet, saying, "Master, if only you had been here, my brother would not have died." When Jesus saw her sobbing and the Jews with her sobbing, a deep anger welled up within him. He said, ''Where did you put him?" "Master, come and see," they said. Now Jesus wept." Even though Jesus knew that their sorrow would turn to joy after he raised Lazarus, he demonstrated great empathy for them when he also wept.

When should we cry? You and I should be moved to tears by situations that break the heart of Jesus. The tragedies in Georgia and Colorado that took the lives of eighteen people are prime examples. As we learned about the victims and saw the anguish on the faces of those who loved them, the Holy Spirit moved many of us to tears. It's also a stress reliever to be moved to tears occasionally, and crying is certainly nothing to be embarrassed about. Jesus set the standard. Let's follow his lead.

21
Four Underdogs

The woman said, "*I know* that Messiah" (called Christ) "is coming. When he comes, he will explain everything to us." Then Jesus declared, "I, the one speaking to you—*I am he.*" Then, leaving her water jar, the woman went back to the town and said to the people. "*Come, see a man* who told me everything I ever did.
Could this be the Messiah?"
(The Woman at the Well. John 4:25-29)

"Sir," the invalid replied, "I have no one to help me into the pool when the water is stirred. While I am trying to get in, someone else goes down ahead of me." Then Jesus said to him, "*Get up! Pick up your mat and walk.*" At once the man was cured; he picked up his mat and walked. At once the man was cured; he picked up his mat and walked.
The day on which this took place was a Sabbath…
(The Invalid, John 5:7-9)

When they kept on questioning him, he straightened up and said to them, "Let any one of you who is without sin be the first to throw a stone at her." Again he stooped down and wrote on the ground. At this, those who heard began to go away one at a time, the older ones first, until only Jesus was left, with the woman still standing there. Jesus straightened up and asked her, "Woman, where are they? Has no one condemned you? "No one, sir," she said. "*Then neither do I condemn you,*" Jesus declared. "Go now and leave your life of sin."
(The Adulteress, John 8:7-11)

After saying this, he spit on the ground, made some mud with the saliva, and put it on the man's eyes. "*Go,*" he told him, "*wash in the Pool of Siloam.*" So the man went and washed, and came home seeing. His neighbors and those who had formerly seen him begging asked, "Isn't this the same man who used to sit and beg?" Some claimed that he was. Others said, "No, he only looks like him." But he himself insisted, "I am the man." (The Blind Man, John 9:6-10)

March Madness is one of our favorite events of any year! Bracket pools break out all over America, and productivity drops as we follow our brackets. An estimated seventy million brackets were completed in 2021 by March Madness fans who tried to predict the teams in the Final Four and hoped for a perfect bracket. Sorry, but the odds of a perfect bracket are about five quintillion (that's 18 zeroes) to one.

These were four great moments for underdogs in the NCAA basketball tournament. In 1966 Texas Western started an all-Black Five in the championship game, and their pivotal win helped spur the full integration of college basketball. In 1983 NC State Coach Jim Valvano led his nine-loss Cardiac Pack to a string of thrilling last-minute upsets and culminated with his mad dash to hug Dereck Whittenberg after the win over Houston and Phi Slama Jama. In 1985 the tournament expanded to sixty-four teams, and 8-seed Villanova played "The Perfect Game" to defeat heavily favored Georgetown by two points in the finals. Last but not least, in 2018 we fell in love with Loyola (Ill.) and their chaplain, Sister Jean, when the mid-major Ramblers made the Final Four! What a treat it will be to see Sister Jean, 101 years young, on the sidelines again when Loyola faces Georgia Tech in arguably the most-anticipated first-round game of this year's tournament.

Sometimes people who don't know basketball pick better brackets than the basketball junkies. The challenge is to pick the surprise teams for the tournament. The mass appeal of the tournament is fueled by the buzzer-beater wins of the underdogs that upset the favorites. A 12-seed upsetting a 5-seed is fairly common, and a 13 over a 4 or a 14 over a 3 happens occasionally. Rarely does a 15 defeat a 2. A 16-seed had never defeated a 1-seed until 2018 when UMBC defeated Virginia, which bounced back a year later to win the championship! The underdogs who pull the stunning upsets are called bracket busters because they blow up your brackets!

Just as the odds of winning are great for the underdogs, the odds were stacked against the underdogs when Jesus walked the earth. In a

Jewish and Roman world that made outcasts of females, the weak, the sick, the least fortunate, and those with special needs, Jesus supernaturally helped four underdogs pull monumental upsets!

Jesus asked a Samaritan woman held in low esteem for a drink of water and promised her living water if she would only believe. Because she believed that the Messiah would come, Jesus admitted to her that he was the Messiah, and many Samaritans were converted after her testimony.

Beside the pool near the Sheep's Gate in Jerusalem, Jesus raised up a man who had been crippled for thirty-eight years, telling him to "pick up his mat and walk."

Then Jesus made mud paste and gave sight to a man who had been blind since birth. Not only that, but he did it on the Sabbath, which infuriated the Pharisees.

Last but not least, Jesus told a self-righteous mob of Pharisees and teachers of the law to throw a stone at an adulterous woman *if any of them had never sinned.* His action rescued her, and Jesus told her to sin no more.

These two women and two men, all seemingly without hope, received the greatest victories of their lives, but Jesus was even more concerned about their spiritual health.

Two of these upsets by the underdogs featured physical healing miracles, and all four were life-changing transformations. Because Jesus is the same yesterday, today and forever (Hebrews 13:8), he is still in the miracle business of rescuing the marginalized and transforming their lives. Jesus is and will always be a champion for societal underdogs, and believers have that same power of the Holy Spirit to be champions and supporters for the poor, the oppressed, and the suppressed. Follow the example of Jesus and give an underdog the hope that is in Christ Jesus!

22

Enduring

More than that, we rejoice in our sufferings, knowing that suffering produces endurance, and endurance produces character, and character produces hope.

Romans 5:3-4 (NIV)

To persevere is to persist steadfastly in pursuit of an undertaking, task, journey, or goal, even if hindered by distraction, difficulty, obstacles, or discouragement. To endure is to continue to carry on, despite obstacles or hardships; to experience and deal with something that is painful or unpleasant without giving up. I believe the difference between perseverance and endurance is that endurance means carrying on despite hardships, personal loss and pain.

Enduring also means denoting or relating to a race or other sporting event that takes place over a long distance or otherwise demands great physical stamina. Lengthy sporting events include the Baja 1000 24+ hour race, and who will soon forget the LSU-Texas A&M seven OT, five-hour football game which ended with a basketball score, LSU 74 A&M 72!

My favorite endurance contest was at Wimbledon in 2010 between John Isner (L) and Nicholas Mahut (R). Isner and Mahut played an astounding 138 games in the fifth set with Isner winning 70-68! Note: There was no tiebreaker in the fifth set at Wimbledon then. The two men played a total of 183 games, the equivalent of fourteen tiebreaker sets, over eleven hours and three calendar days! Think of the exhilaration and relief of the Wimbledon champions after only five sets! Thinking of their mental strength and physical endurance, Roger Federer said, "It's beyond anything that I've ever seen or could imagine."

Perhaps during these past twelve months you have had experiences beyond what you've ever seen or could imagine. Was there a time when you could not find the strength to pull yourself out of a rut? Share with someone how God and your inner circle helped you endure.

The apostle Paul is a prime example of endurance. Recall that Saul persecuted Christians before Jesus changed him from Saul to Paul on the road to Damascus. Jesus made it clear to Paul that he was his "voice of choice" to share the good news with the Gentiles, and he would experience "hard suffering" as he lived out his calling. Paul made his case for the "Suffering Hall of Fame" when he wrote the following:

"They say they serve Christ? But I have served him far more! (Have I gone mad to boast like this? I have worked harder, been put in jail more often, been whipped times without number, and faced death again and again and again. Five different times the Jews gave me their terrible thirty-nine lashes. Three times I was beaten with rods. Once I was stoned. Three times I was shipwrecked. Once I was in the open sea all night and the whole next day. I have traveled many weary miles and have been often in great danger from flooded rivers and from robbers and from my own people, the Jews, as well as from the hands of the Gentiles. I have faced grave dangers from mobs in the cities and from death in the deserts and in the stormy seas and from men who claim to be brothers in Christ but are not. I have lived with weariness and pain and sleepless nights. Often, I have been hungry and thirsty and have gone without food; often I have shivered with cold, without enough clothing to keep me warm. Then, besides all this, I have the constant worry of how the churches are getting along (2 Corinthians 11:23-28)."

Paul's love for Christ and his unwavering devotion to the gospel allowed him to push forward through these many hardships. The author of Hebrews inspired us by using this breathtaking example of the endurance of Jesus and the cross.

"Therefore, since we are surrounded by so great a cloud of witnesses, let us also lay aside every weight, and sin which clings so closely, and let us run with endurance the race that is set before us, looking to Jesus, the founder and perfecter of our faith, who for the joy that was set before him endured the cross, despising the shame, and is seated at the right hand of the throne of God. Consider him who endured from sinners such hostility against himself, so that you may not grow weary or fainthearted" (Hebrews 12:1-3).

Jesus demonstrated his unconditional love for humankind and endured the cross for the joy of knowing that he was making the way for everyone to have access to God's gift of grace, eternal life in heaven.

We may never suffer to the extent that Paul and Jesus did for the gospel, but we will suffer. Rejoice that "...suffering produces endurance, and endurance produces character, and character produces hope (Romans 5:4)." Perhaps you have used the expression "I'm at the end of my rope," or "I'm at rock bottom," or "I'm at the bottom of my well." Rest assured that the bottom of Jesus's well is so much deeper than ours! Ask Jesus for the living water from his well and receive the strength to endure one day at a time.

23

What Price Are You Willing to Pay?

Let your light so shine *before men*, that they may see your good works and glorify your Father in heaven.

Matthew 5:16

I came across an article about the late Peter Norman, the Australian sprinter who finished second in the 200-meter race at the 1968 Mexico City Olympics. Norman had the fifth-fastest time in the world coming into the Games, but he discovered that his stride had lengthened in the thin air of Mexico City. He blazed the last fifty meters, passing a startled John Carlos from the USA to earn the silver medal behind gold medalist Tommie Smith from the USA.

But the real drama occurred after the race on the medal stand. With heads bowed and black-gloved fists raised in the air, an iconic photo of Norman, Smith and Carlos, protesting racism and segregation, circled the globe.

Recall that 1968 was a period of great unrest following the assassinations of Rev. Dr. Martin Luther King, Jr. and Senator Robert Kennedy. Racial protests and riots, peppered with protests of the Vietnam War, occurred across America. The year concluded with the Apollo 8 crew taking turns reading from the Book of Genesis as they circled the moon at Christmastime, and the memorable photo of our beautiful planet was taken from the spaceship.

Regarding the 200-meter race, Smith and Carlos were the overwhelming favorites to finish 1-2, but the upstart Norman spoiled the outcome. Following the race, the two American sprinters prepared to stage their silent protest on the medal stand by wearing black socks with no shoes and raising black gloves in the Black Power Salute. However, Carlos forgot to bring his gloves from the Olympic Village.

Norman suggested that each American wear one glove, and their problem was resolved. Smith has his right fist, and Carlos raised his left fist.

Because Norman passed Carlos down the stretch, he stood with his back to Smith and Carlos on the platform during the playing of the National Anthem. Therefore, he could not see them, yet he knew they had followed through because he heard someone singing the anthem, and the person stopped singing after their arms went up.

But their problems had just begun. Smith and Carlos were sent home in disgrace and banned from the Olympics for life. Both men received death threats back home in America. However, they were treated as returning heroes by the Black community. Norman was staunchly against racism and had seen racial oppression by his government, which allowed children of Aboriginal descent to be taken from their parents and given to white parents for adoption. He empathized with the stance that his competitors were bravely taking. Norman took his stance by wearing a button on the left lapel during the medal ceremony that read "Olympic Project for Human Rights." Smith and Carlos wore the same button that recognized the project that was founded in 1967 by Dr. Harry Edwards, who created Sociology in Sport and has been a leading activist for human rights in sports for over fifty years.

Each athlete paid a heavy price and was persecuted for making this public stand against racism. Norman was hated by some Australians and was passed over by the Australian Olympic Committee (AOC) for the 1972 Munich Games, despite the fact that his 200-meter time in 1968 would have won gold in Munich. At the 2000 Sydney Games, the presence of Norman, arguably the greatest Australian sprinter ever, was downplayed. Norman's nephew said, "He suffered to the day he died."

Norman died of a heart attack in 2006. His pallbearers included two Americans, Smith and Carlos, who traveled 15,000 miles round-trip to deliver the eulogy and to carry the coffin of the man who stood with them before men in Mexico City. Smith said, "He paid the price. This was Peter Norman's stand for human rights. He just happened to be a white guy, an Australian white guy, between two Black guys in the victory stand believing in the same thing."

Over fifty years after the Mexico City Olympics, the battle to end systemic racism continues. When you take a stand to denounce racism, you may become unpopular among some of your friends and family members. What price are you willing to pay? Jesus Christ paid the price for all humankind, and he teaches us to do what is just and honorable and brings glory to His Father.

Peter Norman never had another shot at Olympic gold, but his light shone far brighter than a gold medal in the eyes of his two comrades in Mexico City. As Christ followers we are supposed to let our light shine before men. Let your light so shine before men, that they may see your good works and glorify your Father in heaven (Matthew 5:16).

24

Moving Up the Spiritual Depth Chart

Love is patient, love is kind. It does not envy, it does not boast, it is not proud. It does not dishonor others, it is not self-seeking, it is not easily angered, it keeps no record of wrongs. Love does not delight in evil but rejoices with the truth. It always protects, always trusts, always hopes, always perseveres. Love never fails...

1 Corinthians 13:4-8

I asked football players to describe their high school journeys that typically begin with the scout team. Each journey was unique but going from scout to a backup to a starter required discipline and commitment.

I compared the football depth chart journey to the spiritual depth chart journey. We begin our spiritual journey when we are received into the family of God as his child through faith in Jesus Christ. The second phase in the journey is to become a disciple of Jesus Christ, but many never move forward from that initial phase. Often, they lack the discipline to become holy and set apart. Discipleship requires daily discipline being in the word of God, praying for others, being obedient, and cleansing from sin. But if we are to become all that God wants us to become spiritually, it's the third phase, which is to become disciples who make disciples, that is so critical. Jesus gave us The Great Commission, "Go therefore and make disciples of all the nations, baptizing them in the name of the Father and of the Son and of the Holy Spirit, teaching them to observe all things that I have commanded you; and lo, I am with you always, even to the end of the age" (Matthew 28:19-20).

I believe that unconditional love for others in our hearts is the key to climbing the spiritual depth chart. God personifies this selfless and sacrificial love, which was named agape (ah-gah-pay) by the Greeks. The love of God in our hearts allows us to point others to him. God loving us does not depend on how we love Him. No matter where you are on the depth chart in God's kingdom, or whether you are even on the depth chart, God's love for each person never changes. But by consistently loving our friends, teammates, family members, and co-workers through the power and presence of the Holy Spirit, who is God in us, we can direct people to God, the source of eternal and perfect love. Jesus said, "A new commandment I give to you, that you love one another: just as I have loved you, you also are to love one another. By this all people will know that you are my disciples, if you have love for one another" (John 13:34-35).

Some athletes told me they had experienced the lie from Satan that if you get serious about being a Christian, the fun in your life will disappear. But actually the opposite is true! Each move up the spiritual depth chart affords you greater freedom and opportunities because you are operating closer to God's will and plan for your life!

There are three plateaus of the spiritual depth chart: a child of God, disciple, and disciple maker. When you become a child of God, that commitment puts you on God's team for eternity. Becoming a disciple requires you to put in spiritual reps, sort of like football players putting in their reps Monday through Thursday. Being a disciple maker means that you are impacting others for God's kingdom. Disciple making is where the greatest joy and satisfaction occurs for believers. The disciple makers are like the starters who get their paydays under the Friday night lights! The great news is that God can have an unlimited number of starters on his team.

The football journey is temporary, but the spiritual journey is for eternity! Agape love propels you up the depth chart in the kingdom of God. "And now abide faith, hope, love, these three; but the greatest of these is love" (1 Corinthians 13:13). The ability to love others is a skill that we develop, and it allows us to see others with God's eyes, even those who look different, have different values, or are simply hard to love.

Are you a scout team member or backup on the spiritual depth chart? If so, I encourage you to pray about moving to the next level in your spiritual journey.

25

Depth Chart

The mother of Zebedee's children (James and John) came to Jesus with her sons. She got down on her knees before Jesus to ask something of Him. He said to her, "What do you want?" She said, "Say that my two sons may sit, one at Your right side and one at Your left side, when You are King." Jesus said to her, "You do not know what you are asking. Are you able to take the suffering that I am about to take?
(*Are you able to be baptized with the baptism that I am baptized with?)" They said, "Yes, we are able." He said to them, "You will suffer as I will suffer. But the places at My right side and at My left side are not Mine to give. Whoever My Father says will have those places." The other ten followers heard this. They were angry with the two brothers.

Matthew 20:20-24

All football players and coaches are aware of the depth chart. I married a wonderful woman who knows the names on the depth chart for her favorite teams. It was the beginning of a marriage made in heaven.

In this scripture the mother of James and John pushed Jesus to move her sons up the apostle depth chart, to make them 1's (first team) and relegate their peers to the 2's (second team). Her prodding was noise coming from outside the bubble. Jesus told her plainly that the Head Coach, his Father, would make the final decision on any depth chart moves. This drama made Jesus's other followers angry at the brothers and spurred division in the ranks.

An athlete expressed disappointment that he did not move up the depth chart after his excellent performance at a scrimmage. It reminded me that when our primary concern becomes moving up the depth chart or the org chart, that focus takes us away from our mission to perform as well as possible day after day. If we focus on making the plays that help our team, excellence will be recognized eventually. Our positions on the depth chart or the org chart will take care of themselves. It's not something that can or should be forced.

Stay focused on the daily tasks at hand. When you move up the depth chart, rejoice and give God the glory. If your name doesn't move up the chart as you expect, remain encouraged. It's always better to move up too late than too soon. When you move up later, you are more apt to stay there.

Baseball Hall of Famer Lou Gehrig rode the bench behind starter Wally Pipp, a Yankee first baseman who became ill one day. Gehrig, who had fully prepared and patiently waited, replaced Pipp in the lineup. Gehrig took full advantage of the opportunity and started every game for the next fifteen seasons!

Worrying about your place on the depth chart? Just perform as well as possible each day, be the best teammate you can be, and seek God's guidance. God is always there to help you, no matter where you are on the depth chart.

26

Equal Seating

So God created man in His own image, in the image of God he created him;

Genesis 1:27

The tributes to the late Henry Aaron flooded my mind with memories. This is a memory from a baseball game played in August 1962. At age seven, I attended the last minor league baseball game ever played at Lovett Field in Dublin, Georgia. The Class D Dublin Braves disbanded after one season. After the game ended, a team representative dumped bats, balls and used equipment on the mound. Kids scrambled to pick up the treasures. I saw a boy pick up an entire sack of used baseballs. That sack looked like a gold mine!

A scene from that evening is emblazoned in my mind. It is the same image each time that I think about it. From my seat behind the screen I saw a small set of bleachers halfway down the right field line. These bleachers looked old and rickety with three or four rows of seats. They were filled with thirty-five or forty fans, who were all Black. I recall a few Black children running and playing near the bleachers.

Those bleachers represented segregated seating. Many baseball teams were integrated before baseball fans in that era in the South. I saw segregated water fountains at Belk's Department store in Dublin, and no one explained why. *It's just the way things were*, seven years after Rosa Parks refused to give up her seat on the Montgomery bus, one year before Rev. King's "I Have a Dream" speech in Washington D.C, and over two years before former U.S. Representative John Lewis narrowly escaped death in Selma.

I don't recall asking about the seating, and I don't recall anyone explaining it to me. What an indelible impression it could have made on a young child if someone had said, "*Danny, see the group of people sitting down the right field line? The reason they are sitting there is because they are Black, and that's not right. They should be sitting up here with us.*"

That group of Black baseball fans sitting in the worst seats in the house is symbolic of Black America's plight. Statistics demonstrate that Black folks have the worst seats in the house when it comes to economic wealth, job opportunities, technology, reliable internet access, affordable healthcare, and most recently, a disproportionately higher COVID-19 infection rate, mortality rate, and vaccination rate so far. Henry Aaron worked to level the playing field in his community. Christians should be compelled to level the playing field and work to make the best seats in the house accessible. Black America is not asking the white community to sit in the bleachers down the right-field line. I believe the Black community wants all of us to be able to sit *together* and receive the same opportunities.

King David was loyal to a young boy named Mephibosheth after he was traced to the lineage of Saul's family. He gave Mephibosheth, his dear friend Jonathan's son, a seat at his table for the rest of his life. How can we give marginalized communities a seat at the table? The church should be where people come together and live out the teachings of Jesus Christ, which includes loving people as Christ would love them and helping them gain equal access to the best seats in the house.

27

Stacking Pennies

...A man reaps what he sows...whoever sows to please the Spirit, from the Spirit will reap eternal life. Let us not become weary in doing good, for at the proper time we will reap a harvest if we do not give up. Therefore, as we have opportunity, let us do good to all people...

Galatians 6:7(b)-10(a)

A college football player told me that his position coach encouraged him and his teammates to think about stacking pennies, to put one good workout on top of another one. Try to get 1% better each day.

A penny could represent a good session in the weight room, an efficient practice session, a meaningful study session, or a productive day in the workplace. One penny is worth a little, but when coaches and athletes collectively stack dozens of good sessions over several months, that's a lot of pennies!

As you watch athletes lift in a weight training session, you notice the ones who are stacking good sessions, and the ones who are slacking. It becomes obvious in physical or virtual classrooms which students are putting in the demanding work, and which students sadly are falling behind.

Take a moment to consider your daily spiritual effort. Are you stacking or slacking? Are you stacking spiritual pennies that will eventually deepen your relationship with God? If you believe the pennies that you and your athletes are stacking will make your team much improved, it's logical that if you place a similar effort on your spirituality, the growth will also pay off handsomely.

Recall the acronym RPO. Not Run Pass Option, but Read the Bible, Pray for others, and Obey. Each verse that you comprehend, each prayer request, each name that you lift in intercessory prayer, and each time you choose good over evil, is like pennies stacked in your spiritual bank. When you need to make a withdrawal, you should have plenty of collateral to draw from when you need it most.

You can decide today to start stacking more spiritual pennies. As you stack these spiritual pennies, you should experience a difference in the way you love your spouse, your children, your athletes, your students, your fellow coaches, and yourself. At the end of the day, isn't it all about loving God and loving others as yourself? That's the essence of the New Commandment that Jesus gave his disciples.

FCA leader Manny Maldonado wrote about how he thought Rev. Martin Luther King, Jr. pursued love. "What I love most about Dr. King was he did it by pursuing love day in and day out. It was a daily choice. It wasn't a quick fix. It's still not a quick fix. This is why we remember his legacy."

28

Skipping Past?

"Father, forgive them for they don't know what they are doing."

Luke 23:34

What activity comes to mind when you hear the term Hell Week? Many people think of special forces training when candidates endure sixteen to twenty hours of intensive physical training in adverse conditions for five to seven consecutive days. A candidate must pass this rigorous physical, mental and emotional test to attain the special forces rank.

Author JD Walt offered Holy Week would be more aptly named Hell Week. This week many Christians will go straight from Palm Sunday, which was filled with Hosannas, to Easter Sunday, when traditionally we purchase new outfits, hunt for Easter eggs, attend an Easter service, and celebrate with our families. Those activities are special, but Christ followers should not miss the momentous events that happened in the valley between those two mountaintops.

Skip Past?

In March Madness many teams used zone defenses. One of the best weapons against the zone defense is the skip pass, which occurs when the ball is passed over the top of the zone to a non-adjacent player. A skip pass is an essential play in winning basketball. But when we practice another skip, the "skip past" Hell Week straight to Easter, we miss the very heart and meaning of God's redemptive love story through the cross of Calvary.

Imagine two tall mountain peaks and a valley between the mountains. The peaks represent Palm Sunday and Easter Sunday. There is no way to get from Palm Sunday to Easter without coming down the mountain and walking through the valley, which represents the hell that Jesus went through during Holy Week.

Five Crucial Events

Consider these five events during Holy Week to appreciate the incredible love sacrifice that Jesus made for each of our lives.

1) The Last Supper (John 13:18-27, 30)

Jesus remarks as he and his disciples are sharing the Last Supper. "I am not referring to all of you; I know those I have chosen. But this is to fulfill the passage of Scripture: 'He who shared my bread has turned against me.' "I am telling you now before it happens, so that when it does happen you will believe that I am who I am. After he had said this, Jesus was troubled in spirit and testified, "Very truly I tell you, one of you is going to betray me." His disciples stared at one another, at a loss to know which of them he meant.

One of them, the disciple whom Jesus loved, was reclining next to him. Simon Peter motioned to this disciple and said, "Ask him which one he means."...Leaning back against Jesus, he asked him, "Lord, who is it?" Jesus answered, "It is the one to whom I will give this piece of bread when I have dipped it in the dish." Then, dipping the piece of bread, he gave it to Judas, the son of Simon Iscariot. As soon as Judas took the bread, Satan entered into him. So Jesus told him, "What you are about to do, do quickly."...As soon as Judas had taken the bread, he went out. And it was night.

After Judas left the Upper Room, Jesus shared the New Commandment, which is to love God, others, and yourself, with his remaining eleven disciples (John 13:34-35).

2) The Unlawful Arrest (John 18:2-7, 12-14)

Following the Last Supper, Jesus and his disciples crossed the Kidron Valley and entered the Garden of Gethsemane. Jesus struggled mightily as he prayed because he knew he must suffer an excruciating death for the sin of all humankind. But Jesus prayed to His Father, "Not my will, but Your will."

Now Judas, who betrayed him, knew the place, because Jesus had often met there with his disciples. So Judas came to the garden, guiding a detachment of soldiers and some officials from the chief priests and the Pharisees. They were carrying torches, lanterns and weapons. Jesus, knowing all that was going to happen to him, went out and asked them, "Who is it you want?" "Jesus of Nazareth," they replied. "I am he," Jesus said. (And Judas the traitor was standing there with them.)

When Jesus said, "I am he," they drew back and fell to the ground. Again he asked them, "Who is it you want?" "Jesus of Nazareth," they said. Jesus answered, "I told you that I am he. If you are looking for me, then let these men go."...Then the detachment of soldiers with its commander and the Jewish officials arrested Jesus. They bound him and brought him first to Annas, who was the father-in-law of Caiaphas, the high priest that year. Caiaphas was the one who had advised the Jewish leaders that it would be good if one man died for the people.

The soldiers and religious officials took Jesus to Pontius Pilate, the Roman governor. Pilate determined that Jesus had done nothing wrong, but he relented to the pressure from the Jewish leaders when he released Barabbas and sent Jesus to be scourged.

3) The Scourge and the Verdict (John 19:2-7, 12)

In the Praetorium courtyard, Roman soldiers tied Jesus to a "whipping post" and lashed him thirty-nine times with a cat-o-nine tails, which ripped hunks of flesh from his body, caused excessive bleeding and excruciating pain, and left Jesus virtually unrecognizable.

The soldiers twisted together a crown of thorns and put it on his head. They clothed him in a purple robe and went up to him repeatedly, saying, "Hail, king of the Jews!" And they slapped him in the face. Once more Pilate came out and said to the Jews gathered there, "Look, I am bringing him out to you to let you know that I find no basis for a charge against him." When Jesus came out wearing the crown of thorns and the purple robe, Pilate said to them, "Here is the man!"

As soon as the chief priests and their officials saw him, they shouted, "Crucify! Crucify!" But Pilate answered, "You take him and crucify him. As for me, I find no basis for a charge against him." The Jewish leaders insisted, "We have a law, and according to that law he must die, because he claimed to be the Son of God."…From then on, Pilate tried to free Jesus, but the Jewish leaders insisted that Jesus be crucified, shouting "Take him away! Take him away! Crucify him!"

Pilate gave Jesus to them to be crucified, and the journey to the cross began on the Via Dolorosa.

4) The Via Dolorosa to Golgotha (Mark 15:21-32)

The Via Dolorosa wound through Jerusalem. In agony, Jesus dragged his heavy cross as thousands of people watched on both sides of the narrow street. Consider that five days earlier his many followers cheered Jesus as he rode on a donkey's colt. As he dragged the cross that was his death sentence, a young father came to his aid.

A certain man from Cyrene, Simon, the father of Alexander and Rufus, was passing by on his way in from the country, and they forced him to carry the cross. They brought Jesus to the place called Golgotha (which means "the place of the skull"). Then they offered him wine mixed with myrrh, but he did not take it. And they crucified him. Dividing up his clothes, they cast lots to see what each would get. It was nine in the morning when they crucified him.

The written notice of the charge against him read: the King of the Jews. They crucified two rebels with him, one on his right and one on his left. Those who passed by hurled insults at him, shaking their heads and saying, "So! You who are going to destroy the temple and build it in three days, come down from the cross and save yourself!" In the same way the chief priests and the teachers of the law mocked him among themselves. "He saved others," they said, "but he can't save himself! Let this Messiah, this king of Israel, come down now from the cross, that we may see and believe." Those crucified with him also heaped insults on him.

5) The Crucifixion and Death (Mark 15:33-39)

At noon, darkness came over the whole land until three in the afternoon. And at three in the afternoon Jesus cried out in a loud voice, "Eloi, Eloi, lema sabachthani?" (which means "My God, my God, why have you forsaken me?"). When some of those standing near heard this, they said, "Listen, he's calling Elijah." Someone ran, filled a sponge with wine vinegar, put it on a staff, and offered it to Jesus to drink. "Now leave him alone. Let's see if Elijah comes to take him down," he said. With a loud cry, Jesus breathed his last. The curtain of the temple was torn in two from top to bottom.

The curtain was torn in two, signifying that God's people were no longer separated from him. When the Jewish people lost a loved one, they tore their clothes in mourning. Perhaps God tore the curtain because he mourned the loss of His Son.

And when the centurion, who stood there in front of Jesus, saw how he died, he said, "Surely this man was the Son of God!" Jesus' lifeless body was taken down from the cross before sunset according to Jewish tradition by Joseph, a rich man. Joseph anointed his body for burial and placed it in a freshly hewn tomb, which was sealed with a large stone.

Why did Jesus go through Hell Week? First, Jesus knew that he must fulfill the prophecies so that all humankind could be rescued for eternity, and he stayed alive on the cross for six hours in excruciating pain to demonstrate his perfect love. Second, he knew that each of us would go through Hell Weeks of our own when life seems overwhelming. Yet we can turn to Jesus, who did not opt out of Hell Week, giving us eternal hope because he overcame death. Let's recognize and appreciate the suffering that Jesus endured as God's perfect sacrifice as we anticipate the celebration on Easter Sunday.

29

Walking with Jesus

They asked each other, "Were not our hearts burning within us while
He talked with us on the road and opened the Scriptures to us?"
Luke 24:32

Most days part of my daily routine is to walk twice around my
neighborhood as I try to get in 10,000 steps. Usually I meet at least one
dog and the dog's owner. All of the dog owners in our neighborhood
leash their dogs, except one man. I have turned around and gone the
other way on numerous occasions when I saw them.

But my perspective changed on my walk last Saturday morning as
I spoke with a friend on the phone. He shared a saying that made me
consider how well-mannered dogs exhibit Christlike characteristics
such as obedience and loyalty. As I listened to his story, the man and
his leash-free dog, a handsome Golden Retriever, were coming down
the street.

In that moment I sensed God's presence. The dog ambled a few
feet behind the man. Usually the dog walks beside him, and sometimes
he walks a few feet in front of him. But without fail, he is always by
the man's side. I had never appreciated his steadfast obedience to his
owner.

After I came around the circle, I saw them again. I commented
about how well-behaved his dog is. The gentleman nodded, laughed
and said, "He won't even chase squirrels!" Note: There are many
squirrels in our neighborhood! For the Golden, it was all about walking with his owner.

Only hours after the resurrection, two disciples of Christ are walking to a village called Emmaus about seven miles from Jerusalem.

Suddenly Jesus appears beside them, and the knowledge that it is Jesus is hidden from them. He inquires why they are downcast.

One of them, named Cleopas, asked him (Jesus), "Are you the only one visiting Jerusalem who does not know the things that have happened there in these days?" "What things?" he asked. "About Jesus of Nazareth," they replied. "He was a prophet, powerful in word and deed before God and all the people. The chief priests and our rulers handed him over to be sentenced to death, and they crucified him; but we had hoped that he was the one who was going to redeem Israel. And what is more, it is the third day since all this took place" (Luke 24:18-21).

Jesus tells them everything about himself in the scriptures. As they approach the end of their journey, they insist that Jesus stay with them and have a meal. After Jesus breaks the bread, his identity is revealed, and Jesus disappears. They said to each other, "Were not our hearts strangely warmed as he revealed the scriptures to us?"

We never know when the presence of God will be revealed to us through everyday circumstances. When it happens, will we see it? We must develop a heart like Christ to see these glimpses of God in our lives.

The breaking of the bread was symbolic of the sacrifice of Christ's broken body just three days earlier. His death on the cross and resurrection makes it possible for us to walk with Jesus personally, just like the Golden Retriever and my neighbor. How are you responding to the opportunities for encounters with the risen Lord? Are you avoiding Jesus or walking with him?

When God reveals himself to us through circumstances, it can change our hearts. Now I look for the Golden Retriever and my neighbor on my daily walks!

30

The Two and the Ten

Joshua, son of Nun, and Caleb, son of Jephunneh, who were among those who had explored the land, tore their clothes and said to the entire Israelite assembly, "The land we passed through and explored is exceedingly good. If the Lord is pleased with us, he will lead us into that land, a land flowing with milk and honey, and will give it to us. Only do not rebel against the Lord. And do not be afraid of the people of the land, because we will devour them.
Their protection is gone, but the Lord is with us.
Do not be afraid of them."

Numbers 14:6-9

The Israelites, free after four hundred years of bondage in Egypt, prepared to enter Canaan, the land flowing with milk and honey that God had promised to their ancestors. Moses sent twelve leaders, one from each tribe, on a forty-day scouting report. He wanted to know what the inhabitants of the land and their cities looked like and if the land was fertile. The men returned with glowing reports of a land filled with rich produce. They even brought back a branch filled with grapes that were so plentiful that it took two men to carry the grapes that were draped over a pole.

But here came the buts, which demonstrated the unbelief of the ten men who reported, "**But** the people who live there are powerful, and the cities are fortified and very large" (Numbers 13:28). They had seen descendants of the giant Nephilim people. Then Caleb silenced the people before Moses and said, "We should go up and take possession of the land, for we can certainly do it."

But the men who had gone up with him said, "We can't attack those people; they are stronger than we are." The negative report about the land quickly spread among the Israelites. The ten men said, "The land we explored devours those living in it. All the people we saw there are of great size…We seemed like grasshoppers in our own eyes, and we looked the same to them" (Numbers 13:30-32).

All of the Israelites continued to grumble against Moses, Aaron and the Lord. Joshua and Caleb tore their clothes and said to the entire Israelite assembly, "The land we passed through and explored is exceedingly good. If the Lord is pleased with us, he will lead us into that land, a land flowing with milk and honey, and will give it to us. Only do not rebel against the Lord. And do not be afraid of the people of the land, because we will devour them. Their protection is gone, but the Lord is with us. Do not be afraid of them" (Numbers 14:6-9).

Joshua and Caleb believed that the Lord was with them, and that their strength and God's strength could overcome any foe that they would face. Today the names of those ten leaders are non-descript because their faith in God was weak, even after the miracles they had seen in Egypt. I suspect that very few babies were ever named after these men. Joshua and Caleb made it to the Promised Land, but the ten immediately died from a plague.

It takes courage, humility and conviction to stand up for Christ when we are the minority voice. We decide each day if we will speak boldly for God and realize the bountiful promises that he planned for us. My prayer for coaches and athletes is that they will seize the hope and a future that God created for them. God allows us to go through trials that serve to strengthen us, yet it is HIS strength that helps us overcome the challenges. God gives us the same strength that he gave Joshua and Caleb, which allowed them to be courageous. When we stand strong in our faith like Joshua and Caleb, God can use us to change someone else's world.

Here are five takeaways from the story.

1. **Speak up when you hear false reports**. Christians cannot remain silent any longer.
2. **Develop and maintain a "can do" attitude.** Joshua and Caleb believed that God would perform another miracle, just as he had done in Egypt.

3. **Trust God completely.** Caleb and Joshua understood who held their futures. We may not know our futures, but we can know the Living God who holds our futures.

4. **God gives each of us "hope and a future"** (see Jeremiah 29:11). We can each claim our hope and a future by trying to live in God's will daily. Scripture never tells us that realizing this hope and a future will simply be handed to us. Relying on God's strength and yoking ourselves to him is necessary to overcome the obstacles on our walk.

5. **Commit to daily RPOs** (Read, Pray, Obey) that help align our lives with God's will.

Keep persevering through the obstacles and confusion in this chaotic world. Partner with a fellow believer who will stand tall with you for Christ. It's all worth it!

31

Discipleship Impact! Part 1

My football athletes and I completed a nine-week study of the virtues
of 1 Timothy 6:11. I invited the athletes to share how our discussions
helped them grow in their faith.

John Michael DiRoberto (Roswell HS '20, Wofford College)

"My discussions with Rev Dan have helped me grow my faith in
multiple ways. When you are moving out of your house and living on
your own at college, you really have to learn to adapt and work
through new situations. A lot of that comes with not only maturity, but
through the word of God. Back at home, I wasn't able to be as disciplined. There's nothing or nobody to blame for that, but that's just how
it was."

John Michael explained how he now relies on the Word of God.
"To be able to face multiple challenges, I've relied on leaning into the
Word. Playing college football is not easy, and one of the main support
tools I've had going through this experience has been God's Word.
Through readings and multiple PowerPoint sessions with Rev Dan,
I've learned a lot of lessons. One of those lessons was about endurance
and perseverance. We've been over multiple situations where Jesus
had to endure and persevere. Endurance comes in my everyday life
here as a student-athlete. In my opinion, endurance ties to perseverance because the end result of enduring something is part of the overall
perseverance. Rev Dan and I went over a good example of endurance
that I had in high school. I endured a lot of pain when it came to injuries. But now, I look where I've come and notice that I've persevered
through it all. Without trials and tribulations, no person can grow."

John Michael shared how he has learned to grow despite disappointment. "One of the most devastating times I've had in football was

when I was told by a doctor that I couldn't play in the Walton game due to injury, especially because the game was on TV. I still think about that day. But I had to endure and overcome the fact that it happened. Now I look towards my faith and hope in situations like those. I think about how God has put me in a place where I'm meant to be for his purpose so that I can honor him on bigger stages like playing on ESPN. Not only does this learning apply to football, but to my life outside of football as well."

He explained how his prayer life has grown. "Not knowing answers to things really helps me lean on God. Through regular meetings and praying for others, some of my questions have already been answered. These disciplines have helped me mature and build my faith. I've become more reliant on the Word and pray much more often. I've learned new ways to pray, and to give thanks instead of praying for my wants. As Rev and I talked about, praying for your wants isn't bad, but when praying through God's will, he will answer and give you what you need, which is far more important than what you want."

John Michael shared some concluding thoughts about his faith journey. "My faith has grown a lot in the past two months at Wofford. I think about how there is always time for God because God is more important than anything else going on. Sometimes I stop what I'm doing and turn to the Word during tough times or even less eventful times. Being thankful is one of the most important parts of my relationship with God. Not only that, but the answers are there the more I pray and obey. I've learned God has a plan for me, and I've found myself more encouraged than I've ever been. Overall, my faith has taken over a big part of my life, and I've learned that faith and belief are very important."

Riley Easterly (Roswell HS '20)

Riley shared his appreciation for our discussions about faith. "The faith talk that we had was one that was very helpful to me because it is a daily challenge to have faith and rely on God, even when we think we are in control, so it was a good reminder to let go and let God."

Riley is interested in helping others know God. "I was able to help my friend start going to Bible study at his college because I was telling him what this discussion was doing for me as well as meeting with my small group."

Riley concluded, "Our discussions have helped me grow my faith by learning more about God, how mighty he is and that I want to be on "God's first team."

Note: The reference to God's first team was our discussion about the spiritual depth chart that you can read in this book. Riley's sincere desire is to become a disciple making disciples!

Connor Patterson (Pope HS '21)

"My discussions with you have helped me grow in my own faith immensely. When we first began meeting, I had only recently truly given my life to Christ. Our weekly discussions have helped me get to know God more and understand our relationship with him more and more. They have also just helped me be in a better place. I enjoy sitting down and talking about our weeks before we get into the lesson. Learning about the love and grace of God with you has been a great experience, and I don't think I would be this far in my journey without our weekly meetings. I am very grateful that we are able to talk every week!"

Trey Roth (Roswell HS '21, University of Georgia)

"Over the years, our discussions with Rev Dan have greatly helped me grow my relationship with Christ and with life in general. These discussions showed me how passionate people are about Christ and have motivated me to get to their level of relationship. In turn, these discussions allowed me to help spread my love of Christ with others."

32

Discipleship Impact! Part 2

Jeffery Lubin (Roswell HS '19, Anna Maria College)

The Faith Journey

Jeffery shared a story from this semester when he helped a class-mate with her faith journey.

"Rev Dan and I have been spending some time every week talking and learning about the words of Christ that have deepened my under-standing of the world around me. One day in my theology course, my professor put us into groups of two and asked us to talk about whether we believe in God or not. I was paired with a young lady who was skeptical about God. She stated, 'Why should I believe in God if he lets mothers lose their babies to cancer?' and "Why does God let all the bad things happen to us?'"

Jeffery explained, "I responded that we are given free will and that we could not truly appreciate living without feeling pain, that the pain that we have been through only makes us better, and we realize it when we are happy and look back. Maybe this never crossed her mind before, but she seemed to really understand what I said on a deeper level than I even meant it to be."

Jeffery concluded, "When our class came back together, a student asked the same question, and she recited exactly what I said and told our professor that I had explained that to her."

A pastor once told me that doubts lead to questions, questions lead to answers, and answers lead to increased faith. Well done, Jeffery!

The Test

Jeffery endured a 20-day COVID-19 quarantine this semester. He was contacted after a student tested positive, and Jeffery was moved to another dorm. He and I were on our weekly Zoom call when he received the news that he had tested positive. Jeffery was again moved to a different dorm where he rode out the extended quarantine. About his experience, Jeffery said, "I think it helped because I had some outside communication with others than just classes. We would talk about old high school days, and it gave me something to think about. It wouldn't have been possible (to stay faithful) if I weren't open to learning more about Christ."

Fortunately, Jeffery had a mild case, but he had to pass an EKG before returning to spring football practice. His faith was tested again when the initial attempts returned false results, but finally the EKG worked properly! Regarding the delay in the EKG results, Jeffery shared these thoughts, "Once I realized my nurse was getting bad results, I instantly started speaking to God and started hoping for the best."

The Reward

Early in the morning before Jeffery got on the team bus to travel to Endicott College, he and I prayed the following prayer together: *"We can do all things through Christ who strengthens us. If God is for us, who can be against us?"* Jeffery started at safety for Anna Maria College on a cold, rainy morning with temperatures in the mid-thirties. He was excited and thankful to play this next game in his college career almost eighteen months after his last college game in 2019. Praise the Lord that he received this reward following his hard work and perseverance!

Duncan Reavis (Blessed Trinity Catholic HS '21,
University of Georgia)

"The discussions have been so impactful for me during this semester because they have helped calm a lot of stress over college decisions and senior year. They have helped me stay consistent in my faith journey and encouraged me to grow in my prayer life and pray for others more. For example, I pray for someone in my contact list each day of Lent, which is an idea I originally got from you. I have taken some pieces of the lessons and shared them with friends of mine who have needed encouragement."

Several weeks after Duncan updated me, a coach told me that on the same day that he had a family emergency, Duncan texted him that he was praying for him on that day. The coach shared that he was at peace the remainder of the day, knowing that Duncan prayed for him.

Harrison Duncan (Roswell HS '21, The Citadel)

"During my final season of high school football, I had to play through a brutal injury that sidelined me every game. The rehab, strengthening, soreness and pain, on top of a tough academic load and extracurricular activities became a weight on my shoulders that never stopped growing. I had to pick between physical therapy and extra help sessions, which became a daily choice. Through Reverend Dan Farr and the FCA weekly meetings, I was able to take a minute and reflect on my situation while using the discussion of the week to help both myself and my teammates. Learning the RPO (Read, Pray, Obey) helped me further my relationship with God, as well as learn more about the Bible and faith. These meetings helped me get through the tough times with God's help and the help of my FCA brotherhood!"

Matthew Ford (Roswell HS '20, Grinnell College)

"Our weekly FCA discussions have helped me significantly over the past year. Being able to meet online consistently has given me much needed stability in my thrown off schedule. Discussing scripture with someone one-on-one has allowed me to really see how the Bible and its lessons apply to everyday life. Taking the time to dissect scripture makes the material much easier to digest, and it leaves a larger impact in my mind. These sessions have become a highlight of my week and have made me feel more comfortable than ever in regard to worshipping, praying, and reading."

33

Who Controls Your Mission on Earth?

"Houston, we have a problem."
Apollo 13 Commander Jim Lovell

I can quote many lines from *Apollo 13 The Movie*. "Houston, we have a problem," was altered for the movie and is a popular meme.

The movie plot is about how three astronauts, who were on NASA's third moon-landing mission in April 1970, were rescued after an explosion damaged their spacecraft. Hundreds of people at NASA Mission Control and three brave astronauts improvised a breathtaking return to Earth which saved the lives of Jim Lovell, Fred Haise, and Jack Swigert.

Tom Hanks portrayed Commander Jim Lovell. Prior to the Apollo 13 flight, Lovell was asked if he had ever encountered danger as a pilot. He recalled flying a fighter jet over the Pacific at night when his instrumentation went out, leaving him in pitch black darkness. He would have been forced to ditch his plane had he not spotted the trail of phosphorescent green algae that was churned by his aircraft carrier. He followed the green trail, the third point that he needed, to the carrier and completed his mission.

To execute the mission on earth that God has given us, we need a Third Person, the Holy Spirit, whose role in our lives is often underestimated and misunderstood. The Trinity consists of God, Jesus, and the Holy Spirit, who have never been separated and have always been connected before time began. Each has distinct functions but work seamlessly together. God is our Father and Creator. Jesus is God's Son whom God sent to save us from our sin and to teach us how to live. The Holy Spirit, which lives within us the instant that we receive Jesus into our lives, can help us in many ways that are detailed in the next two paragraphs.

After Jesus ascended to heaven, the Holy Spirit took his place on earth. *"But the Helper, the Holy Spirit, whom the Father will send in My name, He will teach you all things, and bring to your remembrance all things that I said to you"* (John 14:26). The Amplified Bible refers to the Holy Spirit as the Helper, Comforter, Advocate, Intercessor, Counselor, and Strengthener. The Holy Spirit helps us with our daily problems. We certainly have problems that need to be solved! The Holy Spirit helps us pray when we don't know how to pray or what to pray for (see Romans 8:26). The Holy Spirit powerfully reinforces our prayers to Jesus, who intercedes for us to God so that all three receive our prayers!

The Holy Spirit is eternal, holy, loving, truthful, all-knowing, all-powerful, and is in all places. The Holy Spirit has emotions, feelings, and a will. The Holy Spirit helped create the universe, helped generate Jesus Christ as a human, and inspired the Scriptures (see 2 Timothy 3:16-17). The Holy Spirit teaches, testifies, guides, convicts, regenerates, intercedes, and commands. The Holy Spirit can reason and think faster and more powerfully than all search engines combined.

The Apollo 13 astronauts would have been lost forever without Mission Control. We would be lost forever without the presence of the Holy Spirit. God means for every believer to experience the transforming power of the Holy Spirit, but we must yield control to the Spirit.

Will you allow the Holy Spirit to take control? When the Spirit controls us, we avoid giving into temptation, enjoy freedom and joy, produce the fruit of the Spirit, live as fully as God intends us to live, and courageously battle with a sense of boldness. When we allow the Holy Spirit to coach us continually, the Holy Spirit helps us complete our mission on earth to impact others for Christ.

34

I Chose You First!

You did not choose Me, but I chose you…

John 15:16

One of the most publicized weeks of the sports year is the NFL Draft, which occurred last week in Cleveland after being held virtually in 2020. NFL owners and general managers selected players who will hopefully make a significant difference in their teams for years to come.

Prior to the draft, aspiring athletes underwent a series of strenuous exams and workouts at the NFL combine and at Pro Days on college campuses across the country. A player hoped to impress one team so favorably that he is drafted in one of the first few rounds.

In 2021 Alabama and Ohio State tied for the most players drafted with ten, followed by UGA and Notre Dame with nine. Three of the 2020 College Football Playoff (CFP) teams were in the top four teams in terms of number of players drafted. Because LSU had fourteen draft picks in 2020 and Alabama had ten in 2021, including six first rounders, there appears to be a correlation between a high number of players drafted and a team's chance to win the CFP.

There is virtually no chance that a player can pick the team that drafts him. The owners and general managers control the draft. The player doesn't choose the team. The team chooses the player.

God chose us before we chose him. He chose us to be his children before time began. "We love God because He first loved us" (1 John 4:19). He wants to spend a lot of time with us, both here on earth through the Holy Spirit which lives inside each believer, and in heaven, where God will prepare a permanent and everlasting home for us.

But we must choose to follow Christ and remain in him. God appoints us to bear fruit and keep on bearing fruit that will remain and be a lasting demonstration of our love for him. An NFL player must produce for the relationship with his team to continue, but God loving us is not dependent on our productivity. However, Jesus challenges us to remain connected with him so that we will bear much fruit that lasts. John 15:5 says, "I am the vine; you are the branches. If you remain in me and I in you, you will bear much fruit; apart from me you can do nothing."

The average NFL career spans less than four years. When a player no longer produces, his relationship with the team ceases. Those who know Christ and are known by Christ should be grateful that if we have a low fruit-bearing season, we are still on God's team for eternity! But it is our responsibility as disciple makers to allow God to prune our non-fruit bearing habits and refine our good habits that produce even more fruit for his kingdom.

No matter how selfishly or pridefully we act, God still thinks we are the greatest thing going. Using a term for the last NFL draft pick, we will never become "Mr. Irrelevant" in his eyes. God makes us to be fruitful when we allow him to work through us and glorify him.

35

Student-Athlete Profile: Trey Roth

Senior Trey Roth was the starting nose guard for the 2020 Roswell Hornets. He started the season at offensive guard but unselfishly moved to help out the defense. I found out about the move when one of the boys on the scout team told me that he went up against Trey on defense, who did not call attention to the fact that he switched positions. That exchange is an indication of Trey's unselfish heart.

His work ethic on the football field and in the weight room is exemplary. Trey trained relentlessly to become stronger and improved his footwork, technique and speed to become a starter his senior season. When he was a sophomore on the scout team, a coach commented that Trey has the heart "of an All-American."

Trey has been highly active in our year-round FCA football huddles for three years. He is one of our most devoted disciples of Christ. Trey displayed spiritual leadership for his football team by introducing the speaker at the pregame meal and organizing the optional pregame prayer.

Trey Roth excelled in the classroom with a 3.8 unweighted GPA and a 3.98 weighted GPA. His ability in the classroom and on the field enabled him to receive his first college offer from a prestigious D-III college! Trey and I met virtually, and I asked him these three questions.

Dan: I could tell that you were thrilled after making your first varsity start on September 18. What have been your thoughts and emotions about this fall season when it appeared you might not have a senior season, and that the season could be interrupted at any time?

Trey: Going into this fall, I was filled with both excitement and anxiety. I knew that this would be my first real opportunity to prove myself but there is always that fear that we might get shut down. Something that has helped me throughout this tough process is to be focused on the things I can control. I've realized that if I dwell on the what if's, it will take over and suffocate my thinking.

Dan: What has our FCA huddle meant to you during your high school career?

Trey: The FCA huddle with my team means the world for me. These huddles show who my brothers really are, knowing that they will have my back no matter what, plus it has strengthened my relationship with Christ.

Dan: What difference has your relationship with Jesus Christ made in your life?

Trey: A relationship with Christ has been life changing for me. He has always been there for me through thick and thin. Even when I might drift away from him, he is always there for me when I need him.

Update: Trey played club rugby for UGA against numerous SEC rugby teams and is a second-year student at UGA.

36

Student-Athlete Profile: Harrison Duncan

Harrison Duncan was a senior inside linebacker at Roswell High School. It has been my distinct honor and pleasure to know Harrison for the past three years as a friend, a student-athlete, and brother in Christ. He frequently participated in our FCA football weekly discipleship huddles throughout the calendar year, and it has been a pleasure to interact with him on a consistent basis. Harrison reflects the light of Christ through his personal interaction, his engaging smile, and the way he lives his life. I have watched him live out his faith through his smart decision making, positive attitude, excellent leadership, and respectful demeanor.

Harrison is a doer of his faith. He created a fundraiser that raised enough money to buy two soccer goals for a lower-income neighborhood in Roswell. He and his senior teammates installed the goals, held a "grand opening" event for the neighborhood, and played soccer with the neighborhood kids!

Harrison is a very loyal, caring person and has a deep affection for his teammates. Having demonstrated great heart and leadership as a junior, Harrison was selected as a team captain for his senior season. I watched him bring his teammates together and encourage them after a coaching change was announced. Harrison's leadership was a significant reason that the team stayed on the same page despite the protocol restrictions and related obstacles.

Harrison is highly respected by his teammates and coaches. I was at weightlifting class when he attempted a personal record (PR) in the power clean. As he grabbed the bar, his teammates quietly surrounded him in a perfect half-circle, and they celebrated with him when he accomplished the lift. The way they locked in spoke volumes about their love for their teammate!

I admired Harrison's demeanor when he was sidelined with an injury during his junior year. His positivity never wavered even though he missed a number of games. Compared to many other teenagers that I have seen come back from injuries, his resilience and cheerful outlook was remarkable. In my opinion, it reflected his belief in God and his trust that God would see him through adversity. Harrison worked relentlessly to become stronger and returned as a starting inside linebacker his senior year!

He is a role model in every way and showed his teammates how to compete successfully and how to be a great person while you are doing it. Football is a year-round commitment in the highest classification in Georgia; yet Harrison performed equally well in the classroom with an unweighted average of 3.6.

Harrison is selfless and focuses on the team's success rather than personal statistics. His dedication to the team was apparent throughout practice and through his excellent habits on and off the field. Harrison's strong work ethic, leadership skills, teamwork, perseverance, and discipline will make him an outstanding collegian.

Harrison shared how FCA helped shape his life. "The Roswell FCA football ministry has been a second family to me. It already has my brothers in it, but FCA creates a deeper bond with my teammates, and has created my lifelong friends! The program has also provided a Bible study environment, where I am able to learn from the scripture, and develop deeper understanding of the Bible. These past three years with FCA have been a game changer for both me, and our team, helping us come together as one before each game!"

Update: Harrison is a second-year student at The Citadel in Charleston, South Carolina.

37

A Role Model for Our Time

And the Pharoah said to his servants, "Can we find such a one as this, a man in whom is the Spirit of God?"

Genesis 41:38

In the Old Testament, God is often referred to as the Father of Abraham, the Father of Isaac, and the Father of Jacob, who had twelve sons. Joseph was the youngest and was Jacob's favorite. Jacob gave him a coat of many colors. When he was seventeen, Joseph infuriated his brothers when he told them about his dream in which their sheaves bowed to his sheaf. Jacob had another dream that the sun, the moon, and the eleven stars bowed to him. Jacob took note.

His envious brothers threatened to kill him but instead sold him into slavery. His brothers drenched his multi-colored coat in goat's blood and gave it to Jacob, who wept and mourned the apparent loss of his son. Joseph was sold by the Midianites to Potiphar, the captain of the Egyptian guard and an officer of Pharaoh, the ruler of Egypt.

But the Lord was with Joseph, and he was a successful man. Because Joseph found favor with God, Potiphar made him the overseer of his house. However, Potiphar's wife attempted to seduce young Joseph, who resisted her advances. She accused him of attacking her, and Joseph was unjustly thrown into prison.

But God gave Joseph favor in the prison. The prison keeper gave him authority over all the prisoners. With God's help Joseph correctly interpreted the dream of redemption for Pharaoh's butler and the dream of death for Pharaoh's baker.

After Pharaoh learned about Joseph's interpretation, Pharaoh asked him to interpret his dream which involved seven blighted cows and seven blighted grain stalks which devoured seven plump, healthy cows. Joseph explained that the dream meant that there would be seven years of prosperity followed by seven years of famine. After interpreting Pharaoh's dream, Joseph was released from prison and was made the governor of Egypt at the age of thirty. Pharaoh recognized that the Spirit of God was with Joseph.

As the governor of Egypt, Joseph directed the gathering of seven years' worth of grain. During the seven years of plenty, he built storehouses and stored enough grain for the seven drought years. When all countries came to Egypt for grain, Joseph became the world's most prominent grain broker.

Meanwhile, in the land of Canaan, Jacob heard that there was grain in Egypt. He sent ten of his sons to Egypt to buy grain, but he did not send Benjamin, the youngest remaining son, lest calamity befall him as had befallen Joseph, his youngest. When Joseph saw his brothers, he turned away from them and wept.

Joseph gave his brothers grain, money and other supplies to take back to Canaan, but he insisted that they bring Benjamin back to prove that they were not spies. In other words, come back with Benjamin or you will see me no more.

After they ran out of grain, Jacob sent eleven sons, including Benjamin, back to Egypt. Joseph slaughtered an animal and held a feast for his brothers. Joseph said, "I am Joseph; does our father still live?" The answer was yes. Again Joseph wept when he saw them. He was especially moved to see Benjamin, weeping on his neck.

He sent them back with grain and provisions for the second time. Joseph insisted that his father come back to Egypt along with the families of his brothers. Pharaoh was supportive and promised them the fat of the land. The brothers returned to Canaan and told Jacob, "Joseph is still alive, and he is governor over all the land of Egypt."

Jacob agreed to come to Egypt, and his sons returned a third time, this time taking Jacob, their families, their livestock and belongings. Altogether there were sixty-six who settled in the land of Goshen, seventy including Joseph and his family.

Joseph ruled throughout the seven years of the famine, accumulating wealth by exchanging bread for land and money. Jacob died at age 130 and was taken back to Canaan for burial. Joseph died at age 110, and before he died, he said to his people, "God will surely bring you out of this land."

Indeed God did bring them out of Egypt. Jacob's twelve sons were the patriarchs of the twelve tribes, which became a great multitude. The Hebrew nation was placed into bondage by the new pharaoh and remained in slavery for four hundred years. Moses led his people out of Egypt, but they remained in the wilderness for forty years due to a lack of faith. After Moses died, Joshua became their leader and led the people across the Jordan River to the Promised Land.

Brad Lomenick summarized eight key leadership characteristics that Joseph demonstrated.

1. Principled - he had character and integrity. He was honest. He was tempted at multiple times, and he resisted.

2. Humble - the power and prestige of his position working for Pharaoh never changed him.

3. Disciplined - Joseph had the proper long term perspective, even while in jail for a crime he didn't commit.

4. Faithfulness - while in jail and throughout all of the turmoil, Joseph remained faithful to God and never wavered from his commitment to follow Him.

5. Grace and mercy - Joseph showed grace and mercy to his brothers, even though they had sold him into slavery.

6. Competence - he did his job with excellence. Whether as a servant, or the interpreter of Pharaoh's dream, or as the manager of the family sheep flock.

7. Wise - Joseph was wise beyond his years. He was thirty when he stepped in to help set up Egypt for the famine and demonstrated a seasoned perspective with decision after decision.

8. Strategic - Joseph was a planner. He instructed the officials to prepare for a famine, even though it was years away, gathering up food to store, even during the seven years of "plenty."

Joseph's life is a great roadmap for how to live our lives today. Joseph also put the vision that God gave him into action, and he demonstrated compassion for his brothers after estrangement for over twenty years. Let's consider how we can live out our lives more effectively according to the model that Joseph established. Read Genesis Chapters 37 through 50, one chapter per day for fourteen days, to experience Joseph's journey more fully.

38

Mark the Occasion

So Joshua called together the twelve men he had appointed from the
Israelites, one from each tribe, and said to them, "Go over before the
ark of the LORD your God into the middle of the Jordan. Each of you
is to take up a stone on his shoulder, according to the number of the
tribes of the Israelites, to serve as a sign among you. In the future,
when your children ask you, 'What do these stones mean?' tell them
that the flow of the Jordan was cut off before the ark of the covenant
of the LORD. When it crossed the Jordan, the waters of the Jordan
were cut off. These stones are to be a memorial to the people
of Israel forever."

Joshua 4:4-7

On May 11, 2021, Washington Wizard guard Russell Westbrook
broke Oscar Robertson's NBA record with his 182nd triple-double in a
game against the Atlanta Hawks. Westbrook immediately rushed to the
official holding the game ball. Hawks announcer Bob Rathbun said,
"He wants the ball to mark the occasion."

When I was a student, Georgia defeated Auburn at Auburn to win
the SEC Championship. I was among the Georgia fans who piled onto
the field after the game. There was a plastic forty-yard-line sideline
marker under the Georgia bench. I marked the occasion by stuffing the
marker under my jacket. That marker became the coffee table center-
piece in our Athens apartment!

For generations Americans have marked the occasions of major
sports achievements and championships with trophies, banners, retired
numbers, retired jerseys, rings of honor, parades, T-Shirts, caps, game
balls, rings, memorabilia and banquets. Joshua found a unique way to

mark the occasion after he led the Israelites across the Jordan River into the Promised Land.

Joshua and Caleb bravely told Moses and the grumbling Israelites that they should occupy the Promised Land that God had given them. However, the people of Israel were fearful and instead spent forty years in the wilderness. Following the death of Moses, Joshua became their leader and led them across the Jordan River. Here is how he did it.

The Lord told Joshua, "Moses my servant is dead. Therefore, the time has come for you to lead these people, the Israelites, across the Jordan River into the land I am giving them" (Joshua 1:2). Joshua ordered the officers to tell the Israelites to get their provisions ready. He identified forty thousand fighting men from the Reubenites, Gadites, and Manasseh to help the Israelites take possession of the land.

Joshua and the Israelites camped near the Jordan River, which had overflowed its banks at harvest time. There were the priests with the Ark of the Covenant, which contained the Ten Commandments tablets, the fighting men, and the Israelites. As soon as the priests entered the water, God backed up the river on both sides, just like he had done in the Red Sea. The priests stood in the riverbed until the fighting men and the Israelites passed through safely. As soon as the priests stepped onto dry ground, the river immediately went back to flood stage.

Then the Lord told Joshua to choose twelve men, one from each tribe, to take up twelve stones from the middle of the Jordan where they crossed over and place them at their campsite that evening. The twelve stones served as a sign. "In the future, when your children ask you, 'What do these stones mean?' tell them that the flow of the Jordan was cut off before the Ark of the Covenant of the Lord. These stones are to be a memorial to the people of Israel forever. Joshua set up the twelve stones that had been in the middle of the Jordan at the spot where the priests who carried the ark of the covenant had stood. And they are there to this day" (Joshua 4:6-7). Joshua marked the occasion of the Israelites crossing over the Jordan, symbolically going from death to new life.

Consider the life-altering events that have occurred in your lifetime such as births, graduations, weddings, jobs, big games and championships. Perhaps there have been failures, setbacks and disappointments which forced you to persevere, endure and overcome.

In which remarkable events in your life do you know that God was with you? When we acknowledge God's presence, that situation becomes a spiritual marker to mark the occasion.

Checking off answered prayers and remembering times when God brought you through gives you confidence when you experience the next big moment or obstacle. It's amazing to look back and see that God's mercy and grace went before us even when we did not realize it. That's how much he loves us!

Just as sports teams document major victories and commemorate titles, remembering the spiritual markers encourages us to stay centered on God and stay on his path. "The steps of a good man are ordered by the Lord, and He delights in His way" (Psalm 37:23). Let's remember to thank God when we mark our next occasion.

39

Life Is a Transfer Portal

But when the fullness of the time had come, God sent forth His Son, born of a woman, born under the law, that we might receive the adoption as sons.

Galatians 4:4

The college football world was stunned to receive the news that Mike Leach, the head football coach at Mississippi State, suffered a massive heart attack and passed away on December 13, 2022. Coach Leach battled pneumonia during the regular season.

After I stay with my grandson on Monday afternoons, I usually listen to music on the way home, but I tuned into the last hour of the Paul Finebaum Show because I wanted to get my latest fix on the College Football Playoff.

If you are not familiar with the Paul Finebaum Show, it's a four-hour call-in show hosted by Paul Finebaum that is almost exclusively about SEC football. The show is replete with loyal callers who describe themselves as "die-hard" Alabama or Auburn or Tennessee or Georgia fans. Many complain about somebody else's team while they tout their own. Callers have nicknames such as I-Man and Legend, who perhaps stirs up more emotion from listeners than any other caller.

But on this occasion, instead of the usual ranting and raving, caller after caller paid tribute to Coach Leach, who is incredibly popular across college football after coaching in the Big 12, Pac 12 and SEC. One man said that he had been angry with God after losing his mother and father, but lately he had been praying more and that he was praying for Coach Leach and his family. A staunch Ole Miss fan said she was praying for him, and she uttered two words that "I never expected I would ever say, 'Hail State.'"

Another man shared that when he was a Washington State graduate student while Coach Leach was the WSU head coach, he walked up to him outside a theatre in Pullman, thinking "What have I got to lose?" He spent the next thirty minutes talking to Leach, who spent time asking him about his graduate program and his life. I heard from others who shared how Mike Leach took the time to talk and express genuine interest in them. A Tony Dungy devotion reminded me that responding to life's interruptions and freely giving your time to others is a true expression of God's love.

But Legend was the caller who made the strongest impression on me. After he recalled a conversation that he had with Finebaum and Leach, he told Paul, "Life is a transfer portal." He alluded to the process whereby college athletes can exercise a one-time, penalty-free transfer to another college.

Life is a transfer portal. Those five words are a stark reminder that we pass from one portal to another throughout our lives. We move from infancy to childhood to high school to post-secondary education to a career to retirement to our final location on earth, changing physical locations along the way. From there we enter the eternal transfer portal to a destination that is determined by our faith commitment, or lack thereof, to Jesus Christ.

Jesus did not come through the transfer portal as the people of Israel expected. The Jewish community expected the Messiah to arrive as a conquering hero who would set them free after centuries of oppression. Instead Jesus arrived as a babe born to a virgin and wrapped in swaddling cloths. Jesus was the Messiah who was supernaturally conceived by the Holy Spirit yet born through natural childbirth in a stable in a nondescript town. For there is born to you this day in the city of David a Savior, who is Christ the Lord. And this will be the sign to you: You will find a Babe wrapped in swaddling cloths, lying in a manger (Luke 2:11-12).

Even today Jesus doesn't come when we expect him to come or in the manner that we expect. I heard a sermon that there is nowhere that Jesus has not been, and He brings his light to any situation. His light appeared repeatedly in the unlikely place of that call-in show. A pastor remarked, "We don't have the answers, but we know The Answer."

As believers prepare their hearts during Advent to celebrate the arrival of the Christ child, remember that the light of Jesus shines at Christmastime every year, but his light is with us every day.

Let's join countless others as we celebrate the iconic legacy of Coach Mike Leach, a true innovator who lived life to the fullest and blessed the entire landscape of college football.

40

He Was Just So Doggone Human!

"Pardon your servant, Lord," Moses replied. "Please send someone
else."

Exodus 4:13

My athletes, coaches and I completed a series on the life of Joseph
and began a series on the life of Moses. When you leave Genesis, you
come to Exodus and the story of Moses, the most famous man in the
Old Testament. I noted the similarities and differences of both men.

Joseph was the youngest of twelve brothers who were born in Canaan. He was a dreamer, and some jealous brothers sold him into slavery. Joseph was later sent to prison although he was a man of integrity.
Joseph was anointed with the Spirit of God and developed leadership
skills after being placed over all of the prisoners. Joseph's interpretation of dreams led to his appointment as the governor of Egypt at age
thirty by the "good" Pharaoh, who totally supported Joseph's work.
Joseph saved Egypt and many countries from a great famine. His father Jacob moved his sons and families to Egypt at Joseph and Pharaoh's request. Joseph rose from humble beginnings, overcame a painful twenty-five year separation from his family, and became a global
superstar!

Several generations later Moses was born in Egypt and was
adopted by a "bad" Pharaoh's daughter, who rescued him from certain
death. Moses grew up with many privileges in the royal court, but he
lost it all at age forty after angrily killing an Egyptian who was beating
a Hebrew. The word soon got to Pharaoh, and Moses fled to Midian to
save his life. He protected some young women watering their flocks
and received favor from their father Jethro, the Priest of Midian. Jethro
blessed Moses with a steady job and a wife, who bore him a son. He

also helped prepare Moses for his calling from God to rescue the Israelites from bondage. I suspect Jethro gave Moses a lot of good coaching! Moses was never a slave, but he experienced the hurt of his fellow Hebrews.

When God told Moses that he had been chosen to lead his people out of Egypt to the Promised Land, Moses offered many excuses. *I am not sharp enough, I do not speak well enough. I am so unworthy that I cannot even look at you. Who am I that I should go to Pharaoh? Please send someone else.* Moses was not exactly a profile in courage.

But God stuck with Moses and continued to instruct him and give him powers to demonstrate to the Israelites that God had indeed sent him. God used Moses to bring glory to his kingdom by using someone who lacked faith.

God allowed Moses to mature in a foreign land for forty years. When Moses was ready, God called him out of the Midianite bullpen and said (paraphrasing), "You will be my closer when I bring the Red Sea down on the Egyptian army in the bottom of the ninth."

Why wouldn't God choose a Joseph instead of a Moses to lead his people to freedom? Perhaps because Moses was just so doggone human, that God could put his full power on display so that Egypt and the Israelites would know, beyond the shadow of a doubt, that it was God who led the Israelites to freedom.

Has your life story been more like Joseph or Moses? My hat is off to you if you are more like Joseph. Keep doing what you are doing! I spent much of my life in the wilderness, then matured in my faith as I supported coaches and athletes. How many times have you blown it by reacting instead of responding? How many times have you doubted? Many of us are more like Moses than Joseph.

God can lead us to the freedom that can only be known through a relationship with His Son, Christ Jesus. He can use anyone in his kingdom work who is willing to give his or her whole heart and to trust him. Even though you may be so doggone human, God can use you to change others. God is much more concerned with our availability than our ability. Are you available?

41

Lord of the Ring – The Sequel

Trust the Lord with all your heart, and do not rely on your own understanding. In all your ways acknowledge Him, and He shall direct your paths.

Proverbs 3:5-6

William Muller is an outstanding student-athlete at Roswell HS (Class of 2022). He was seeded in the top five for 7A State competition in the shot put and discus, the only athlete to accomplish this double! William excels in the classroom with a 98.8 grade average (on a scale of 100) and completed four Advanced Placement (AP) classes during spring semester.

William became a fan of throwing after watching the Olympics as a child. He was not a natural-born thrower. In fact, he was undersized in middle school. After William hit his growth spurt in eighth grade, he was tall and thin. He lifted weights to improve his physique and become stronger, and that's when I met William. I observed a humble, hard-working young man. William gained seventy pounds since the end of his freshman year and now stands 6' 2" and 230 pounds!

William was mentored by Roswell teammate Zach Peterson (Class of 2020), who went on to throw hammer at the Naval Academy. Zach encouraged William and introduced him to his local throwing club. William has a great deal of respect for Zach, and William became the team leader of the Roswell throws group, which he said has been "like a little family to me."

His sophomore high school season ended abruptly in early March 2020 due to the pandemic. Although he missed his high school season, he continued to work extensively with his throwing club. The pause gave him time to get stronger and improve his technique.

William's goal was to throw the shot 55 feet ever since the coach at Army shared that standard in a letter to William. If William could throw 55 feet, it would open the possibility of attending prestigious West Point!

But he placed pressure on himself to perform at this high level on top of the stress of being "cooped-up" in the past year. After throwing 52 feet, 9 inches in March, William had tailed off going into region where he only threw 49 feet. He had very little working for him going into Sectionals at McEachern High School.

Sensing that William was feeling pressure, I sent him the video of Zach's testimony. In the video Zach explained to me that he "gave his throwing to God" and made him "Lord of the Ring" in the middle of his region competition. I hoped that Zach's story would give William needed inspiration. The night before Sectionals, William watched the video. He recalled, "The next morning I woke up refreshed, and it felt like a weight had come off my shoulders."

He took a knee before the Sectionals competition and said, "one more prayer." His first throw was 53 feet, but there was a mix-up by an official, and his throw was disallowed! William told me, "I was really frustrated!" But his coach eyed him, as if to say, don't lose your focus. Focus your energy on something positive. William's next throw was 54' 7", a Personal Record (PR) by two feet that would please the Army coach!

After achieving his goal which propelled him to State, William shared how he felt. "Ecstatic! It felt amazing! I said, 'Thank you Lord! I've been waiting so long!'" He added, "I stressed the whole season and was down going into region. After I gave God my throwing, it was like twenty pounds came off my back."

I asked William what he learned from this experience that he can apply to his faith. He had the following advice: "You have one life to live. Trust God with your life. God's looking out for you. Let him take over."

In the summer of 2021 William competed in two tremendous competitions, the USA Track and Field age-group nationals and the Junior Olympics! He received an invitation from the U.S. Military Academy, but he was unable to clear his medical exam. In the spring of 2022 William won the Georgia 7-A state championship in the shot and enrolled at the University of Alabama in the fall of 2022!

42

Hit the Pause Button

The earnest prayer of a righteous person has great power
and produces wonderful results.
James 5:16 TLB

Our daughter Jillian became a fan of international soccer when she stood in Barcelona's Catalonia Square with an estimated twenty-five thousand people and watched on a big screen as Spain defeated Germany in the 2008 Euro Cup final. She texted me this past Saturday that the Euro Cup was underway. I saw that Denmark and Finland were playing, which is not quite like France vs. Germany, so I changed channels. When I went back, the game had been halted for an injured player, but the mood was clearly different than usual on the field and in the broadcast booth. Christian Eriksen, a twenty-nine-year-old Danish midfielder, had collapsed, and his teammates were either in shock or in tears. The scene became absolutely riveting, and one announcer said that you could hear a pin drop in the Copenhagen stadium.

When I realized the situation was life-threatening, I texted Jillian. "Awful thing has happened to Denmark's best player at Euro Cup...pray for him...looks like they are giving him CPR..." She texted moments later, "Oh goodness!! Praying for him – that's so awful." Each of us hit the pause button to pray.

I texted back, "Danish team captain...29 years old...LMU's Hank Gathers situation" (Note: In 1990 Gathers collapsed during a Loyola Marymount basketball game and died two hours later at the hospital). "Game has been suspended. Thousands remain in the stadium awaiting word." Then came the tremendous news, "From UEFA...Eriksen has been stabilized!"

There were so many heroes. The medical team saved his life with decisive action. Eriksen "was gone" before he was resuscitated, said

Denmark's team doctor, Morten Boesen. "We got him back after one defib. That's quite fast," Dr. Boesen said.

Christian's teammates formed a human circle by locking arms with their backs to Christian to give privacy to their fallen teammate. Denmark's goalkeeper consoled Eriksen's distraught fiancée who came out of the stands.

It is possible for much good to come out of dire situations. Inquiries in Denmark about how to use a defibrillator rose sevenfold. Soccer fans from nations around the globe united to pray for Christian's life and thanked God that his life had been spared. Putting aside busyness and disagreements in a moment that we see much too infrequently, the world came together to pray as one for Christian.

Hit the pause button where you are. Close your eyes and ask God to reveal to you who in your family, your community or across the world needs prayer. The gift of prayer from God was never designed to be used just in emergency situations. Coach Andy Trevers wrote that his prayer is that we would make prayer our first response, not our last resort. Rev. Dennis Kinlaw wrote, "The most sacred and creative thing, the greatest work that any person can ever do, is to thank God, to praise him, and to pray."

I also thanked Coach Trevers for pointing out that there may have been people who prayed to God for the first time. Maybe those same people thought, If God saved Christian Eriksen, maybe he will help me in my predicament, and began to know God through the stirring of the Holy Spirit.

Before you leave home in the morning, hit the pause button, thank God for the day, and pray specifically for the people and situations that God places on your heart. James 5:16 (TLB) reminds us, "The earnest prayer of a righteous person has great power and produces wonderful results." You will be doing the work of a saint!

Footnote: UEFA paid tribute to Eriksen before Denmark's next game. A giant Denmark shirt with Eriksen's name and No. 10 shirt was unfurled on the field to a massive roar of approval from the fans. Such giant match shirts are unfurled for both teams before every game, but this was the first time a giant shirt carried a player's name. The Belgian national team presented Eriksen with a framed #10 Belgian jersey. The jersey was signed by all of the players and bore Christian's name.

At the ten-minute mark, because Eriksen wears #10, the Denmark and Belgium sides paid tribute to Eriksen and his miraculous recovery, and the sellout crown in Copenhagen paid tribute with a full-minute standing ovation. Eriksen is in a nearby hospital, and it was expected that he could hear the ovation from his hospital room. There could not have been many dry eyes in the house!

Denmark's team doctor reported that Christian will have a defibrillator implanted to help prevent future heart episodes. The device will be placed under Eriksen's skin to monitor his heart rhythm. The device tracks a person's heartbeat and can send electrical pulses to restore a normal rhythm as needed.

43
God Only Knows

God only knows what you've been through
God only knows what they say about you
God only knows the real you
There's a kind of love that God only knows.

God Only Knows by For King and Country

It saddened me to watch NBA star Ben Simmons struggle during the Hawks-Sixers series. The first overall pick in the 2016 NBA draft, Simmons, 24, will long be remembered for the following play in the fourth quarter of Game Seven. With the Sixers down by two, Simmons whirled around his defender and had a clear path to a dunk. Instead of dunking, he passed to a teammate because he did not want to get fouled and go to the free throw line, where he was shooting 35% in the series. The lack of expression on his face was evidence of the immense pressure that he had placed upon himself. Harsh criticism by basketball experts, a lack of support from the Sixer organization, and multiple trade rumors quickly followed.

I noted that Simmons was the third young sports star that has experienced recent mental duress. First, Naomi Osaka, 23, a four-time Grand Slam tennis champion, withdrew from the French Open and Wimbledon, citing a fear of press conferences that triggered her mental health issues. Osaka received criticism initially but eventually received significant support from numerous tennis legends who properly acknowledged that her mental health was the top priority.

Second, Matthew Wolff, 22, the 2019 NCAA individual golf champion, a winner on the PGA TOUR at age 20, and runner-up in the 2020 US Open, left the Tour for two months after his game went completely awry. Wolff spoke about increased expectations from himself and others that led to his decline. Fellow golf pro Bubba Watson described the anxiety that he experiences on a regular basis and offered advice to Wolff to help him. Wolff played well in the 2021 US Open and considered it a personal victory that he was even able to compete.

Mental health struggles are not new, but these three athletes are so young! Consider the pressure on high school athletes who compete for a limited number of college scholarships. For the fortunate recipients, the pressure increases as soon as they hit campus and begin to compete with older athletes who received an extra year of eligibility. The pandemic triggered an even greater struggle to keep those scholarships.

We will never know everything that these athletes are going through, but God only knows. My prayer is that each struggling athlete will turn to God for advice and counsel, strength and support. Here are some suggestions for how we can help them.

Touch base with athletes to see how they are doing and offer to pray specifically for them. A well-timed and thought-out call or text can be a powerful stress reliever.

Be a good listener who does not judge. Allow young people the space to express their feelings freely about the stress that they are experiencing from expectations placed on them by themselves or by others.

Be alert for signs of stress, anxiety and depression. No one is immune to anxiety and depression, but believers have inherent advantages through the power of the Holy Spirit to help them with their daily problems.

Help them fight their battles through consistent support, prayer, and presence. Text them appropriate Bible verses and encouraging words to give them hope and strength. Michael W. Smith wrote, "This is how I fight my battles. It may look like I'm surrounded, but I'm surrounded by You." Assure young people that God is always there to battle for them, even when God seems far away to them.

Encourage young people to define their inner circle, the people in whom they can confide. It is a privilege to be a member of a young person's inner circle!

Remind them that God knows exactly what they are going through, and that Jesus felt their pain here on earth. King and Country sings, "God only knows what you've been through, God only knows what they say about you, God only knows how it's killing you, But there's a kind of love that God only knows."

Finally, pray and pray some more! As you pray, believe that the young person will be blessed and protected. Pray as the apostle Paul taught us in Philippians 4:6, "Do not be anxious about anything, but in every situation, by prayer and petition, with thanksgiving, present your requests to God."

Mental health issues in sports are not going away. Thank God for the privilege to bear the burdens of young athletes who are struggling and try to love them unconditionally.

Here are more of God's promises that we can stand on.

- Fear not, for I am with you. Do not be dismayed. I am your God. I will strengthen you; I will help you; I will uphold you with my righteous right hand (Isaiah 41:10).
- Let him have all your worries and cares, for he is always thinking about you and watching everything that concerns you (1 Peter 5:7).
- Because God will be right there with you; he'll keep you safe and sound (Proverbs 3:26).
- How precious it is, Lord, to realize that you are thinking about me constantly! I can't even count how many times a day your thoughts turn toward me; they outnumber the grains of sand! And when I waken in the morning, you are still thinking of me (Psalm 139:17-18)!

44

God's Gift of Wisdom

The fear of the Lord is the beginning of wisdom.

Proverbs 9:10

Ever wish that you had a do-over for a decision you made? Of course! My father coached high school basketball for thirty seasons, and in retirement he would reflect more often on unwise decisions that cost him games more often than the victories.

King Solomon was considered the wisest man in the Old Testament. Solomon prayed to God and asked him for wisdom so that he could govern Israel effectively.

Consider this humble prayer that Solomon presented to God and see God's response. "And your servant is in the midst of your people whom you have chosen, a great people, too many to be numbered or counted for multitude. Give your servant therefore an understanding mind to govern your people, that I may discern between good and evil, for who is able to govern this your great people?" It pleased the Lord that Solomon had asked this. And God said to him, "Because you have asked this, and have not asked for yourself long life or riches or the life of your enemies, but have asked for yourself understanding to discern what is right, behold, I now do according to your word. Behold, I give you a wise and discerning mind, so that none like you has been before you and none like you shall arise after you." 1 Kings 3:8-12

Wisdom is one of the greatest gifts that we can ever receive from God. It's the gift that keeps on giving. Note that 1 Kings 3:10 says, "It pleased the Lord that Solomon had asked this (for wisdom)."

Read this sentence aloud and substitute your name for Solomon's.

It pleased the Lord that (your name) asked for wisdom.

I think that it's awesome that I could please God by merely asking him for wisdom, one of his greatest gifts. God will freely give us wisdom throughout our lifetime when we remain in relationship with him and his son Jesus and *remember to ask*. Wisdom helps us make the best choices, large or small, keeps us out of situations that result in undesirable consequences, and helps us recover from bad situations.

What are you wrestling with that seems unsolvable or insurmountable? Ask God for wisdom to help you with and through that situation. Let's give him thanks for being there for us and give him all glory, honor and praise for all he has done for us. Just ask him!

45

Sloshing

But how can I ever know what sins are lurking in my heart?
Cleanse me from these hidden faults.

Psalm 19:12

The entire country of England was optimistic as their team faced Italy in the Euro Cup Final. The English team sent their fans around the world into delirium by scoring in the third minute. Italy tied the game 1-1 in the second half, and the game went to penalty kicks (PKs) after 120 minutes.

England took a 2-1 lead in PKs, but Marcus Rashford and Jaydon Sancho, who were inserted into the lineup just before the second extra period and did not have time to get into the flow of the game, missed. A friend shared that when Rashford hit the post, the air went completely out of a group of English fans at a local sports bar. After Bukayo Saka missed the fifth and deciding kick, England's fate was once again sealed as had happened so many times since 1966.

Unfortunately, many frustrated and disgruntled fans lambasted those three young players on social media with stereotypical racial epithets for missing the kicks AND being Black. Although the English Football Association, the Prime Minister of England, and their teammates quickly came to their defense and condemned the slurs, they could not stop the actions which created an ugly cloud that overshadowed a great sporting event after England came out of COVID lockdown.

What were the conditions of the hearts of those people who posted slurs after the missed kicks? They were *the same before and after* the kicks. Those racist positions existed regardless of whether the kicks had been made. The sins concealed in their hearts would eventually spill out.

The late Rev. Dennis Kinlaw shared a story about a professor who asked one of his students to come forward and shake his arm while the professor held a cup filled with water. The student shook his arm, and water flew everywhere! The professor asked the student why water spilled onto the floor. The student replied, "Because I shook your arm!" The professor explained, "No, the reason was that there was water in the cup. If there had been no water in the cup, there would have been no spillage."

When you suffer an unexpected loss, or things don't go your way, or you lose your temper after a player runs a drill wrong, what sloshes out of your heart? Matthew 12:34 (TLB) reminds us, "Out of the overflow of the heart, the mouth speaks." You can no more put words back in your mouth than the professor could put all of that water back into his cup. Proverbs 4:23 advises, "Above all else, guard your heart, for *everything you do* flows from it."

Ask God to help you deal with any sin that creates "sloshing" and hinders your witness for his kingdom. The great news is that there is forgiveness for our sins through confession because of Christ Jesus, who made all things possible through the cross.

46

Ring the Bell!

The bells will be heard when he enters the Holy Place…

Exodus 28:35

Becca and I took our daughters Allison and Jillian to numerous UGA football games when they were children. Gameday was much simpler then. We drove past the UGA Arches on Broad Street and took the first right. If we arrived ninety minutes before game time, we parked curbside on the side street that borders North Campus.

Becca and I set up our tailgate picnic on the lawn while Allison and Jillian played on the low-hanging branches of stately magnolia trees. But our favorite activity was ringing the chapel bell. After a win, UGA fans ring the chapel bell until midnight, and when the Dawgs defeat their arch-rival, fans have been known to ring the bell all night long!

We waited for our turn, and I eased the rope down so that Allison or Jillian could wrap themselves around it. I would grab the rope, give it a hard pull, and the recoil lifted us into the air! I managed four or five consecutive pulls. What a joyride! We looked forward to the exhilaration of ringing the bell after a Georgia win!

On July 7, 2021, our family celebrated a different kind of victory after I completed my twenty-eighth and final treatment for prostate cancer. This condition was under surveillance for two years, and my urologist informed me that it was time to act.

Becca and I chose the Emory Proton Therapy Center located in midtown Atlanta. I cannot say enough good things about Emory's medical staff during my treatment cycle. When Becca asked me how it was going during the first week of treatment, all I could say was, "Everybody is so nice!" Not only did the technicians make me feel at ease, but after I shared my preference for Contemporary Christian Music (CCM) during treatment, they played CCM each time that I entered the treatment room. Frequently I heard my favorite songs, *Oceans* by Hillside United and *Between You and Me* by DC Talk, which became my walk-up song, sort of like a batter walking up to home plate!

In the Old Testament Aaron the priest wore a holy garment laced with golden bells which could be heard as he entered the Holy Place. The good news of the Gospel is that through Christ's death and resurrection, we are no longer restricted to worshipping God in only one place. A holy place can be anywhere that we convene with our Father and His Son. The treatment table became my holy place as I listened to the lyrics and remembered that I was covered in prayer.

I saw the bell each day in the lobby, but I could not ring it until I completed my treatment. I was pleased for other men who rang the bell, which gave me hope that it would eventually be my turn! Often, we are tempted to ring the bell prematurely, but God needs us to go the distance to complete a work in us so that we can encourage others. Men with cancers much more severe than mine inspired me with their courage and strength. I was lifted by their positivity and tried to return the favor.

I am very thankful that God gave me the strength to continue my virtual and on-campus ministry schedule. I am so grateful for the prayers from my family and friends. Becca even sent me multiple Bible verses each morning before I left for treatment. Here are some of those verses that can help you endure until you ring the bell on the other side!

- Look to the Lord and His strength; seek His face always (1 Chronicles 16:11).
- Cast all your anxiety upon Him because He cares for you (1 Peter 5:7).
- Rejoice always, pray continually, give thanks in all circumstances; for this is God's will for you in Christ Jesus (1 Thessalonians 5:16-18).
- Finally, be strong in the Lord, and in His mighty power (Ephesians 6:10).
- But they that wait upon the Lord shall renew their strength. They shall mount up with wings like eagles; they shall run and not be weary; they shall walk and not faint (Isaiah 40:31).

- So do not fear, for I am with you; do not be dismayed, for I am your God. I will strengthen you and help you; I will uphold you with my righteous right hand (Isaiah 41:10).
- For the joy of the Lord is your strength (Nehemiah 8:10).
- Do not be anxious about anything, but in every situation, by prayer and petition, with thanksgiving, present your requests to God. And the peace of God, which transcends all understanding, will guard your hearts and your minds in Christ Jesus (Philippians 4:6-7).
- But My God will supply all your need according to His riches in glory by Christ Jesus (Philippians 4:19).
- God is our refuge and strength, our ever present help in trouble (Psalm 46:1).
- The LORD watches over you—the LORD is your shade at your right hand; the sun will not harm you by day, nor the moon by night. The LORD will keep you from all harm, He will watch over your life; the LORD will watch over your coming and going both now and forevermore (Psalm 121:5-8).
- Give thanks to the Lord, for He is good. His love endures forever (Psalm 136:1).
- And we know that in all things God works for the good of those who love Him, who have been called according to His purpose (Romans 8:28).

47
Guard Your Yard

Keep your heart with all vigilance, for from it flow the springs of life.

Proverbs 4:23 (ESV)

College basketball analyst Jimmy Dykes uses creative terminology and witty sayings when he describes action. One of his favorite terms is "guard your yard," which means to defend your assigned area on the court. Whether you are playing man-to-man or zone, do your job and guard your space.

If your opponent with the ball is slower than you, pressure your opponent aggressively and try to force a turnover. If both of you are similar in quickness, give your opponent a full step (three feet) when you establish your guarding position. However, if your opponent is much quicker than you, give your opponent two full steps (six feet minimum) to keep from giving up a layup or a dunk.

Out of all the COVID variants thus far, the Omicron variant is the most contagious. If you are fully vaccinated, continue to give yourself ample space and protection around unvaccinated people. Fully vaccinated people get COVID from this variant, though typically the in a milder form. We who are vaccinated must continue to "guard our yard."

Here is a second illustration. The majority of Fortune 500 companies use a metric called the Net Promoter Score, which measures the enthusiasm of a company's customer base on a ten-point scale, where 1 is low and 10 is high. Promoters give a score of 9 or 10, passives give a score of 7 or 8, and detractors give a score of 6 or less. Companies focus on maintaining promoters and moving passives toward becoming promoters. Promoters of the vaccine can pray that the Holy

Spirit will make *key information points uniquely available to passives* so that they confidently and safely move forward with receiving the vaccine and saving lives.

Join me in praying that children under five, who are currently ineligible to receive the vaccine, can become eligible in the days, weeks and months ahead. Our prayers make a dramatic difference because there is great power in prayer. James 5:16 reminds us that the fervent prayer of a righteous person has great power and wonderful results. If you sincerely hope that the vaccine spreads more rapidly, pray daily for the passives that you know and those who are ineligible to become eligible. Keep a mask on you in case you are "pressed" unexpectedly. Protect your health and the health of your loved ones by guarding your yard!

48

Is God Number One in Your Heart?

I am the Lord, and there is no other. There is no God besides me.

Isaiah 45:5

Georgia was crowned 2021 college football national champions and number one in the land following their win over Alabama. The next day the "way too early" preseason poll revealed the pollsters' choice for number one in 2022. There are even online blogs which daily track each team's ranking in recruiting for the 2023 and 2024 seasons!

Speaking of number one, if you ranked your interests and passions weekly in 2021, how many weeks would your relationship with God occupy the top spot? Your work, family, school, favorite teams, hobbies, social media, blogs, the Internet, and TV broadcasts can all vie for number one in your life.

Consider the number of hours you spend weekly in each area that did not include God. God can be number one on Sunday morning, but by Monday morning, has he slipped in your poll? How about on Friday evening after the world has dragged you through the mire? Has the enemy separated you from your relationship with God and pushed him further down your poll?

How many first-place votes for your relationship with God would family members, close friends, and co-workers give you? God can quickly be displaced from the top if you lose focus on him. If God consistently falls behind idolatrous things, which is anything that becomes more important to you than God, your relationship with God will suffer.

Idolatry can also occur as the result of falsehoods which occupy your mind and your heart. When falsehoods conflict with Christ's teachings, Christians need to resolve this conflict. In the very last chapter in the Bible, Jesus warns that there is no room in God's kingdom for "everyone who loves and practices lies" (Revelation 22:15). Christians need to understand Scripture so that we do not become deceived.

A disciple of Christ represents Jesus in words, deeds, actions and thoughts. Guard your heart so that you consistently reflect the love of God. "God Is love" (1 John 4:8). Love God. Love your neighbors as yourself. Place your trust in God, His Son, Jesus Christ, and God's will for your life.

Satan attempts to grab a toehold in your life and make it a foothold, which can lead to a stronghold that can possess you. John 8:44 reveals the following about Satan: "...not holding to the truth, for there is no truth in him. When he lies, he speaks his native language, for he is a liar and the father of lies."

An example of the practice of lies are the murders and heinous atrocities against the Black residents of the Tulsa, OK neighborhood of Greenwood that were covered up for almost one hundred years by the city of Tulsa. But construction has begun on a Greenwood museum whose artifacts and stories will display the truth for generations to come, and the truth will help Tulsa residents move forward. I encourage you to watch a documentary on Greenwood such as Tulsa Burning: the 1921 Race Massacre on the History Channel.

But there is hope for living a life based upon the Truth, Jesus Christ. "Then you will know the Truth, and the Truth will set you free (John 8:32)", and "Therefore, if the Son makes you free, you shall be free indeed (John 8:36)." Follow Christ and demonstrate daily how he is more important than anything to you.

"Because you belong to Christ Jesus, God's peace will stand guard over all your thoughts and feelings. His peace can do this far better than our human minds" (Philippians 4:7). Protect your heart and keep God number one by being careful of your intake and gaining discernment through the understanding and application of Scripture with help from the Holy Spirit.

49
Swallow Your Pride

Pride lands you flat on your face;
humility prepares you for honors.

Proverbs 29:23 (MSG)

Remember the Titans was a movie about the T.C. Williams Titans high school football team from Alexandria, Virginia. The movie was released in 2000 and is one of the all-time classic football movies. Our daughters Allison and Jillian were extras in a crowd scene that was filmed at the Sprayberry High School stadium in Marietta, Georgia. They came home after midnight with *Remember the Titans* T-Shirts, which would be a collector's item today. Few people envisioned how popular the movie would become.

Two scenes from the movie stood out to me. The first scene was when Coach Bill Yoast, the defensive coordinator, benched Alan, a Titan defensive back. Alan's dad, Mr. Bosley, was irate as Sheryl, Coach Yoast's daughter, explained, "He's getting beat like he stole something!" To his credit Alan swallowed his pride and humbly supported his coach's decision. Alan would receive a second chance in the state semifinal game.

The second scene also involved Coach Yoast, the defensive coordinator whose ego clashed occasionally with Head Coach Herman Boone. In the locker room at halftime of the state championship game, Coach Yoast walked up to Coach Boone and said, "Herman, I sure could use your help. Ed Henry (the opposing head coach) is kicking my (butt) out there." Coach Yoast swallowed his pride and asked for help.

Gymnast Simone Biles displayed humility after her disastrous first vault in the Tokyo Olympics women's gymnastics team competition. She could have possibly landed flat on her face due to a case of the "twisties," which makes a gymnast lose track of body rotation. Simone admitted to her coaches and teammates that she just didn't have it. Simone, the GOAT of gymnastics, told her team that she needed help on the biggest stage in sports. Paraphrasing, she told them, "I'm giving you my position." Biles swallowed her pride and found herself surrounded by love within her inner circle.

With her frank confession about her mental state of mind, Simone Biles showed young athletes that you should speak up when you don't have it all together. On the NBC telecast former Olympic champion Michael Phelps, who has also experienced mental struggles, shared his foundation's motto, "It's okay not to be okay."

Are you experiencing a stretch when you are not ok? Who among us has had a stretch that wasn't ok during the pandemic? It's okay to be vulnerable and tell someone about it!

God only knows what you've been through, God only knows what they say about you, God only knows the real you. Swallow your pride and admit it when you are not okay in the following five areas: emotionally, mentally, morally, physically or spiritually.

A coach described life balance as a wheel supported by five spokes. When our life is in balance, the wheel rolls smoothly. But when a spoke is broken or missing, the wheel won't look right, and it's going to roll rough. Are you rolling rough today? Proverbs 29:23 from The Message states, "Pride lands you flat on your face; there is honor in humility." Swallow your pride and humbly tell someone, "I'm broken." Tell God. He is always there to help when you swallow your pride and turn to him.

50
Discover an Extra Gear!

Now to him who is able to do immeasurably more than all we ask or imagine, according to his power that is at work within us.

Ephesians 3:20 NIV

The Olympics always delivers exceptional stories, even when the stands in Tokyo were virtually empty. Track and field events were my favorite events of the Tokyo games. The highlights of track and field were the showdowns between Norwegian Karsten Warholm and Rai Benjamin for the men, and Sydney McLaughlin and Dalilah Muhammad for the women, in the 400-meter hurdles. Both races obliterated the world record (WR)! Warholm broke his WR by 0.76 seconds and McLaughlin broke her WR by 0.44 seconds. Benjamin and Muhammad, the runners-up, easily broke the previous WR.

As great as the McLaughlin/Muhammad race was, the race between Warholm and Benjamin was even more electrifying, and I almost missed it! I fell asleep on the sofa, woke up, told my wife that I was going to bed, and headed upstairs. But I looked back at the TV and saw that the men's 400-meter hurdles race was about to begin, so I scrambled downstairs to watch. I'm glad that I did because the following day one writer called it "the best race in Olympic history."

Warholm's race strategy was typical, which was to run as fast as possible the entire race and hold off any challengers down the home stretch. In the last one hundred meters, Benjamin made up significant ground and was a few feet behind Warholm as the men cleared the last hurdle. Usually the runner gaining ground continues that momentum through the finish line. Not this time because the extraordinary happened! Warholm found an extra gear, accelerating through the last twenty meters and pulling away from Benjamin to win in a new world record time of 45.94!

I asked a local sprint coach, "How did Warholm find an extra gear?" He explained that Warholm "has an amazing training program and a desire to succeed like no other." Warholm has found an extra gear against Benjamin before. I searched "Warholm extra gear" on the Internet and found this recap in a European track and field article, "In 2019 Karsten Warholm ran the second-fastest time in history when he held off a late challenge from American champion Rai Benjamin to clinch the men's 400 metres hurdles at the Diamond League finals on Thursday. Benjamin appeared to be gaining near the finish line before Warholm found an extra gear and pulled away again to win in a time 0.14 seconds outside American Kevin Young's world record of 46.78 set in 1992." Warholm ran 46.92 in 2019 and an astounding 45.94 in Tokyo, almost a full second faster!

When you have pushed as hard as you possibly can, and you still haven't reached the finish line, how can you find an extra gear? Our power is finite, but God's power is infinite. The apostle Paul described the equivalent of an extra gear in Ephesians 3:20 (NIV), telling his readers, "Now to him who is able to do immeasurably more than all we ask or imagine, according to his power that is at work within us. Immeasurably more than anything we ask or imagine is pretty amazing!

The Message describes the extra gear as follows: "God can do anything, you know—far more than you could ever imagine or guess or request in your wildest dreams! He does it not by pushing us around but by working within us, his Spirit deeply and gently within us" (Ephesians 3:20-21). The Amplified Bible translation provides further emphasis. "Now to Him who is able to [carry out His purpose and] do superabundantly more than all that we dare ask or think [infinitely beyond our greatest prayers, hopes, or dreams], according to His power that is at work within us, to Him be the glory in the church and in Christ Jesus throughout all generations forever and ever" (Ephesians 3:20-21).

If we are about to conclude that we've done all that can possibly be done, God promised us an extra gear to accelerate through the finish line, not simply collapsing over the line in sheer exhaustion. Are the pressures of a trial, a project, or a family crisis gaining ground and breathing down your neck? Trust the Lord because he has an extra gear!

51

Slinging It!

David said to the Philistine, "You come against me sword and spear and javelin, but I come against you in the name of the Lord Almighty, the God of the armies of Israel, whom you have defied. This day the Lord will deliver you into my hands, and I'll strike you down and cut off your head...All those gathered here will know that it is not by sword or spear that the Lord saves; for the battle is the Lord's, and he will give all of you into our hands." Reaching into his bag and taking out a stone, he slung it and struck the Philistine on the forehead. The stone sank into his forehead, and he fell face down on the ground. So David triumphed over the Philistine with a sling and a stone; without sword in his hand he struck down the Philistine and killed him.

1 Samuel 17:45-47, 49-50

Virtually everyone is familiar with the story of David vs. Goliath. The triumph of the underdog has been shared in many pregame talks before important sports contests. But could David have really killed Goliath with a sling and a stone? How fast would the stone need to travel? How much would the stone need to weigh? How could David score a kill shot on the first attempt under immense pressure?

Goliath was nearly ten feet tall and wore one hundred twenty-six pounds of armor. He talked trash for forty consecutive days and challenged Israel to a "Best on Best" duel. But David, who split his time between tending sheep and bringing food to his three oldest brothers on the battlefield, defended Israel and the Lord God Almighty. David yelled, paraphrasing, "Who does he think he is, trash talking *us* like that?"

David volunteered to face Goliath, but King Saul thought he was too young and too small. However, David had trained for this moment by killing lions and bears that attacked David's flock. He believed God would deliver him from Goliath, just as God delivered him and his sheep from those predators.

It was time for the showdown. David's armor was too heavy, so he removed it and faced Goliath with a sling and five stones. Here is some background on "slingers." Judges 20:15-16 described this specialty position in the Benjaminite army, "At once the Benjaminites mobilized twenty-six thousand swordsmen from their towns, in addition to seven hundred able young men from those living in Gibeah. Among all these soldiers there were seven hundred select troops who were left-handed, each of whom could sling a stone at a hair and not miss." I cannot tell you why they were all left-handers, but everybody knows that a left-hander's ball just moves differently than a righty's! It is a reasonable assumption that these slinging skills were passed down from generation to generation.

So how fast was the stone going when it crashed into Goliath's forehead? I found this recap. In 2013, tests were conducted at the University of Nebraska to evaluate the effectiveness of the sling throughout history. When using a leather or cloth sling with a sling stone that matched the archaeological record for Iron Age (the date of the story of David and Goliath), it resulted in a velocity of the stone reaching between 50-55 m/s (meters per second and roughly 120-125 mph) with a range of accuracy at 65 yards (195 feet). Due to the training needed to obtain true accuracy, its use was limited to those, like the Benjaminites, who were especially skilled with the sling shot.

To give you an idea of how David's fastball could have stacked up against today's athletes, here is a comparison. Fastest recorded football thrown at NFL Combine – Tyrod Taylor 60 mph; Fastest recorded baseball thrown - Adonis Chapman 105 mph; Fastest home run exit speed – Fernando Tatis 116 mph; David's stone estimated by the University of Nebraska – 120 to 125 mph; Fastest recorded tennis serve – Sam Groth 163 mph; Fastest recorded jai alai ball – 187 mph; Fastest driver golf ball speed – Bryson DeChambeau 203 mph.

Goliath was slowed by his armor and could not dodge the baseball-sized stone which sizzled through the air toward his forehead. *Smack*! David successfully took the biggest shot of his life and saved Israel from the wrath of the Philistines.

Here are a few questions to ponder from David vs. Goliath. I suspect that there were slingers that King Saul could have summoned from his bullpen. Why didn't anyone besides David step up and take the shot against Goliath? Because only David trusted God to fight his battle and deliver him victoriously.

Think of a situation when you trusted God to help you take a big shot, either on or off the field. How did you muster the courage to take on your Goliath? Perhaps due to past failures, you are hesitant or lack confidence to take the next big shot. Where and how do you need God to help you take that shot? Stand on God's promise found in Joshua 1:9, "Have I not commanded you? Be strong and courageous. Do not be afraid; do not be discouraged, for the Lord your God will be with you wherever you go." God is always there to help you take your biggest shots. Remember that being well-prepared is essential and that your battle is the Lord's. Trust him with the outcome.

52

Be Somebody's Jonathan!

Saul's son Jonathan became one in spirit with David
and loved him dearly.

1 Samuel 18:1

The story of David and Jonathan is a story about brotherly love, right doing, and loyalty. After David slew Goliath, the lame duck King Saul became insanely jealous of David after the Hebrew women sang, "Saul has slain thousands and David ten thousands." Driven by an evil spirit, Saul attempted to kill David on numerous occasions. Jonathan, Saul's son, was keenly aware of the royal depth chart which showed David as number one in line for the throne and Jonathan as number two. Despite all of the power, wealth, and prestige that Jonathan would have gained if David died, Jonathan developed a deep and abiding friendship with David and was fiercely loyal to him.

As found in 1 Samuel 20:1-4, David asked Jonathan, "How have I wronged your father, that he is trying to kill me?", and added, "Yet as surely as the Lord lives and as you live, there is only a step between me and death." Jonathan replied, "Whatever you want me to do, I'll do for you."

Jonathan reassured David that he would protect him. He risked his life by "testing the water" to find out if his father was indeed after David's life. Saul hurled a spear at Jonathan, who was righteously indignant about his father's behavior and treatment of his beloved friend.

Jonathan helped David with the plan that would determine Saul's motive. Jonathan shot three arrows and announced, "Look, the arrows are beyond you," which were the code words to let David know he was now a fugitive. Jonathan already knew that David could never return to the palace, but these words must have hit David almost as hard as he struck Goliath. The scripture from 1 Samuel 20:41-42 tells us, "...David got up from the south side of the stone and bowed down before Jonathan three times, with his face to the ground. Then they kissed each other and wept together—but David wept the most. Jonathan said to David, "Go in peace, for we have sworn friendship with each other in the name of the Lord, saying, 'The Lord is witness between you and me, and between your descendants and my descendants forever.'" That must have been some bro hug as they departed!

Just as Jonathan cared for David, David cared for Jonathan and his family after ascending to the throne. David and Jonathan met only once more, shortly before Jonathan's death, yet their incredible bond lasted.

How many ways did Jonathan help David? He had David's back when Saul lashed out in jealousy and rage. He risked his life and protected his friend despite the power of the throne that he could have gained. Jonathan lived out this commandment that Jesus shared centuries later, "Greater love has no one than this; to lay down one's life for his friends" (John 15:13). He joined with David in spirit which connected these two friends who had strong personal relationships with God. Jonathan loved David unconditionally despite their vastly different social, economic, and political backgrounds. The two men openly expressed their love for each other. He helped develop and carried out David's request to determine Saul's intentions. Surely Jonathan prayed often for David's safety.

What if we actually lived out Jonathan's character traits for family members, fellow coaches, and friends? Think about who your Jonathan is. Now, whose Jonathan can you be? Jackson Browne penned this lyric in his hit song, Somebody's Baby, "She's gonna be somebody's only light..." Who is going through a trial and needs encouragement and help? You can be somebody's Jonathan, the light that somebody needs.

53

Mercy and Grace

I cry out to God Most High, to God, who vindicates me. He sends from heaven and saves me, rebuking those who hotly pursue me—God sends forth his love and his faithfulness.

Psalm 57:2-3

David and his band of warriors were on the run from King Saul, who was focused on taking David's life. As David and his men hunkered down in a cave, Saul walked in to take care of his business. David's men pleaded with him to take Saul's life, which was there before him on a silver platter. But David, who was next in line for the throne, rebuked his men, saying, 'The Lord forbid that I should do such a thing to my master, the Lord's anointed, or lay my hand on him; for he is the anointed of the Lord' (1 Samuel 24:6).

David gave Saul grace when he spared his life. He refused to place himself on the throne, waiting for God to place him at the appropriate time. Instead of getting revenge and talking trash to Saul, David bravely confronted him. He bowed and said to Saul, "Some urged me to kill you, but I spared you; I said, 'I will not lay my hand on my lord, because he is the Lord's anointed.'… May the Lord be our judge and decide between us. May he consider my cause and uphold it; may he vindicate me by delivering me from your hand" (1 Samuel 24:10, 12).

Saul responded, "You are more righteous than I," he said. "You have treated me well, but I have treated you badly. You have just now told me about the good you did to me; the Lord delivered me into your hands, but you did not kill me. When a man finds his enemy, does he let him get away unharmed? May the Lord reward you well for the way you treated me today. I know that you will surely be king and that the kingdom of Israel will be established in your hands. Now swear to me by the Lord that you will not kill off my descendants or wipe out my name from my father's family" (1 Samuel 24:17-21).

Saul was deeply repentant, weeping aloud and calling him son. He acknowledged that David did not kill him when he was delivered into David's hands. How many men in a thousand would have spared Saul's life? In what must have been sweet music to David's ears, Saul finally admitted that the kingdom of Israel will go to David. Saul saved face when David mercifully gave Saul his word that Saul's descendants and family name would survive.

Dr. Charles Stanley explained the difference between mercy and grace. Mercy is not getting what you deserve. Grace is getting what you do not deserve. Here is a marvelous example of granting both mercy and grace. Jay Carty, the co-author of a devotional book with Coach John Wooden, gave this example of mercy and grace. Paraphrasing, an athlete broke numerous team rules. His coach disciplined him with twenty sprints. After the athlete completed ten sprints, the coach said, "You can stop." Cancelling the last ten sprints was mercy. After ten sprints, his coach says, "You can stop. I will run the last ten for you." The coach's sacrifice for his athlete was grace.

Our Lord and Savior Jesus Christ embodied mercy and grace for six hours as he painfully labored through thousands of breaths on that cross. "He himself bore our sins in his body on the cross, so that we might die to sins and live for righteousness; by his wounds you have been healed" (1 Peter 2:24). Jesus gave us mercy by absorbing the punishment for our sins. Jesus gave us grace through his sacrifice, which created the way to eternal life with him.

54

Close Encounters of the Holy Kind

The steps of a good man are ordered by the Lord,
and he delights in his way.

Psalm 37:23

Ron Washington is the highly respected third-base coach for the Atlanta Braves with over fifty years in professional baseball as a player, manager and coach. A third-base coach typically only gets noticed when a runner is called out at the plate.

When a third-base coach holds up both hands, that is the signal for the runner to stop. The runner has two choices, slam on the brakes and scamper back to third, or run through the stop sign. If the runner runs through the stop sign, either he didn't see the coach or he thought his judgment was better than the coach's judgment.

David ran through one stop sign and would have run through a second one except for a "close encounter of the holy kind" with Abigail, the beautiful, intelligent wife of the rich, surly, mean Nabal. David had protected Nabal's shepherds and his flock of three thousand sheep from Philistine raids. He needed to feed his army and asked Nabal to compensate him and his army for their valuable service.

David sent ten young men from his army to inquire, but Nabal rejected David's request, acting as if he did not recognize David's name, which was famous across Israel. David reacted angrily to the news and told his men they were going to kill Nabal and every man who worked for him. Although David did not seek vengeance from Saul in the cave, he failed to act properly toward Nabal. One of Nabal's servants pled David's case to Abigail. Unbeknownst to Nabal, she and his servants quickly gathered food and provisions for David's army and journeyed to deliver them.

Their encounter is described in 1 Samuel 25:20-31. As she came riding her donkey into a mountain ravine, there were David and his men descending toward her, and she met them. David had just said, "It's been useless—all my watching over this fellow's property in the wilderness so that nothing of his was missing. He has paid me back evil for good. May God deal with David, be it ever so severely, if by morning I leave alive one male of all who belong to him!"

When Abigail saw David, she quickly got off her donkey and bowed down before David with her face to the ground. She fell at his feet and said: "Pardon your servant, my lord, and let me speak to you; hear what your servant has to say. Please pay no attention, my lord, to that wicked man Nabal. He is just like his name—his name means Fool, and folly goes with him. And as for me, your servant, I did not see the men my lord sent. And now, my lord, as surely as the Lord your God lives and as you live, since the Lord has kept you from bloodshed and from avenging yourself with your own hands, may your enemies and all who are intent on harming my lord be like Nabal. And let this gift, which your servant has brought to my lord, be given to the men who follow you."

Delivering her closing plea humbly, respectfully, and convincingly, Abigail concluded, "Please forgive your servant's presumption. The Lord your God will certainly make a lasting dynasty for my lord, because you fight the Lord's battles, and no wrongdoing will be found in you as long as you live. Even though someone is pursuing you to take your life, the life of my lord will be bound securely in the bundle of the living by the Lord your God, but the lives of your enemies he will hurl away as from the pocket of a sling. When the Lord has fulfilled for my lord every good he promised concerning him and has appointed him ruler over Israel, my lord will not have on his conscience the staggering burden of needless bloodshed or of having avenged himself. And when the Lord your God has brought my lord success, remember your servant."

When he sought vengeance, David ignored the first stop sign, the guidance of the Holy Spirit. Perhaps David and his men could have taken any of several paths, but they could not possibly avoid Abigail and her servants in the mountain pass. That meeting in God's perfect timing was the second stop sign that God placed in his path. Abigail diffused the situation by bringing the supplies to David's army that he needed. Just as Saul listened patiently to David, David listened patiently to the fervent plea of a woman during a time in history when women were not properly respected.

David's reply is captured in 1 Samuel 25:32-34. David said to Abigail, "Praise be to the LORD, the God of Israel, who has sent you today to meet me. May you be blessed for your good judgment and for keeping me from bloodshed this day and from avenging myself with my own hands. Otherwise, as surely as the LORD, the God of Israel, lives, who has kept me from harming you, if you had not come quickly to meet me, not one male belonging to Nabal would have been left alive by daybreak."

How can we recognize the seemingly chance encounters that are designed by God to help us? How do we spot God's stop signs to pull up and wait, and those times when he passionately waves us forward with his blessing? We must first believe that these encounters actually take place in our everyday lives. Our obedience is dependent on the condition of our relationship with him and the rule of the Holy Spirit in our hearts at any given moment.

Oswald Chambers addressed random events in his classic, *My Utmost for His Highest*. Chambers wrote, "Never believe that the so-called random events of life are anything less than God's appointed order. Be ready to discover His divine designs anywhere and everywhere." Furthermore, Chambers stated, "A saint realizes that it is God who engineers his circumstances." He added, "Yet we never realize that all the time God is at work in our everyday events and in the people around us. If we will only obey, and do the task that He has placed closest to us, we will see Him."

Before exclaiming "What a small world!" after an encounter, remember that it is God alone who engineers close encounters of the holy kind. May we realize much more often when God places someone or something in our lives that helps us stay on track, and may we give him the glory!

55

From the First Snap

Then (Jesus) said to them (the twelve disciples): "Whoever wants to be
my disciple must deny themselves and take up their cross daily
and follow Me."

Luke 9:23

I received a tweet that featured Notre Dame Head Coach Brian
Kelly awarding a game ball to JD Bertrand, a Blessed Trinity Catholic
HS (Roswell, Georgia) graduate and linebacker for the Fighting Irish.

After Notre Dame's narrow victory over a two-touchdown underdog Toledo squad, Coach Kelly highlighted JD's intensity level as follows: "brought the intensity level ...that everybody has to see...," "you
could see his intensity level every snap...," and "that's the type of intensity that is needed from the first snap, not when the game is on the
line." Coach Kelly sent his players a clear message that they needed to
play with intensity from the first snap.

"From the first snap" can also indicate the intensity level of a disciple of Christ, a person who has made a total commitment to be like
Christ and to work purposefully to transform lives and expand God's
kingdom. God desires that we represent him honorably from the moment that we wake up in the morning until we fall asleep at night. If
we consistently incorporate RPO'S (Read the Bible, Pray often, Obey,
and Serve others) into our daily game plan, when a family member or
friend is experiencing an issue, then we will be prepared to rise to the
occasion for that person!

I watched a powerful video, *The Problem of Discipleship*, by
Mark Clark, a pastor in Vancouver, BC, and captured a number of his
remarks which are in quotes. "The bar of discipleship is high. The call
of discipleship is costly. Discipleship must cost us something. Becom-

ing a disciple is difficult." Think of the thousands of hours it takes to become a great student-athlete, coach, teacher, and professional. Clark emphasized that becoming a disciple of Christ was never supposed to be easy and hoped that every new Christian could understand the difficulty.

Clark emphasized three main components of being a disciple: deny yourself, take up your cross daily, and follow Jesus. First, "To deny yourself in a find-yourself culture is very challenging. We must deny the impulse for material goods to have precedence in our lives." Second, the Romans used crosses to kill people. God used this horrible tool of death for eternal purposes. Jesus took up his cross and carried it to Golgotha, where he died on the cross for our sins and was resurrected on the third day. What does it mean for us to take up our crosses daily? It means to make Jesus our top priority each day. Third, Clark emphasized the importance of what you follow and who leads you. Disciples passionately follow Jesus, are led by him, and live out his teachings and share them with others.

From "the first snap" on an ordinary day, what is our level of intensity to live that day as a disciple of Christ? Clark shared that mastering a discipline or skill requires ten thousand hours. If we devote only one hour per week, that is a 200-year pace! How many hours are we spending each week to become disciples so that we can love others as Jesus loves them? Is Jesus the master of our time? Let's schedule time daily in our calendars to be with the Master.

Becoming an effective disciple is heavily dependent on cultivating a daily relationship with Jesus Christ and the quality and consistency of our RPO'S. Our growth as disciples ceases when we abandon the RPO'S. Let's vow to take up our crosses daily with intensity from the first snap!

56
Strength Under Control

"Blessed [inwardly peaceful, spiritually secure, worthy of respect] are the gentle [the kind-hearted, the sweet-spirited, the self-controlled], for they will inherit the earth."

Matthew 5:5 AMP

Mahatma Gandhi founded the nonviolent freedom movement in India and was most instrumental in freeing his country from British rule in 1947, one year before he was assassinated in 1948. In 2014 I toured the majestic Aga Khan Palace, which features the Gandhi National Memorial, in Pune, India. Gandhi was imprisoned for his protests in this palace for twenty-one months between 1942 and 1944. In a nondescript gift shop on the back of the property, I bought a copy of Gandhi's autobiography for thirty rupees (forty cents) and read it on my return flight. I discovered that Gandhi considered Jesus's Sermon on the Mount a most powerful doctrine that appealed deeply to him. However, he never converted to Christianity because he was turned off by the self-righteousness of some Christians that he met in South Africa.

The Sermon on the Mount begins with the Beatitudes, which notes eight types of blessed people that represent the characteristics of a Christlike person. I have often struggled to adequately understand and explain the concept of gentleness or meekness, one of the eight. "Blessed [inwardly peaceful, spiritually secure, worthy of respect] are the gentle [the kind-hearted, the sweet-spirited, the self-controlled], for they will inherit the earth" (Matthew 5:5 AMP).

According to the Henry Commentary, the gentle (meek) "quietly submit to God, can bear insult, return a soft answer, and keep possession of their souls. Meekness promotes comfort and safety, even in this world." Even that commentary did not put me at ease. I thought, *Gentle still seems a little weak.* However, the Guzik Commentary completed the meaning for me. Guzik stated that "meek in Greek means strength under control," which was my breakthrough for understanding gentleness!

You may be entering the "second season" when the last half of the schedule means more. How are you displaying strength under control? The world applauds and champions the intense, fiery, win-at-all-cost approach, but the Spirit helps you protect and nurture relationships with your student-athletes. Continue to be kind-hearted, sweet-spirited, and exhibit strength under control. Quietly submit to God, bear insults and setbacks with class, return soft answers, and keep possession of your soul. When you consistently exhibit strength under control, which you and your athletes need in the waning moments of a close contest, your coaching legacy will last far beyond this season's outcome and the seasons to come.

Gandhi appeared frail due to his many fasts, but he remains a sterling example of strength under control over seventy years after his passing. Regarding Gandhi's rejection of Jesus, it is so important that we represent Christ to others through love, mercy, grace, and compassion. When we strive to emulate the Beatitudes and demonstrate strength under control, God can use us in powerful, eternal ways.

57
Walk the Halls

"Blessed are the poor in spirit, for theirs is the kingdom of heaven.
Blessed are those who mourn, for they will be comforted.
Blessed are the meek, for they will inherit the earth.
Blessed are those who hunger and thirst for righteousness,
for they will be filled.
Blessed are the merciful, for they will be shown mercy.
Blessed are the pure in heart, for they will see God.
Blessed are the peacemakers, for they will be called children of God.
Blessed are those who are persecuted…,
for theirs is the kingdom of heaven.

Matthew 5:3-10 NIV

It has been traditional for decades for high school varsity football players to wear their game jerseys to school on Friday game days from August through November, possibly into December.

If a team achieves the goals they set in preseason, players will have from six to ten more opportunities to wear their jerseys on Fridays.

Two things are obvious. The player is on varsity and his team plays that evening! A player doesn't have to notify his teachers and classmates that he is on the team.

If you are a player, do you need a number 1 jersey and "Christ" on the back for people to identify you as a Christian, a member of God's team?

Is it possible for your faith in Jesus to be as apparent to others, as it is apparent that you are a football player when you wear your team's jersey? It is possible when you consistently live out the following eight Christlike characteristics:

- Poor in spirit – totally reliant on God's power; walk humbly.
- Mournful – repentant for sins; constantly seeks cleansing of the Spirit.
- Gentle – kind-hearted, sweet-spirited, meek, strong and under control.
- Hunger and thirst for righteousness - actively seek right standing with God; yearn for righteousness to play out in the world.
- Merciful – patiently bear afflictions while helping those in misery.
- Pure in heart - integrity, moral courage, and godly character.
- Peacemakers – love, desire and delight in peace; keep and recover peace.
- Persecuted – endure suffering and painful circumstances, willing to sacrifice.

Which ones are holding you back? Game plan it with God. Play to your spiritual strengths and attack those weaknesses through scripture, persistent prayer, and fellowship with other believers. "Iron sharpens iron" (Proverbs 27:17).

As you walk the halls and throughout your day, strive to represent Christ in all you do. May you have the reputation of a person who places God first each day and doesn't need crosses, bracelets, or T-Shirts to announce your faith. Let the life you live for Jesus go before you! "In the same way, let your light shine before others, that they may see your good deeds and glorify your Father in heaven" (Matthew 5:16).

58
Love Them Like Jesus!

"You have heard that it was said, 'You shall love your neighbor (fellow man) and hate your enemy.' But I say to you, love [that is, unselfishly seek the best or higher good for] your enemies and pray for those who persecute you,

Matthew 5:43-44 AMP

It would be easy to read Matthew 5:44 and simply check the box that we love our enemies. But where is the proof? The Enduring Word commentary points out, "To truly fulfill this law we must love, bless, do good and pray for our enemies – not only our friends. Love our enemies; bless them as we can (judgment is not here yet)."

Consider who our enemies are. Who have we refused to love? Perhaps there are persons that have rubbed us the wrong way, have taken cheap shots, gotten under our skin, wronged us, engaged in petty disagreements, acted selfishly, and failed to act for the higher good.

If I love someone, does it mean that I must also like them? After reading an article on goodfaithmedia.com, I believe that Jesus loves and likes everybody. Jesus never hated anyone, even the people who persecuted and killed him. "Father, forgive them, for they do not know what they are doing." Jesus dislikes a person's wrongful actions and hates all sin. Jesus always separates the sin from the person. Are we capable of achieving that same separation through the work of the Holy Spirit, which is God in us?

"But I say to you, love [that is, unselfishly seek the best or higher good for] your enemies and pray for those who persecute you," (Matthew 5:44 AMP). How can we ever hope to love the people who make us angry and tie our stomachs in knots when we hear their names or voices? Will we hold grudges for the wrongs they committed against us or against society? While studying the Sermon on the Mount, I admitted that I didn't love some people and attempted to change my heart.

Ask God to help you find positives about a person you dislike, even if you consistently disagree with their motives and sinful actions. Look for common ground such as similar likes, interests, family ties, and stages in life. One positive is that we are all created in God's image. "God created mankind in his own image, in the image of God he created them; male and female he created them" (Genesis 1:27).

Jesus said to pray for those who persecute you. Prayer is a wonderful place to start! Ever keep a prayer list of people that you haven't loved as you should? Print the names of up to five people who have persecuted you, directly or indirectly, on a note card. Note: *You don't have to know the person*. The person can be in the news or social media. The person can even be yourself, a young man reminded me, since sometimes we can be our own worst enemy.

Place the list where you will see it each day. Commit to pray for these five people. You might be thinking, *How should I pray for them*? Pray for their souls. Pray for their families. Pray for them to seek the higher good and the best interests of others. Commit to pray for twenty-one consecutive days because twenty-one days can create a habit that lasts for a lifetime.

After twenty-one days of prayer, examine your list. Are there names that you can eliminate because you genuinely love them? Did your list shrink, grow or remain the same? Why? Now examine your heart. Are you praying for more people and loving more people like Jesus? I encourage you to share your findings with another believer.

On the fifth day of my commitment, I discovered that praying for these people has improved my attitude toward them. I hope that I allow God to mold and shape my heart so that I harbor no ill will.

Consider this next step. Is there a relationship that needs to be reconciled? Minister Quentin Jones preaches the need for more love, forgiveness, and reconciliation (LFR), which is making peace. After praying consistently for these people, may love, forgiveness and reconciliation flow freely.

Prayer changes us and increases our love, and we can use this increased love to forgive and reconcile. Here are several verses in support of LFR.

Jesus replied: "'Love the Lord your God with all your heart and with all your soul and with all your mind.' This is the first and greatest commandment. And the second is like it: 'Love your neighbor as yourself' (Matthew 22:37-39).

"A new command I give you: Love one another. As I have loved you, so you must love one another. By this everyone will know that you are my disciples, if you love one another" (John 13:34-35).

"For if you forgive other people when they sin against you, your heavenly Father will also forgive you. But if you do not forgive others their sins, your Father will not forgive your sins" (Matthew 6:14-15).

"So if you are presenting your offering at the altar, and *while* there you remember that your brother has something [such as a grievance or legitimate complaint] against you, leave your offering there at the altar and go. First make peace with your brother, and then come and present your offering" (Matthew 5:23-24).

"All this is from God, who reconciled us to himself through Christ and gave us the ministry of reconciliation: that God was reconciling the world to himself in Christ, not counting people's sins against them. And he has committed to us the message of reconciliation" (2 Corinthians 5:18-19).

59

Prepare and Share

For wisdom is a protection *even as* money is a protection,
But the advantage of knowledge is that wisdom shields *and* preserves
the lives of its possessors.

Ecclesiastes 7:12

After the pandemic began in March 2020, I could no longer spend time on high school campuses. I used the extra time to compile a Ziploc bag full of pregame talks and stories to create a book. One entire Saturday I searched the Internet for a cover photo which blended football, spirituality, and brotherhood.

After viewing hundreds of photos, I saw this photo of two Texas high school football players clasping hands and praying after a game in the fall of 2019. The two athletes had been teammates on a 7-on-7 team that summer, and the White athlete prayed for the Black athlete's mother who was battling Stage Four cancer. I showed Becca the photo and announced, "This is the one!" She immediately agreed, and this photo graced our book cover. It seemed that the Holy Spirit led me to the photo. It was exactly what I was looking for!

In August 2020 Ty Jordan tweeted that his mother had died following her battle with cancer. Jordan, a University of Utah running back, was named 2020 AP Pac-12 Newcomer of the Year and Pac-12 Offensive Freshman of the Year. On Christmas Night, December 25, 2020, ESPN announced that Ty Jordan had died of an accidental gunshot wound that may have been self-inflicted. Gage Smith, who prayed with him, said, "Seeing the type of person that kid is and seeing his heart for other people, that's what I want people to remember about him...As good as he was, you would want to remember the type of person he is."

Then on September 25, 2021, exactly nine months later, came the shocking news that Aaron Lowe, a University of Utah football player, had died in an apparent homicide at a party following Utah's home game. Aaron and Ty were high school teammates in Mesquite, Texas, and had become the best of friends. The Utes family credited Lowe with persuading Jordan to commit to Utah. Lowe switched his jersey number from No. 2 to No. 22 to honor Jordan's legacy. Fittingly in August 2021, Aaron Lowe received the first Ty Jordan Memorial Scholarship, which is awarded to a student-athlete who exemplifies the inspiring qualities that Jordan displayed through his work ethic, positivity and perseverance through adversity.

Like Jordan, a scholarship has been established in Lowe's name at the University of Utah. "Aaron was an amazing son, brother, friend and set an example for his teammates as a leader on the Utah football team. He was loved by all. The Aaron Lowe Memorial Scholarship will be awarded to a student-athlete in the football program who exemplifies the inspiring qualities Aaron displayed through his determination, dedication, and leadership," the scholarship page reads.

Gene Wojciechowski aired a video tribute to Lowe and Jordan on ESPN College Gameday. The ESPN story documented how the grief-stricken Utah football team had traveled to West Mesquite, Texas, for both funeral services. Utah Head Football Coach Kyle Whittingham, who has a photo of both young men on his desk to remind him of the fragility of life, made the first contribution to the Lowe scholarship. The University of Utah created a memorial Portal 22 in Rice-Eccles Stadium and will retire the number 22.

I was stunned on Christmas night when the photo of Ty and Gage praying flashed on the screen. A teenage athlete texted me, "Isn't that the photo on your book?" I struggled to make sense of these tragic stories with a clear linkage to the young man on my book cover. What do I do with this unusual circumstance? How can this inexplicable loss of life and resulting sadness and grief for Ty's family, Aaron's family, their friends, the young man who prayed for Ty, the Utah team, and the Mesquite community happen?

My men's group discussed the long odds of miracles and unusual events. The odds are astronomical that I would select this photo, that a young man in the photo would die from a gunshot wound, and his high school and college teammate would also die from a gunshot wound in an unrelated incident. It was time to share this story.

After my first draft of this devotion, the Atlanta Journal-Constitution reported that a young teen was allegedly shot and killed by an older teen at a house party after midnight. Perhaps you will read this account and be prompted by the Spirit to help young men become more aware of the dangers in society. Raising awareness can help young men make better choices when they truly connect with the risk and potential consequences. Studies show that a young Black male is almost six times more likely to die from a homicide than from a suicide. If you have influence in the lives of young athletes, share the story of these two young men and add your perspective.

As Christ followers who have gained wisdom and knowledge from a plethora of life events, we have valuable perspectives to share. In his book *Uncommon Life*, Coach Tony Dungy encourages us to invest in others. He wrote, "Whatever God has poured into your life is something you can pour into others' lives. You have received from (God) freely; freely give to whoever needs your encouragement, your advice, and your love."

Our wisdom will be of limited value unless we prepare and share. "But the advantage of knowledge is that wisdom *shields and preserves the lives of its possessors*" (Ecclesiastes 7:12). Sharing your wisdom and experiences are invaluable for young people who believe they are infallible and bad things won't happen to them. Offer them shields that will preserve their lives. Prepare and share, and God will bless it for the greater good.

60

A Second Chance to Love Them Like Jesus

I will give you a new heart and put a new spirit in you; I will remove from you your heart of stone and give you a heart of flesh.

Ezekiel 36:26 NIV

As I walked through my neighborhood, I was troubled by negative thoughts about the things that were not happening in my life. Then I heard the song, "God Only Knows," that helped sustain me during my prostate cancer treatments. The Spirit reminded me of all the wonderful things that were happening and "flipped the field" on my attitude! I slept more peacefully.

Then I read and discussed Matthew 5:44," ...love your enemies and pray for those who persecute you." I accepted the 21-day challenge to pray for five people against whom I had been harboring ill will, bitterness, or resentment. I challenged other brothers in Christ to accept the challenge. Here are some of our experiences and thoughts.

For me, it felt strange the first few days to pray for people that I previously would not have prayed for, but now it seems natural. The Holy Spirit led me to pray more specifically, most notably Ezekiel 36:26, "...I will remove from you your heart of stone and give you a heart of flesh."

What I discovered is that God softened my heart. Some mornings after I awakened, the first thing that I did was pray through the list of persons while lying in bed. When I saw or heard these people or their names, my heartbeat didn't quicken, and my emotions did not race. When I learned about an improper action by one of these people, I was much more able to separate the action from the person for which I was praying.

Others shared these thoughts about the impact of the prayer challenge. *I am (hesitant) to try it...I forgave the person and put it behind me...I missed some days but prayed on other days...I added a couple of names to my list...I would describe it as a softening of my heart...I contacted someone and said you need to let it go...I find myself praying for the people on my list at random times...I took exception to the actions of the people that I am praying for...(praying) gave me a healthier perspective...I added two people from social media who irritated me...I can see them in a different light."*

If you were too busy or weren't quite ready the first time, here is a second chance to accept the 21-day prayer challenge. If you list the people that you struggle to love and make praying for them a daily priority, there is a great chance that you will be a little more like Jesus in three weeks.

Here is the chorus from Zach Williams' song, Less Like Me. *A little more like mercy, a little more like grace, a little more like kindness, goodness, love and faith, a little more like patience, a little more like peace, a little more like Jesus, a little less like me.*

As the holidays approach when family members typically gather, praying for your relative(s) who are hard to love may be just the thing you need to make the gathering more peaceful, relaxing and enjoyable. Love 'em a little more like Jesus!

61

Bloom Where You Are Planted!

Not only so, but we also glory in our sufferings, because we know that
suffering produces perseverance; perseverance, character;
and character, hope.

Romans 5:3-4

Remember the Sports Illustrated cover story that dubbed Jeff
Francoeur, "The Natural," after he batted .400 in his first month with
the Atlanta Braves in 2005? However, he was humbled the following
season after starting two for 32. After going hitless in an extra-inning
game, he told the audience at a Fellowship of Christian Athletes (FCA)
banquet that he walked three miles in the rain to his San Francisco ho-
tel and gave his baseball career to the Lord that same night. Francoeur's career was replete with difficulties before he retired from
baseball. He has since blossomed as an analyst on Braves telecasts and
was the feature analyst during the 2021 Braves-Dodgers National
League Championship Series (NLCS).

Francoeur was accompanied to the banquet by a member of the
Braves organization, third-base coach Brian Snitker. As a baseball lifer, Snitker had also experienced ups and downs over thirty-three years,
first as a minor-league catcher and later as an instructor for Braves minor league teams after being hired by Hank Aaron. Twelve years later
Braves Manager Brian Snitker's resilience paid off with a World Series championship! He acknowledged his wife Veronica's (Ronnie)
role in raising their children when he was absent during those long
baseball seasons. Brian shouted to Ronnie, "Honey, we did it!" after
Game 6 in Houston as their daughter Erin and their grandsons stood
next to her. During the World Series the Snitkers received publicity
because their son Troy is a hitting coach for the opposing team.

After seven years as a third-base coach with the Braves, Snitker thought that his chance to manage in the big leagues had disappeared when he was sent down to manage the Gwinnett Triple-A team in 2013. Surely there were many days that he had thoughts such as, *Why am I going through all this? Is this worth spending all this time away from my family?* As I reflected on Snitker's career, I thought of Romans 5:3-4, "Not only so, but we also glory in our sufferings, because we know that suffering produces perseverance; perseverance, character; and character, hope."

Snitker was pleasantly surprised in 2016 when he was awarded the Braves interim managerial job after forty years in baseball. As one broadcaster said, Snitker wasn't one of the "flashy new breed with their baseball analytics." He was simply a lifer who was dedicated to the Braves organization and persevered as he taught young men to be better baseball players and teammates. The Braves front office removed the interim tag from Snitker's job description in 2017 as the team continued its climb from mediocrity. Snitker proved to be a steady hand at the helm as he guided the Braves to the NLCS in 2020 and led them to the World Series in 2021. The Braves front office made four crucial player acquisitions at mid-season, and Snitker meshed these new personalities as the Braves played almost .700 ball in the last three months.

Before the World Series began, Snitker paid homage to the late Hank Aaron and to Phil Niekro, Don Sutton, and former Braves owner Bill Bartholomay, who all passed in 2020 or early 2021. He stated, "I've said many times there's a lot of bragging going on in heaven right now with all those guys. I can't imagine how all of (those) guys, how proud they would be of everybody." The Braves paid tribute to Aaron before World Series Game 3 by honoring Hank's memory and his wife, Billye Aaron. After the game Snitker reflected. "I got to hug Billye," and following a lengthy pause to gather his emotions, added, "and tell her how much I miss Hank."

Brian Snitker embodies every person with a big dream who wondered if it would ever come true. Just as Moses toiled for forty years in a foreign land as God developed his character that would prepare him to lead his people out of Egypt, Brian served for forty years before he received his big opportunity. In coaching or whatever profession you choose, one of the toughest challenges is to keep believing until your big opportunity comes.

Be encouraged by Snitker's journey to keep believing because you can achieve your wildest dreams and receive blessings that you never anticipated. Are you willing to let God help you become the best version of yourself? Hebrews 12:1 offers this encouragement, "…let us run with perseverance the race marked out for us." May you persevere as you develop your Christlike character that brings others encouragement and hope in your workplace and in your life. Bloom where you are planted!

62
Lasting Impressions

Who Himself bore our sins in His own body on the tree, that we, having died to sins, might live for righteousness, by whose stripes you were healed.

1 Peter 2:24

My dear friend, Coach A.G. Crockett, shared this coaching story with me. Rockdale County played Dodge County for the 1984 Class AA girls basketball state championship. Dodge County scored with a few seconds remaining to take a one-point lead, and a Dodge County player called a timeout. Unfortunately, her team was out of timeouts, and a technical foul was called. Traci Waites, a three-time Parade All-American from Rockdale County and one of the most talented players in the history of the state of Georgia, made both free throws, and Rockdale County won the state championship.

The Dodge County girls were distraught, particularly the girl who called the extra timeout. To Dodge County Coach Dick Kelley's everlasting credit, he told reporters afterward that it was his fault and that he had told the player to call a TO. Coach Kelley couldn't bear the thought of his player having to answer those questions, so he took responsibility. In the midst of major disappointment and sadness, he took the mistake of his player and put it squarely on his shoulders. Perhaps Coach Kelley's demonstration of love and support inspired the returning players, because Dodge County won the girls state championship in 1985 and 1987!

I knew Coach Kelley because Dodge County was adjacent to my home county of Laurens. The impact of that decision was such that Coach Crockett distinctly recalled the story a generation later. A.G. wondered aloud how the seeds that were planted in those players and in the one player who called the timeout have flourished. Who knows how much fruit has come from that day as the women on that 1984 team raise children and grandchildren?

I recalled this story after Eric, a college student, interviewed me about a coach's leadership qualities for his coaching class. I told him that I admire coaches who create positive lasting impressions in young people's lives by embodying the following traits:

1. Maintain consistency and integrity through good years and down years.

2. Pour holistically into the student, the athlete, and the person.

3. Create and provide opportunities that help student-athletes grow emotionally, mentally, morally, and spiritually.

4. Shoulder responsibility for the outcomes of big games.

5. Motivate out of love, not fear nor intimidation.

6. Demonstrate love, empathy and compassion for the athletes who don't make the team.

7. Create a coaching tree of former athletes who become coaches.

8. Teach accountability to athletes, then live it out so that they see what accountability looks like.

9. Give athletes second chances when logic and personal history suggest otherwise.

10. Follow up, pray for, and be available to athletes long after they graduate.

I appreciate the people who shared how my father, Coach Lester Farr, and my father-in-law, Coach Damon Ray, helped them have better careers and become better children, spouses, and parents. What lasting impressions have you created that your athletes will admiringly recall in twenty, thirty, even fifty years?

Just as Coach Kelley took responsibility for his player's mistake, Jesus took responsibility on the cross for our sins. The verse 1 Peter 2:24 tells us that Jesus bore our sins in his own body. Despite the weight of mankind's past, present, and future sins, Jesus Christ expressed his love on the cross for six excruciating hours, died, and rose from the grave on the third day. Jesus made a powerful impression on us for eternity. Let's thank him for making positive lasting impressions on the young people that we serve.

63

Student-Athlete Profile – Ian Matthews

"…whatever you do, do all to the glory of God."

1 Corinthians 10:31

Ian Matthews was a team captain and starting safety for the 2021 edition of the Roswell Hornets football team. He was a selfless, well-respected team leader and talented defender. Ian was one of the team leaders in tackles, and his last-minute interception sealed the win that gave his team a first-round playoff home game. Ian also excelled in the classroom with a 4.0 GPA and planned to study engineering in college.

As he prepared for his team's second-round playoff game, Ian shared what his senior season has meant to him. "I believe for me it has been about proving to myself and others that the past four years has not been a waste of time or a stroll through the park. All of it has been hard work to get better to lead up to this point. People say they remember their senior season forever and that it is one of the most special seasons they ever played. I'd say that is completely true for me."

During the summer of 2021, Ian participated in his church's mission trip to Guatemala. He shared some memories that he took away from that trip. "For me, seeing a small struggling community in the middle of nowhere with such a strong desire to do better for themselves and for their youth was incredible. I honestly just loved being able to do good for others, for those who struggle to do good for themselves."

He described the impact that the Roswell football FCA huddle has had on him and his teammates. "Starting (my) freshman year, FCA has brought this team together. It has helped me to focus spiritually on and off the field. It has shown me the impact that Christ can have on a group of kids who desire a relationship, and, most importantly, it has shown me how easy it is to invite people to learn about Christ. FCA has been a phenomenal way to get to know some of my teammates and encourage them."

Ian shared how Jesus is working in his life through FCA. "I believe Christ has worked through me by guiding me to invite others to come to FCA and to give them a chance to get to know Christ. I also believe that I have been given an opportunity to show younger kids that you can have a relationship with Christ and enjoy high school and football and everything that comes with it."

Liam Stevens, Ian's close friend, brother in Christ, and Class of 2022 teammate, said, "The hardest worker I've ever seen is Ian Matthews. I met Ian seven years ago, and it was immediately clear where his heart was. He had dedicated his life to God, committing himself to be the greatest disciple he could be. His unwavering commitment to the Gospel keeps his head level and always prepared for the next challenge. His strength of character that has stemmed from his discipleship led him to be one of the greatest leaders that Roswell High School has seen."

Ian was our "go-to" person who reminded his senior teammates each week about the Tuesday huddle after practice. He opened each meeting with a prayer and introduced our guest speaker. Two guest speakers commented on Ian's humility and positive attitude. Our fall huddle would not have been nearly as impactful without Ian's heart and leadership. I believe that God will use Ian in even greater ways to expand his kingdom.

64

Celebration of a Lifetime

One day at a time, sweet Jesus!

One Day at a Time, Cristy Lane, 1974

At 1:15 a.m. on February 10, 2013, I heard Dad's walker scrape across the tile floor in his bathroom. I hopped out of bed and stood at his bedroom door to make sure he didn't stumble going back to bed. He sensed my presence and asked me to turn on the light. I told him that it was Sunday, February 10, and I said, "Happy one-hundredth birthday!" He exclaimed, "I'm a hundred years old!" He went back to bed, and I couldn't get back to sleep because I was so excited for him!

At the nine o'clock service at Cadwell-Rentz United Methodist Church, there were nineteen family members representing four generations. My niece, April, beautifully sang *One Day at a Time*, my dad's favorite song that he had mentioned frequently for the past several months. He often said, "Have you ever heard that song, *One Day at a Time*? " I shared a devotion about his bountiful tomato harvests, and Pastor Paulk concluded his sermon by recognizing Dad for the bountiful harvests that he has produced as a faithful servant, teacher, coach, father, and tomato grower for the community!

Over two hundred people dropped by his home that afternoon to celebrate his birthday. Dad was stylish in his navy suit with a tiny pinstripe. He thoroughly enjoyed chatting and reminiscing with his friends and former students. Ouida Dixon, the star of his 1951 Girls State Championship team at Cedar Grove, was one of the first to congratulate him. I had never met this legendary player who I heard about all my life, and I hugged her with glee. A.D., the center on the 1952 Cedar Grove boys team, introduced himself, and Coach Farr immediately reminded him of a humorous hunting story during A.D.'s high school days.

Dad received more than eighty cards from as far away as California and New Jersey. Many wrote him notes about how he had helped shape their lives. A former student told him that she never understood math until he explained it to her. Another former student, who obviously had serious health issues, kept coming back to sit by Dad. The following day, Dad repeatedly said, "It was quite a day, wasn't it?"

It was an amazing day, not like any that I had ever experienced. Four days later, it was so big that I was still not able to wrap my arms around it. It was "God-size" big. It was beyond the joy of a family reunion on a beautiful day with temperatures in the mid-sixties. Friends spilled out of the house into the front yard to visit and reminisce. There was nothing about the day that we would have changed.

It was an incredible blessing and truly a slice of heaven for my dad, the newest centenarian, to enjoy such a day in good health that so few will ever experience. It was a huge blessing for his three children and the family members who were present for the big occasion.

I searched the scriptures to help me express the joy that surrounded us that Sunday. I found Psalm 16:11, "You will show me the path of life; In your presence is fullness of joy; at your right hand are pleasures evermore." And of course Psalm 118:24, "This is the day that the Lord has made. Let us rejoice and be glad in it." We did indeed rejoice!

65

God's in His Bag!

For to us a child is born, to us a son is given, and the government will
be on his shoulders. And He will be called Wonderful Counselor,
Mighty God, Everlasting Father, Prince of Peace...

Isaiah 9:6 (NIV)

The spark for this devotion came when Craig, one of my student-
athletes, said, "God's in his bag." He morphed the term "in his bag"
after hearing a basketball player say, "I'm in my bag (of tricks)." Envi-
sion the clock winding down in a tie game, and a great ball-handler is
one-on-one with a defender on the perimeter. A capacity crowd is on
its feet as the player begins a series of moves. Cross-over? Step back
three for the win? Power move to the rim and a no-look pass for a slam
dunk?

Consider a professional golfer and his caddie on the tee of the last
hole of a tournament. The caddie must ensure that he pulls the correct
club from the bag. One shot back, the driver comes out. Two shots
ahead, a long iron comes out. Jean Van de Velde held a three-shot lead
on the last hole of the 1999 Open Championship, but he and his caddie
foolishly pulled the driver. He made triple bogey and lost in a playoff.
Jean's caddie should have snapped his driver like Romeo, Roy
McAvoy's caddie, did in the movie *Tin Cup*.

As our pastor says most every Sunday, let's shift gears. Consider
the greatest gift that God ever pulled from his bag. From God's promise in Genesis to the prophet Zechariah in the sixth century B.C.,
prophets foretold the coming of a Messiah who would save the world
from their sin. The prophet Isaiah referred to the Messiah as Mighty
Counselor and Prince of Peace.

Nod your head if you could use some wise counsel at this moment. What positive qualities does an excellent counselor have? Perhaps the person is a great listener, demonstrates compassion, possesses much knowledge, has great wisdom, and gives the right advice at the right time. These are all characteristics of Jesus, who was born in a manger two thousand years ago. The baby grew to be a man who was fully man and fully God, and his name is Jesus. He is alive today and is available for counseling 7/24/365. There is no need to schedule an appointment. There is no time limit, and Jesus has the answers you need.

Sounds too good to be true, doesn't it? But it is true! "And you will seek me and find me, when you search for Me with all your heart" (Jeremiah 29:13). Jesus will meet you where you are. No need to wait for a crisis. Go ahead and schedule time with him daily and make it a priority. Early or late, it really doesn't matter so long as it is uninterrupted, undisturbed time. You can tell the Wonderful Counselor everything. Note: He already knows about it (see Psalm 139). Then wait patiently to receive instructions and follow them.

One primary purpose for seeking wise counsel is to receive peace. Whatever you might be facing in this season—a pressure-packed work schedule, a sickness in the family, a broken relationship, anxiety, or loneliness—the peace of Jesus will comfort you. You don't have to get to the end of your struggle to experience wholeness. Jesus wants to quiet your spirit with His love and perfect your trust in him. You can weather any storm complete in him.

TobyMac sings these lyrics from *Maybe Midnight*, "*Said I've seen my share of troubles, But the Lord ain't failed me yet. We'll keep holding on to the promise y'all, That He's rolling up His sleeves again.*"

Whatever lion-sized problem you are facing, God's rolling up his sleeves and reaching into his bag to give you what you need. Philippians 4:19 assures us, "My God will supply all your need according to His riches in glory by Christ Jesus." God is the giver of "every good and perfect gift" (James 1:17). God's in his bag even before we ask, and he is waiting every minute of every day to give us what we need, if we will only ask.

66

Lay Down Your "Bama"

Jesus told his disciples before they journeyed to Jerusalem, "Whoever wants to be my disciple must deny themselves and take up their cross daily and follow me."

Luke 9:23

After the 2021 UGA-Bama game ended in yet another bitter disappointing loss for Georgia fans, someone in my family said, "Why can't we (the good guys) win just once?" At the time I had nothing. But later I thought, *Everybody has a "Bama" to bear.*

Alabama hired Nick Saban in 2007. After the victorious Dog Pile game in 2007 when Matthew Stafford and Mikey Henderson connected in OT in Tuscaloosa came fourteen years of Bama heartache for UGA fans. Allow me to digress. Number 3 ranked UGA hosted Alabama in the 2008 Blackout Game, but trailed 31-0 at the half and lost 41-30 (we will pick up forty-one later). The 2012 SEC Championship Game featured Number 3 Georgia and "the fingertip deflection." The 2017 National Championship Game featured Number 3 Georgia and is remembered for "Tyler Simmons not offside" and "second and 26." Then there was Number 4 Georgia in the 2018 SEC Championship Game known for the "fake punt." Number 3 Georgia loses to Alabama 41-24 during the pandemic season in 2020.

Then comes the 2021 SEC Championship Game and "If not know, when?" Number 1 Georgia against a supposedly inferior Bama squad. Georgia gives up 41 points again. Loses 41-24 again. Seriously? UGA 6.92 defense PPG sextupled. Look it up. It is a word.

Still can't win the big one. No "kick six" ringtones or 24-point comebacks against Alabama like Auburn. The Bama fan in your neighborhood, office or church who waxes incessantly about their dominance and brashly adds how Kirby should fix his team. The Process. Aflac. Sweet Home Alabama. Yummy rat poison? All this is why UGA fans are feeling so much pain.

Recall the Fenway Park scene in Fever Pitch when Ben's girlfriend Lindsey innocently asks, "What's the curse of the Bambino?" Immediately Ben and his friends call out their team's worst failings over the past eighty-five years including the dominance by the Yankees. Ben concludes the bemoaning with "Buckner" and adds that we need a little (with emphasis) "PER-SPEC-TIVE!" The movie ends on a happy note with the Red Sox's 3-0 comeback against the Yankees in the ALCS and their first World Series title in almost a century!

For those of us who are fans, the perspective is that the outcome of a series of games is not a cross we should bear. To bear your cross is to deal with burdens and problems; to cope with a burden or challenging situation; to deal with one's difficulties. We save our crosses for the real difficulties in life, finding strength through Jesus during the grim times.

Jesus told his disciples before they journeyed to Jerusalem, "Whoever wants to be my disciple must deny themselves and take up their cross daily and follow me" (Luke 9:23). "Whoever does not bear his own cross and come after me cannot be my disciple" (Luke 14:27). "And calling the crowd to him with his disciples, he said to them, 'If anyone would come after me, let him deny himself and take up his cross and follow me'" (Mark 8:34).

Jesus physically bore a heavy cross. "And he went out, bearing his own cross, to the place called The Place of a Skull, which in Aramaic is called Golgotha" (John 19:17). He suffered an excruciatingly painful death as he bore the weight of our sins on the cross before he rose victoriously on the third day.

Bearing your cross is bearing one another's burdens (Galatians 6:2) and being there for your family and friends when they need you. Bearing your cross is about discipleship where a person attempts to place Christ first each day and follow him.

Bearing your cross is not becoming overwhelmed or dismayed or bearing the weight of your team's collective misfortunes. I urge you to "lay down your Bama" and prepare your heart for the coming of Jesus, the Reason for the Season (Advent, not bowl season).

Update: Georgia finally defeated Alabama in the 2021 CFP National Championship game, breaking a seven-game losing streak and giving Georgia its first national championship in forty-one years!

67

The Miracle of All Miracles

"How will this be," Mary asked the angel, "since I am a virgin?" The angel answered, "The Holy Spirit will come on you, and the power of the Most High will overshadow you. So the holy one to be born will be called the Son of God. Even Elizabeth your relative is going to have a child in her old age, and she who was said to be unable to conceive is in her sixth month. For no word from God will ever fail."

Luke 1:34-37

I have seen tens of thousands of pro football plays over the past fifty-five years, but I've yet to see another play like this one. With only a few seconds remaining in the game, a quarterback throws a desperation pass. The safety, the targeted receiver, and the football collide simultaneously. A running back grabs the deflected ball and outruns a flat-footed secondary to win the game.

But that's exactly what happened in the 1972 AFC Championship game played on December 23, 1972, between the Oakland Raiders and the Pittsburgh Steelers in Pittsburgh's Three Rivers Stadium. The score was Raiders 7, Steelers 6 with twenty seconds remaining in the game. The Steelers had never won a playoff game and had only seven winning seasons in their forty-year history.

Pittsburgh quarterback Terry Bradshaw, a Pro Football Hall of Famer, unleashed a desperation pass from the Steeler thirty-yard line. Oakland safety Jack Tatum, a College Football Hall of Famer, drilled Steeler RB Frenchy Fuqua, and the ball flew backwards. Pittsburgh's other running back, the late Franco Harris, a Pro Football Hall of Famer, caught the deflected ball near his shoe tops on the Raider forty-three yard line and outraced the stunned Raiders to the end zone!

Raider Head Coach John Madden claimed that the ball struck Fuqua before Harris touched it. By NFL rule in 1972, two offensive players could not touch the passed ball back-to-back. But that was long before instant replay reviews, and Madden's complaint was to no avail.

NBC broadcaster Curt Gowdy shouted, "You talk about Christmas miracles, this is the miracle of all miracles!" That evening the miraculous play was toasted in a jubilant bar by a Steeler fan who named the play the "Immaculate Reception."

That play was the Immaculate Reception. God blessed Mary, a virgin, with the Immaculate Conception. "How will this be," Mary asked the angel, "since I am a virgin?" The angel answered, "The Holy Spirit will come on you, and the power of the Most High will overshadow you. So the holy one to be born will be called the Son of God. Even Elizabeth your relative is going to have a child in her old age, and she who was said to be unable to conceive is in her sixth month" (Luke 1:34-36).

Mary questioned how something that seemed impossible, a virgin birth, could indeed be possible. God comforted Mary by explaining the details through the angel of the Lord. "For no word from God will ever fail (Luke 1:37)." Six months prior God had done the seemingly impossible for her barren Aunt Elizabeth, who became miraculously pregnant with John the Baptist and reinforced Mary's belief that God could do the impossible for Mary.

God reinforced Mary's belief through Elizabeth's encouragement fueled by the Holy Spirit and her baby leaping for joy! "When Elizabeth heard Mary's greeting, the baby leaped in her womb, and Elizabeth was filled with the Holy Spirit. In a loud voice she exclaimed: "Blessed are you among women, and blessed is the child you will bear! But why am I so favored, that the mother of my Lord should come to me? As soon as the sound of your greeting reached my ears, the baby in my womb leaped for joy. Blessed is she who has believed that the Lord would fulfill his promises to her!" (Luke 1:41-45).

God gave us these immaculate conceptions of Jesus, the miracle of all miracles, and John the Baptist to help us have faith when we cannot see how he will work out the trials in our lives. He gives us words of encouragement through scripture, prayer, the Holy Spirit, and through people whom we trust. God also can use us to help someone who is hoping for a miracle.

Need a miracle as Christmas approaches? Do you know someone who needs a miracle? Ask God to do the impossible. What is impossible for us is possible for God. Never give up hope and give others hope.

68

Six Stones in the Dungeon

You will keep the peace, a perfect peace, for all who trust in You,
for those who dedicate their hearts *and minds* to You.
So trust in the Eternal One forever,
for He is like a great Rock—*strong, stable, trustworthy, and* lasting.

Isaiah 26:3-4 (The Voice)

A devotion by Rev. Dennis Kinlaw features a Scottish dungeon that is carved out of rock. The first ten feet below the ground is a circular shaft that is just wide enough to slip a person down the shaft. The dungeon opens below the bottom of the shaft to a triangle-shaped room. A prisoner was given food and water and left to fend for himself in pitch black darkness. There was no way that he could escape without assistance.

After a prisoner was placed into the dungeon, he would become overwhelmed within several days by the solitary confinement in the darkness. Except for one man who was left in the dungeon for two weeks, and he was still sane. Nobody could figure it out, and the man shared his secret. The man said that when he started to lose his sanity, he would reach into his pocket and pull out six small stones. He moved one stone at a time from one pocket to another. The exercise forced him to concentrate, and he maintained a point of reference in the darkness. Jesus is our unchanging point of reference when trials such as sickness, isolation, bad grades, injuries, lack of money, COVID-19 pandemic, job loss, and failure to meet expectations threaten to engulf us.

The man in the dungeon disciplined himself and stuck to his routine of passing the six stones. Consider what your "six stones" should be as you continue to navigate the challenges during the pandemic. Those six could include investing in your circle of relationships, an early morning devotion time, scripture reading before bedtime, brief prayers throughout the day, regular exercise, and a new hobby or project. When your schedule becomes super busy with school and sports, discipline yourself and stick to these activities, even for a few minutes each day, to maintain life balance and stay centered on Christ.

Regarding the man with the stones in his pocket, you may want to keep a cross in your pocket or wallet. When you start to lose it, clutch the cross for all that you are worth. Just like those stones got that man to the other side, maintaining a strong daily discipline and trusting completely in the LORD Jesus Christ will get you safely to the other side.

Here are six rock-solid promises to stand on.

1. Philippians 4:13 – I can do all things through Christ who strengthens me.

2. Hebrews 13:5-6 – For He Himself has said, "I will never leave you nor forsake you." So you may boldly say, "The LORD is my helper; I will not fear. What can man do to me?"

3. Proverbs 3:5-6 – Trust the LORD with all your heart, and do not rely on your own understanding; in all your ways acknowledge Him, and He shall direct your paths.

4. Isaiah 55:8-9 – "For My thoughts are not your thoughts, Nor are your ways My ways," says the LORD. For as the heavens are higher than the earth, So are My ways higher than your ways, and My thoughts are higher than your thoughts.

5. Jeremiah 29:11 – For I know the plans I have for you, says the Lord. They are plans for good and not for evil, to give you a future and a hope.

6. Joshua 1:9 – Have I not commanded you? Be strong and of good courage; do not be afraid, do not be dismayed; for the LORD your God is with you wherever you go.

Note: Our daughter Jillian and I journeyed to Scotland for the 150th Open Championship at St. Andrews. Before we left, I searched "Scotland bottle dungeon" on the internet and discovered that it is located in a castle in St. Andrews. Jillian and I saw the castle on our first day in St. Andrews!

69

God's Play Sheet

All Scripture is breathed out by God and profitable for teaching, for reproof, for correction, and for training in righteousness, that the man of God may be complete, equipped for every good work.

2 Timothy 3:16-17

UGA's 2021 national championship team will be remembered for its historically excellent defense, which gave up 10.2 points per game (PPG), which was the fourth lowest scoring average in the past twenty-five years. The most casual observer would notice the outlier, which was the 41 points given up in the SEC Championship Game (SECCG), half of their regular season total! I believe complacency was a major factor. But when did complacency begin? It certainly did not begin on the ride from Athens to the Benz.

Georgia played eight consecutive conference games and ended the regular season with two games against non-conference opponents who were massive underdogs. The time between the last conference game against Mizzou and the SECCG was twenty-one days, which happens to be the length of time it takes to create good habits, or in this case, bad habits.

ESPN Reporter Kris Budden was on the UGA sideline for the SECCG, and she stated on College Football Today that members of the defense were "cramping and gassed." Players admitted that they were not at their best physically or mentally. Complacency had set in, and the end result was a humbling defeat.

Dissatisfied and embarrassed by their performance, the defensive unit addressed their complacency with increased focus and much-improved conditioning. When UGA faced Michigan twenty-seven days later, the hungry defense returned to elite status.

Complacency can also be an issue when it comes to reading the Word of God. In the past twenty-one days, how often did you read Scripture and take notes, discuss a passage, encourage someone with a verse, or apply Scripture to a challenging situation? A lack of God's word can lead to a negative attitude, irritability, misinformation, and unnecessary anxiety.

An offensive coordinator (OC) carries a laminated, multi-colored spreadsheet which contains a play for every possible situational, down and distance scenario. Without the play sheet, the OC is at a distinct disadvantage against his opponent. God's play sheet is his Word, which contains a passage of scripture that can be applied to every situation, problem and human emotion. Without God's play sheet, you are at a distinct disadvantage going head-to-head against our spiritual opponent, Satan and his demons. God's Word is timeless, is the Source of Truth, and provides answers to our problems. Scripture gives us strength, healing, direction, guidance, wisdom and the power that comes from God through the Holy Spirit.

If you have become complacent with your Scripture reading, I encourage you to act by diving into this FCA reading plan https://www.bible.com/reading-plans/28946-every, which contains a daily message and supporting verses that will nourish your soul. Let's make 2022 our championship year for reading, studying, sharing, or applying Scripture each day!

70

Win or Lose

Whatever you do, work at it with all your heart, as working for the
Lord, not for human masters, since you know that you will receive an
inheritance from the Lord as a reward.
It is the Lord Christ you are serving.

Colossians 3:23-24

Many are obsessed with winning at all costs, but in any given contest, one team loses 50% of the time. In golf and tennis major tournaments, one participant wins, and all of the others lose. One team wins
the Super Bowl, and thirty-one teams do not. One team wins the College Football Playoff, and 130 teams do not. Because losing is inevitable and tough to swallow, it's important for coaches and athletes to
maintain perspective, remain encouraged, and preserve self-esteem.

Consider the conclusion of a match between two wrestlers. The
referee holds each wrestler's arm and lifts the arm of the victor. It's a
W for the victor and an L for the opponent. It's obvious who won the
match by the scoreboard. Perhaps it was an 8-0 score or 10-9 when the
margin between winning and losing was razor thin.

But does winning a game or match make you a winner, or does
losing make you a loser? There are many factors to consider other than
the final score. How well did you train physically and prepare mentally? Did you encourage your teammates, especially if you were having
a tough day? What did you learn from your failures and mistakes that
you can correct during the next competition? Did you display exemplary sportsmanship even if you received some tough calls? Did you
honor God throughout the competition? Did you give him the glory
win or lose?

How does God view winning and losing? How you compete is more important to God than winning or losing. Colossians 3:23 tells us, "Work willingly at whatever you do, as though you were working for the Lord rather than for people." Whose approval are you ultimately seeking?

Following a 6-7 season in 2010 and losses in his first two games in 2011, UGA Head Football Coach Mark Richt quoted Colossians 3:23 at a news conference. He said that he loved coaching, but his first priority was to serve God, which was a courageous statement during a losing streak. He won his next ten games!

Colossians 3:17 reads, "And whatever you do or say, do it as a representative of the Lord Jesus, giving thanks through him to God the Father." First Corinthians 5:20 speaks of being "an ambassador for Christ." When you compete, is it readily apparent that you are representing your team, school, community, and God?

How can you be victorious when the scoreboard says you were not? Isaiah 41:10 reads, "Don't be afraid, for I am with you." Did you include God during your contest? "Don't be discouraged, for I am your God." Did you stay encouraged, knowing that God was with you? "I will strengthen you and help you." Did you trust that God would give you strength when you needed it? "I will hold you up with my victorious right hand." I have seen a victorious wrestler lift the other wrestler's hand out of profound respect for the heart and fight with which he competed.

Include God in all that you do and follow his direction as you navigate your day. Reflect the light of Christ as you encounter issues and engage with difficult personalities. If you prepared well, gave your best effort, respected everyone through your personal interactions, learned from your mistakes, received and extended forgiveness, and gave God the glory, honor, and praise, at day's end God will metaphorically raise your hand as if to say, "Well done, faithful servant," no matter the outcome.

Put your trust in God and work first to please him. Do that consistently, and you will be a winner in God's eyes. Remember that his approval matters most. God's incomparable, perfect love for you never changes, win or lose. When you are in Christ, you've already won!

71

When a "No" Answer to Prayer Leads to...Yes!!

For Jesus Christ, the Son of God, does not waver between "Yes" and "No." He is the one whom Silas, Timothy, and I preached to you, and as God's ultimate "Yes," he always does what he says. For all of God's promises have been fulfilled in Christ with a resounding "Yes!" And through Christ, our "Amen" (which means "Yes") ascends to God for his glory.

2 Corinthians 1:19-20 NLT

Football fans were treated to arguably the greatest weekend of football in NFL history when all four divisional games in January 2022 were decided after 0:00 on the clock in regulation. Three games were decided by walk-off FGs from the visiting teams, and the fourth game ended with a TD pass in OT by the home team. The average winning margin was less than four points, eclipsing the previous record in 1970. From the blocked punt by the 49ers to the Bengals rookie kicker's game-winner, to the "almost 28-3 repeat" by Brady, to the incredible last two minutes by Mahomes and Allen, there was something special for everyone who loves the game!

The Tuesday before the NFL divisional games, I met with a group of football players. As an icebreaker, I suggested, "Let's pick the NFL winners through the Super Bowl. One point for divisional, two points for conference, and five points for the Super Bowl." I added, "Jot down your picks, and we will talk about them next Tuesday."

Soon a barrage of text messages with their individual picks flooded the group chat. I thought, *That's cool, they bought in, we may have something here.* The following afternoon this text came in. Can I change from the Bengals to the Titans? It had been reported that Titan star RB Derrick Henry would be activated. As I waited to approve the change, here came a reply. "No," wrote his friend. I did not want to take sides, so I let it go. The chat remained quiet, and the verdict was accepted. Because his friend said "No" and the Bengals won three days later, the boy who wanted to change his pick said, "Yes!"

Recall a situation in your life when you asked God to say "Yes," but he said "No." Perhaps you wanted "Yes" but you needed "No" for the long haul. Perhaps the request was outside his will for your life. Oftentimes it is difficult to pray according to God's will. He always answers the prayers of a believer, and his answers are "Yes," "No," and "Not Yet." As we wait for our prayer to be answered, the silence can be particularly challenging. "No" and "Not Yet" can really test your faith.

It is important how you and I respond when God says "No" to our desperate pleas to rescue us from situations that we created or inherited. Remember that God allows trials that test us and help us grow in our faith. Be thankful that God allows these trials that strengthen us; be thankful for the times that God refused to cut us a deal. Oh God, if you will just do this for me, I promise that I will follow you...Dear Lord, if you get me out of this mess, I will never... Our mighty and just God is a chain breaker, not a dealmaker.

As Jesus agonized in the Garden of Gethsemane over his impending death on the cross, he prayed, "Father, if you are willing, take this cup from me." Then Jesus continued, "yet not my will, but yours be done" (Luke 22:42). "An angel from heaven appeared to him and strengthened Him. And being in anguish, he prayed more earnestly, and his sweat was like drops of blood falling to the ground" (Luke 22:43-44).

When you are in anguish and it is difficult to pray according to God's will, God will give you strength from heaven just like he gave his Son. The defiant "No!" from the Romans and Jewish leaders that killed Jesus on the cross led to his apostles saying "Yes!!" after his resurrection on the third day. "The Lord is risen indeed, and has appeared to Simon!" (Luke 24:34).

Remember to pray, "Thy kingdom come, thy will be done. On earth as it is in heaven." Our loving Father prepared the best path for us, but that journey requires the good and the bad, the bitter and the sweet, and the "No and Not Yet" answers and the "Yes" answers. When it seems like God did not come through for you, consider this thought. Did he actually come through and I missed it? When you look back days, months, or years later, you will realize that God has not failed you yet, and he never will!

The apostle Paul wrote, "For no matter how many promises God has made, they are "Yes" in Christ" (2 Corinthians 1:20). If God has made a promise to you, his answer will be "Yes" in his timing. Trust the Lord and his perfect ways and "…wait patiently for him" (Psalm 37:7). "But my God will provide all your need according to His riches in glory by Christ Jesus" (Philippians 4:19).

"No" can be one of God's greatest gifts when you accept his response and realign with his will. It is when God's "No" answer to prayer leads to…"Yes!" as in, "Yes! Father, thank you for the "No" answer to my prayer that prevented me from going down the wrong road and protected my future." Amen and all glory be to God!

72

9 and 8

And whatever you do, whether in word or deed, do it all in the name of the Lord Jesus, giving thanks to God the Father through him.

Colossians 3:17

Leaving home in the morning without reading Scripture and praying is like being two down standing on the first tee. You're at a big disadvantage! Why not read and pray and leave home two up?

Tiger Woods faced Stephen Ames in a PGA match-play event in Carlsbad, California. Ames gave Tiger bulletin board material when he told a reporter that if Tiger hits it all over the place, I have a chance. The quote fired Tiger up. Tiger won the first nine holes and was miffed when he missed a putt on the 10th hole that would have closed Ames out 10 and 8. Tiger didn't give an inch in the 9 and 8 thrashing.

What if our attitude each day was to use the power of God and give the devil a thrashing like that? Your day might look something like this.

1. Read scripture before breakfast – 1 up after 1
2. Prayed for others before breakfast – 2 up after 2
3. Rolled the garbage can to the curb without being asked – 3 up after 3
4. Checked on a friend who was downcast the previous day – 4 up after 4
5. Received your math quiz back – D minus – you cursed under your breath. Oops! 3 up after 5. Before the class ended, you asked God to forgive your anger and cursing, went up to your math teacher and apologized, and set up a tutoring session. Forgiven! 5 up after 5

6. Prayed again for your friend between classes who is struggling – 6 up after 6

7. Shared a verse of scripture with a friend – 7 up after 7

8. Fired your best round in three months during qualifying and gave God the glory – 8 up after 8

9. Prompted by the Spirit, called your grandfather to tell him about the round – 9 up after 9

10.Closed out your day by thanking God for your blessings and shared another prayer for your friend – Match over!

Every day is not always going this smoothly, but why should we settle for 1 up or even with the devil? Why should we give him an inch? Follow through according to the apostle Paul. "And whatever you do, whether in word or deed, do it all in the name of the Lord Jesus, giving thanks to God the Father through him" (Colossians 3:17).

73

Vámonos!

More than that, we rejoice in our sufferings, knowing that suffering produces endurance, and endurance produces character, and character produces hope…

Romans 5:3-4

The excitement that surrounded the NFC and AFC Championship games overshadowed the thrilling, come-from-behind victory by Spain's Rafael "Rafa" Nadal, age 35, in the 2022 Australian Open (AO) final. Nadal came from two sets down for the first time in fifteen years to defeat Russia's second-seeded Daniel Medvedev, age 24, in five grueling sets. Rafa claimed an all-time record 21st men's major championship, breaking a tie with Novak Djokovic and Roger Federer, who tweeted congratulations to the champion.

Nadal became the third-oldest AO champion in the history of the tournament, which began in 1905. My friend who is a tennis expert said that Rafa displayed incredible determination and grit. Pardon the Interruption (PTI) Co-host Tony Kornheiser called it Rafa's greatest win.

Rafa executed a dazzling array of cross-court winners as he captured the second-longest final in tennis major championship history, five hours and twenty-four minutes, which was exceeded by the five-hour, fifty-three minute AO final in 2012 between Nadal and Novak Djokovic.

This 108th edition of the AO had the world's attention since the end of November after the Australian government declared that all contestants must be vaccinated. An unvaccinated Djokovic came to Melbourne and was isolated while his request for an exemption was reviewed. His visa was denied twice, and he returned to Serbia. Nadal voiced his support for the vaccination requirements. It was probably a relief when the tournament began with attendance limited to 50% capacity. On February 2 multiple sources reported that Djokovic will be getting vaccinated.

Nadal's win capped an incredible comeback after he aggravated a foot injury that forced him to withdraw from the 2021 U.S. Open. He went through a lengthy recovery period and worked himself back into top physical condition to play five-set matches. Rafa got COVID in late December after an exhibition match in Abu Dhabi but recovered just in time for the AO.

Rafa's stirring performance in Melbourne was a triumph for all sports fans who value grace, respect, goodness, perseverance, resilience, endurance, and mental strength. Following his match, Rafa graciously praised and encouraged the younger Medvedev, who was extremely disappointed after dropping his third grand-slam final since 2019.

Nadal was effusive in his praise of his support team who helped him get back to the top of his sport. Rafa was the sentimental favorite of the Melbourne crowd and humbly gave the fans homage following the match. He said, "Having the huge support I received during the three weeks is going to stay in my heart for the rest of my life, so many, many thanks."

Rafa fully believed that he would make a comeback, even at the age of thirty-five. "Vámonos" means "Let's Go!" Which of these Christlike virtues can you take from Rafa's game and apply to yours?

The following verses remind me of Rafa's heart and the fighting spirit that fueled his comeback.

- Justice, kindness and humility – "He has told you, O man, what is good; and what does the Lord require of you but to do justice, and to love kindness, and to walk humbly with your God?" (Micah 6:8).
- Perseverance – "And let us not grow weary of doing good, for in due season we will reap, if we do not give up" (Galatians 6:9). Rafa reaped the rewards of his comeback!
- Mental Strength – "More than that, we rejoice in our sufferings, knowing that suffering produces endurance, and endurance produces character, and character produces hope…" (Romans 5:3-4). An AO writer felt that Rafa must overcome a

mental block after going down two sets. If Rafa was going to win, the match would last five sets and exceed five hours. The enormity of the task would discourage most players, but Nadal focused repeatedly on winning the next point.

- Respect – "Let everyone be subject to the governing authorities, for there is no authority except that which God has established. The authorities that exist have been established by God" (Romans 13:1). This scripture reminds us that we must respect the law and submit to those who are in authority. It doesn't mean that we must agree with the law, but we must adhere to it.

- Hope – "Now faith is confidence in what we hope for and assurance about what we do not see" (Hebrews 11:1). Rafa fully believed that he would make a comeback, even at the age of thirty-five. "Vámonos" means "Let's Go!" Which of these Christlike virtues can you take from Rafa's game and apply to yours?

74

Show No Partiality

"…keep these instructions without partiality, and do nothing out of favoritism."

1 Timothy 5:21

In Acts 9, Jesus transformed Saul, a Jew who persecuted Christians, into the apostle Paul and charged him with spreading the Good News of the gospel to the Gentiles, who were the non-Jews that represented over 95% of the world's population. Paul gave Gentiles access to the gospel in Europe, the Middle East, and Asia, and probably advanced the kingdom of God more than any person except Jesus.

In Acts 10, the apostle Peter looked with disdain at the non-kosher animals that appeared in a vision. However, he heard a voice say, "Get up, Peter. Kill and eat." The following day the Holy Spirit summoned Peter to the home of Cornelius, a Gentile and Roman centurion. Peter's subsequent change of heart following this vision led him to declare, "…truly I understand that God shows no partiality, but in every nation anyone who fears him and does what is right is acceptable to him" (Acts 10:34). Peter shared the gospel with Cornelius and his family, who were Gentiles, and each person received Christ. The conversion of this family was a key to the Christian movement that encompasses two billion Christians today.

God created human beings in his own image, so he expects us to show no partiality and treat each other fairly. "For God shows no partiality" (Romans 2:11). "My brothers, show no partiality as you hold the faith in our Lord Jesus Christ, the Lord of glory" (James 2:1). "Therefore, whatever you want men to do to you, do also to them…" (Matthew 7:12, The Golden Rule).

Partiality made the news leading up to Super Bowl LVI when former Miami Dolphins Head Coach Brian Flores filed a racial discrimination lawsuit against the NFL's hiring practices. After the Dolphins fired Flores, the NFL had only one Black head coach and just three minority head coaches. Flores filed the lawsuit after he mistakenly received a text from an NFL head coach who congratulated him for being named the new head coach of the New York Giants. But the text was intended for another coach named Brian, and Flores received the text before his scheduled interview with the Giants. This incident led Flores to believe a coach had already been hired and that his interview was a formality to fulfill the NFL's Rooney Rule, which was created to ensure minority candidates were interviewed for NFL head coaching and senior football operation jobs.

After his lawsuit was announced, the Dolphins and Texans filled their head coaching vacancies with Black men. But the NFL still has only 9% Black head coaches compared to 43% in the NBA. The NFL's implementation of the Rooney Rule has had minimal impact on the hiring of minority head coaches since its inception in 2003. Clearly the NFL is operating "behind the chains."

Many NFL fans cried out for changes to the overtime playoff rule which allows a game to end after a touchdown on the first possession. How many will cry out regarding the shortage of Black NFL head coaches in a league where 70% of the players, but only 9% of the head coaches, are Black?

In an interview with Jay Williams from National Public Radio (NPR), the purpose of his lawsuit. "I'm not thinking about me. I'm thinking about those other coaches who don't feel like they have a voice, and…that younger generation that needs to see more people that look like them in head coaching." When Williams asked if he thought that he would be blackballed, Flores replied, "I hope not…If I never coach again and there is significant change, it will be worth it." Coach Flores and his wife bravely agreed it was a stance that they must take.

Two days after the NFL initially dismissed the lawsuit as being "without merit," NFL Commissioner Roger Goodell informed his thirty-two owners that the league's lack of head coaching diversity was "unacceptable." The NFL released a statement that the goal is to "ensure everyone has access to opportunity." Goodell added, "We understand the concerns expressed by Coach Flores and others this week," and he promised to "reassess and modify our strategies to ensure that they are consistent with our values and longstanding commitment to diversity, equity and inclusion."

Three Dallas-Fort Worth Black head football coaches at McKinney, Cedar Hill and Mesquite high schools shared similar points in an interview. This could be the only head coaching job that I get... I don't want to put undue pressure on myself...I don't want to mess it up for the man coming behind me...My mission personally is being able to go into a situation and be the best that's coached there, regardless of race...For these guys to have the notion that their sons and their daughters could be a coach, that's good for them...Dreams are real.

Race and ethnicity should have nothing to do with someone's opportunity to become a head coach. Ability, attitude, exemplary character, determination, leadership, and passion should have everything to do with it. Hiring the best coaches raises the bar of excellence and leads to more meaningful relationships with student-athletes.

Time will tell if the Flores lawsuit leads to a lasting increase in the number of NFL minority head coaches. If the NFL effectively implements fair hiring practices, it could lead to more Black head coaches in high school football and college football, where only 9% of FCS schools have Black head coaches.

I encourage you to follow this litigation and ask yourself this question. How can I have a positive effect on coaches, athletes, students, my children and grandchildren, co-workers, and peers, so that the playing field is more level for everyone? Black History Month celebrates the contributions of Black pioneers. Perhaps Coach Brian Flores will become the next Black pioneer for justice and equality.

75
The Eternal Crown

Do you not know that in a race all the runners run, but only one gets the prize? Run in such a way as to get the prize. Everyone who competes in the games goes into strict training. They do it to get a crown that will not last, but we do it to get a crown that will last forever.

1 Corinthians 9:24-25

A record seventh consecutive NFL playoff game in 2022 was decided in the last two minutes when Matthew Stafford connected with Cooper Kupp for the go-ahead touchdown in Super Bowl 56, and the sensational Aaron Donald preserved the victory with two dramatic stops. Kupp demonstrated his versatility by running for a critical first down on a jet sweep and making four catches on the final drive.

Kupp's final catch culminated one of the greatest seasons, if not the greatest, by an NFL receiver in history. Kupp won the receiving "triple crown" by catching 178 passes for 2,425 yards, which were both NFL records, and twenty-two touchdowns, which was second all-time. He became only the second player after Joe Montana to be named NFL Offensive Player of the Year and Super Bowl MVP. Kupp became the first receiver since Jerry Rice in 1994 to win the receiving triple crown and Super Bowl MVP award.

That's not bad company for a high school receiver who received only two college offers before selecting Eastern Washington University (EWU), an FCS school that plays its home games on "The Inferno," a red artificial turf field. After setting numerous FCS receiving records, Cooper was the Rams' third-round draft pick in 2017.

On the NBC Super Bowl telecast, Cooper introduced himself as, "Cooper Kupp, EWU," and pronounced it E-WOO. EWU's nickname is the Eagles, but wouldn't the EWU Emus be catchy? After all, an emu can grow to be over six feet tall and can run over twenty miles per hour. That reminds me of Cooper Kupp in the open field!

After Stafford's trade to Los Angeles in early 2022, he and Kupp quickly developed a special bond through their painstaking attention to the details of their craft. It was reported that they met two hours before preseason practice at 6 a.m. to strategize and brainstorm pass routes. I heard an anecdote that Kupp impatiently waited for Stafford to complete a post-practice interview and teased him, paraphrasing, "Well, that took long enough. I need to ask you what you were thinking," pulling up the video of a play from practice on his iPad. Kupp is recognized as one of the best route runners in football, and Stafford trusted him to be in the right place when he threw that no-look pass on the last drive.

Cooper shared these details about his faith when he spoke to the media before Super Bowl 56. "You will find you are most fulfilled, you will find the most joy, when you are rooted in your purpose, and specifically rooted in His purpose for you."

He added, "My motivation coming in every single day is to run the race in such a way as to honor God and the passions and the talents that He's given me. When I'm rooted in that, I am in a great place. I am able to play freely."

Kupp said that goals and honors did not drive him. "It was really about each day being able to wake up and say, 'I want to be the best that I can possibly be for no other reason than that God has put me here, and I want to honor that and respect that to the best of my ability.'"

God blessed Cooper with Anna, an incredibly supportive wife and mother of their two young sons. Cooper and Anna met at a high school track meet, and they married while they were still in college. Anna sacrificed her college track heptathlete career and worked full-time at a restaurant to support their marriage financially. Cooper acknowledged that he would not have achieved his NFL dream without Anna's support. She posted this comment on Instagram following the Rams' Super Bowl victory. "This moment. These moments!!! Thanking God for every one of them. We have prayed for a season to glorify our Savior Jesus Christ and you are doing just that my lovey @cooperkupp. SURREAL!!"

The apostle Paul used references to sports training and competition because the Corinthians were very enthusiastic about their "Super Bowl," the Isthmian Games. Paul wrote, "Everyone who competes in the games goes into strict training" (1 Corinthians 9:25 (a)). According to the Guzik Commentary, Roman athletes trained for ten months before they were allowed to compete in the Isthmian Games. That ten-month interval is similar to the NFL season, which begins with organized team activities (OTA's) in April and ends with the Super Bowl in February.

The following words from 1 Corinthians 9:25 (b) are featured on Cooper Kupp's signature apparel: '...do it to wear the crown that lasts forever." Cooper received countless accolades and numerous awards following his football training this past season, but the crown that he cherishes is the eternal one.

Do you have the daily spiritual self-discipline to pursue the eternal crown? Receiving this crown is not determined by your achievement of earthly goals, which will tarnish and fade into obscurity. Strive to wear the crown that never fades and lasts forever. "So then, just as you received Christ Jesus as Lord, continue to live your lives in him, rooted and built up in him, strengthened in the faith as you were taught, and overflowing with thankfulness" (Colossians 2:6-7). When you are rooted and built up in the Lord through the disciplines of scripture, prayer, obedience, and fellowship with other believers, your faith will be strengthened, and you will be made free!

76

Three Words

Now Jabez was more honorable than his brothers, and his mother called him Jabez, saying, "Because I bore him in pain." **And Jabez called on the God of Israel** saying, "Oh, that you would bless me indeed, *and enlarge my territory*, that your hand would be with me, and that you would keep me from evil, that I may not cause pain!" So God granted him what he requested.

1 Chronicles 4:9-10

Three words. Three words scribbled by a 24-year-old Russian tennis professional on a camera lens on Friday, February 25, 2022, at a tournament in Dubai. Three scribbled words that captured our hearts and brought worldwide attention through sports to a war that was instigated by the tennis pro's government.

No War Please.

Russian Andrey Rublev penned these three words on a video camera lens following his semifinal victory in the Dubai Championships, a tournament which the No. 6 world ranked Rublev won. Before he made his plea via the lens, Rublev stated, "In these moments, you realize that my match is not important. It's not about my match, how it affects me," Rublev said Thursday. "You realize how important (it) is to have peace in the world and to respect each other no matter what, to be united. It's about that. We should take (care) of our earth and of each other. This is the most important thing."

Rublev, an Orthodox Christian who routinely crosses himself on the court, could have stopped there, but instead he doubled down! Several thousand Russian citizens had been arrested for peacefully supporting human rights and protesting the war atrocities by the Russian army. After he won the championship on Saturday night, Rublev tweeted this message with emojis of Planet Earth and a black heart. "Now it's not about tennis. It's not about sport. It's about having peace all over the world. We need to support each other."

Andrey made his plea for peace despite the real possibility of facing persecution by the Russian government. Matthew 5:9-12 reads, "Blessed are the peacemakers, for they shall be called sons of God. Blessed are those who are persecuted for righteousness sake, for theirs is the kingdom of heaven. Blessed are you when they revile and persecute you, and say all kinds of evil against you falsely for my sake. Rejoice and be exceedingly glad, for great is your reward in heaven, for so they persecuted the prophets who were before you." Rublev's compassion and courage spoke volumes for those who think that their voices do not matter.

Have your ever felt that you do not have a voice, or that your voice is so inconsequential that it really doesn't matter what you say or do, or what stand you take? The enemy whispers, *That tweet, that text, that note, that card, that visit, that phone call you are thinking about, It's not going to matter. There's no need because that situation is hopeless.* Yet three little words scribbled in less than ten seconds expressed the sentiments of forty-four million Ukrainians and billions around the globe.

If a 24-year-old tennis pro could bring about that level of awareness, what can I do? How many people do you know? How many followers do you have on Twitter, LinkedIn, Snapchat, Instagram, Meta, Tik Tok, and YouTube? You may influence hundreds or thousands. How can you use your relationships to help humankind? Ask God to show you, and he will!

In the parable of the talents, the first servant received five investments and doubled them. The second servant received two investments and doubled them. The two servants were rewarded with more responsibilities; their territories were expanded. But the third servant buried his investment and was reprimanded for making no effort to grow it. What is your return on investment?

There was a young man named Jabez, who was more honorable than any of his brothers. He prayed to God, "Oh, that you would bless me indeed, and enlarge my territory" (1 Chronicles 4:10). God granted his request. If you want God to expand your territory, honor God by investing in the relationships that he has already given you. It's not about numbers; it's about a lifestyle of building relationships intentionally.

I scribbled this rhyme in my prayer journal. "A little thing from me, can go a long way for thee." The little kindnesses, prayers, and encouragements offered each day will accumulate. Occasionally a little thing, like Andrey's scribble, will be huge for someone or for many others. May Rublev long be remembered for his "No war please" scribble. Continued success on the ATP Tour will increase his opportunities to use the influence of his caring heart.

I invite you to pray this verse for the Ukrainian citizens who cry out for freedom and an end to Russia's brutal treatment and oppression. "He will cover you with his feathers. He will shelter you with his wings. His faithful promises are your armor and protection" (Psalm 91:4). Join me in praying daily until peace is restored.

Three words can make a dramatic difference. No war please. I love you. God loves you. God is good. All the time. Jesus loves you. Died for you. Arose from death. Forgives our sins. Receive God's forgiveness. Accept Christ's love. Jesus saves you.

#UkraineStrong #StandwithUkraine

77

What Is in a Name?

Have I not commanded you? Be strong and courageous. Do not be afraid; do not be discouraged, for the Lord your God will be with you wherever you go.

Joshua 1:9

After four hundred years of bondage in Egypt, the Israelites prepared to enter Canaan, the land flowing with milk and honey that God had promised to their ancestors. Their leader Moses sent twelve men, one from each tribe, on a forty-day scouting trip. He wanted to know what the inhabitants of the land and their cities looked like and if the land was fertile. The men returned with glowing reports of a land filled with rich produce. They even brought back a branch filled with grapes that were so plentiful that it took two men to carry the grapes that were draped over a pole.

But here came the buts, the unbelief of the ten men who reported, "**But** the people who live there are powerful, and the cities are fortified and very large" (Numbers 13:28). They had seen descendants of giants. "We can't attack those people; they are stronger than we are." The negative report about the land quickly spread among the Israelites. The ten men said, "The land we explored devours those living in it. All the people we saw there are of great size…We seemed like grasshoppers in our own eyes, and we looked the same to them" (13:30-32).

All of the Israelites continued to grumble against Moses, Aaron and the Lord. Joshua and Caleb pleaded with the entire Israelite assembly, "The land we passed through and explored is exceedingly good. If the Lord is pleased with us, he will lead us into that land, a land flowing with milk and honey, and will give it to us. Only do not rebel against the Lord. And do not be afraid of the people of the land, because we will devour them. Their protection is gone, but the Lord is with us. Do not be afraid of them" (14:6-9).

Joshua and Caleb believed that the Lord was with them, and that their strength and God's strength could overcome any foe. Joshua and Caleb made it to the Promised Land, but the ten immediately died from a plague. Their names were Shammua, Shaphat, Igal, Palti, Gaddiel, Gaddi, Ammiel, Sethur, Nahbi and Geuel. None of these are household names.

After forty years in the wilderness, it was Joshua, not Moses, who led the Israelites into the Promised Land. Joshua became a great leader! The book of Joshua contains a great go-to verse for any generation, "Have I not commanded you? Be strong and courageous. Do not be afraid; do not be discouraged, for the Lord your God will be with you wherever you go" (Joshua 1:9).

Let's examine how the traits of leadership, commitment and courage that Joshua displayed have also played out in 2022 through another leader, Ukraine's President Volodymyr Zelensky.

As Russian troops and powerful tanks crossed the border, the people of Ukraine could fight or take flight. The underdogs chose to fight the more powerful Russian army! President Zelensky ordered every able-bodied man from age 18 to 60 to stay in Ukraine and help the Ukrainian army battle this foe.

President Zelensky proclaimed, "I am not afraid of anyone....We will fight till the end." Unlike the Israelites who became divided despite the pleas of Joshua and Caleb, the Ukrainians quickly united behind Zelensky. "For all authority comes from God, and those in positions of authority have been placed there by God" (Romans 13:1).

Because Zelensky is Jewish, he was surely familiar with Joshua's story. Both men fought for what is right. Joshua stood up for taking the land that God had promised Israel, but the people of Israel were sharply divided and experienced forty years in the wilderness. Zelensky inspired the Ukrainian people, who quickly united and are battling to overcome the enemy.

What is in a name? Parents name babies after people they admire and respect. Countless generations named male babies after Joshua and Caleb. According to Google, the first names of Volodymyr (Zelensky) and Vladimir (Putin) are the same but are spelled differently. Vladimir was the name of the first Christian ruler of Russia. What will be the popularity of these two names for future generations of Ukrainians and Russians? After Ukrainian husbands are reunited with their wives and children, and they have more children, how many couples will name their baby boys Volodymyr?

Courage, conviction, and perseverance are needed to defeat oppression. The trials have strengthened Ukraine's resolve. May Ukraine survive this onslaught and become a beacon for hope, democracy, and freedom for generations across the free world.

Let's be grounded in scripture reading and prayer to receive inspiration for how to pray and perform acts of compassion for the Ukrainian people. Here are some suggested prayers regarding Ukraine and Russia.

1) God will perform a miracle in Ukraine.

2) President Zelensky is protected so that he can bravely and wisely lead his nation.

3) Food, shelter, and safety for over two million Ukrainian refugees, most of whom are women and children, and all citizens.

4) Ukrainians maintain "can do" attitudes in the face of stiff and dangerous opposition.

5) Many news sources are made available to the Russian people.

6) Freedom of speech will prevail in Russia. The penalty for saying "war" or "invasion" in Russia can now lead to a sentence of up to 15 years in prison.

7) Release all 14,000 Russians arrested for protesting the war and that arrests will stop, and all others unjustly imprisoned.

8) God will guide world leaders to achieve peace and soften President Putin's heart.

9) Trust in God's will and in God's ways, even as the war rages.

10) Russia will release WNBA star Brittney Griner. She was released in November 2022!

11) U.S. astronaut Mark Vande Hei will return safely from the international space station.

78

Build a Solid Foundation

"Therefore everyone who hears these words of mine and puts them
into practice is like a wise man who built his house on the rock. The
rain came down, the streams rose, and the winds blew and beat against
that house; yet it did not fall, because it had its foundation on the rock.
But everyone who hears these words of mine and does not put them
into practice is like a foolish man who built his house on sand. The
rain came down, the streams rose, and the winds blew and beat against
that house, and it fell with a great crash."

Matthew 7:24-27

The early U.S. Space Program sent the first astronauts through incredibly stressful physical and mental tests because no one was certain
of the challenges that space would present. Alan Shepard, the first astronaut in space, described his 15-minute space flight as "anticlimac-
tic" because he had trained to survive much worse conditions. In his
sermon video series entitled Last Supper on the Moon, Pastor Levi
Lusko described this intense preparation as overtraining.

What does it mean to overtrain? Overtraining can be described as
training beyond what is normally required. I looked at overtraining
from these three standpoints: physical, mental, and spiritual. Physical
overtraining for an athlete could include extra weightlifting and speed,
agility, and flexibility drills that are in addition to team workouts and
practices. Football teams train rigorously during off-season workouts
to build stamina and strength for the fourth quarter of games. The
hardest practices occur on Mondays and Tuesdays when teams prepare
for all of the possible situations on game day.

Overtraining can also include intense preparation for a huge personal challenge such as a triathlon, a marathon, Army Ranger training or Navy SEAL training. Who do you know that overtrains physically?

Overtraining mentally could include taking advanced placement classes that are beyond the regular course work and studying rigorously to excel in these courses. This intense preparation opens doors for scholarships at the best schools, leading to productive careers. Strong preparation at the highest academic level requires an immense sacrifice of time and energy. Who do you know that overtrains mentally?

Lusko posed this question, "Why don't people overtrain spiritually?" Overtraining spiritually is perhaps the toughest challenge because there is not always someone to push you and challenge you. Why should I train spiritually? There is a song, Your Time Is Gonna Come, and your time is going to come when you suffer a setback due to disappointment, injury, or a personal or family setback. You must pull yourself out of that situation or rely on other people.

A lack of spiritual training leads to more bad decisions with undesirable consequences. Being physically fit and mentally strong certainly helps, but a solid spiritual foundation supports everything about your life. Spiritual overtraining prepares you for the biggest temptations and trials, and we don't know when they are coming! Who do you know that overtrains spiritually?

A solid base is everything in sports and in life! Perhaps you have experienced mostly mild breezes in your life. What happens when the big gusts of wind come? Is your base built on the rock? Jesus said, "Therefore everyone who hears these words of mine and puts them into practice is like a wise man who built his house on the rock. The rain came down, the streams rose, and the winds blew and beat against that house; yet it did not fall, because it had its foundation on the rock" (Matthew 7:24-25).

Let's consider how Jesus trained spiritually. As a boy Jesus went to temple on the Sabbath, studied the scriptures, learned the prophecies, and prayed. At age twelve Jesus preached to adults in the temple after he was left behind in Jerusalem by Joseph and Mary. When his parents found him, Jesus said, "Did you not know that I must be about my Father's work" (Luke 2:49).

The Bible shares virtually nothing about Jesus during his teen years and young adult life until he was thirty years old. Most likely Jesus worked as a carpenter and cared for his immediate family. As the oldest sibling, perhaps he became the man of the household. Jesus faced similar difficulties that workers face today. He lived out his faith. Because he was faithful in the smallest tasks, he received the greatest task, to save us from our sins.

At age thirty he began his ministry by emerging victoriously from the wilderness after forty days without succumbing to Satan's temptations! For the next three years he performed miracles, healed people, loved them perfectly, and taught what he had walked. At age thirty-three Jesus, fully human and fully God, was victorious over the cross! He overtrained for the biggest moment in history when he bore the sins of an estimated one hundred billion people, past, present and future, withstanding the crushing emotional burden and the excruciating pain of the thirty-nine lashes, the nails, and his spilled blood.

If we will train spiritually with the intentionality that is so often reserved for athletics, academics, and our careers, we can be strong because of God's strength, no matter the trials that we face. Reading God's Word, prayer, obedience, and serving others are four opportunities to overtrain.

• Read the Bible – "The whole Bible was given to us by inspiration from God and is useful to teach us what is true and to make us realize what is wrong in our lives; it straightens us out and helps us do what is right. It is God's way of making us well prepared at every point, fully equipped to do good to everyone" (2 Timothy 3:16-17 TLB).
• Pray – "The prayer of a righteous person is powerful and effective" (James 5:16(b)).
"Don't worry about anything; instead, pray about everything. Tell God what you need, and thank him for all he has done" (Philippians 4:6).
• Obey – "Obedience is better than sacrifice" (1 Samuel 15:22).
• Serve others – "Well done, good and faithful servant" (Matthew 25:21). "Just as the Son of Man did not come to be served, but to serve, and to give his life as a ransom for many" (Matthew 20:28).

Let's honor Jesus's sacrifice by overtraining spiritually. Read extra scripture. Preparation in the Word leads to belief and increased faith. Say extra prayers. Be obedient in life's tiny details. Serve others in new ways that make a difference. Trials, disappointments and setbacks are inevitable. They are going to happen. Overtrain now and give God the glory!

79

Scottie Scheffler, Child of God and Masters Champion

The steps of a good man are ordered by the Lord,
and he delights in his way.
Psalm 37:23

Prior to winning the 2022 Masters, Scottie Scheffler was a name that was familiar to golf fans but was unfamiliar to casual sports fans. All that changed after he won the 86th Masters golf tournament. The Masters win was his fourth in the past eight weeks, the first coming on Super Bowl Sunday when he won a playoff in Phoenix. Scheffler became the first golfer since Arnold Palmer to win three times in a calendar year before the Masters and also to win the Masters. That's good company!

This humble and extremely talented young Texan had become the fastest player to reach number one in the world after winning his first PGA TOUR tournament. Scottie's confidence had grown after his stellar play in the 2021 Ryder Cup. Captain Steve Stricker was roundly criticized by golf experts after making Scheffler a captain's pick, even though he had never won on the PGA Tour. The experts were proven to be oh, so wrong about Scheffler.

Scottie's brilliant play at Augusta was highlighted by two crucial shots on the eighteenth hole on Saturday and on the third hole on Sunday. On Saturday, Scheffler was forced to take a penalty for an unplayable lie after driving wildly into a bush. As the CBS camera operator followed him into the bushes as he pondered his options, his calm demeanor and methodical thought processing was exemplary. Following his drop, he drilled his third shot with a long iron over 240 yards right at the flagstick. He got up and down for an excellent bogey and now led by three going into Sunday's pressure-packed final round.

On Sunday, Scottie's lead was cut to one after the first two holes. Scottie's approach to the par-four third hole was short, and his ball rolled down a steep slope and came to rest forty yards from the flagstick. Then came the shot of the tournament for Scottie. Scheffler pitched his third shot into the slope, and the ball hopped onto the green. Rolling at a significant pace, the ball crashed into the flagstick and fell into the hole for a birdie three! Smith bogeyed the hole, and Scottie regained his three-shot cushion and never looked back. All of those threes seem rather Biblical, don't they?

A Biblical perspective is relevant to Scottie as a person. A high school golfer texted me that he was "super inspired" by Scottie and how "no matter whether he won or lost or never stepped on the golf course again, he understood that he was loved no matter what. He understood that God was going to use him for his kingdom."

Meredith Scheffler, who married Scottie in December 2020, brought her husband wise counsel and peace on Sunday morning after Scottie became very emotional. Feeling the pressure of holding the Masters lead for two consecutive nights, Scottie shared, "This morning was a different story. I cried like a baby this morning. I was so stressed out. I didn't know what to do. I was sitting there telling Meredith, 'I don't think I'm ready for this. I'm not ready. I don't feel like I'm ready for this stuff.' And I just felt overwhelmed."

Scottie continued, "Like Meredith told me this morning, 'If you win this golf tournament today, if you lose this golf tournament by ten shots. If you never win another golf tournament again…I'm still going to love you, you're still going to be the same person. Jesus loves you, and nothing changes.' All I'm trying to do is glorify God and that's why I'm here and that's why I'm in position."

As Scheffler stood on the 72nd tee with a five-shot lead, CBS Broadcaster Jim Nantz shared that Scottie and his caddie, Ted Scott, met at a PGA TOUR Bible Study. Eventually Scott, who was on the bag for Bubba Watson's two Masters victories, became Scottie's new caddie. Scott received well-deserved acclaim for Scottie's rapid ascension that culminated with Scottie's first green jacket. Yes, first, because this team has what it takes to win more! Scottie and Scott go together like a Masters pimento cheese sandwich and an Arnold Palmer, which is half-tea and half-lemonade.

Michael Bamberger wrote, "On Tuesday night of Masters week, in a second-floor dining room in the clubhouse, the Masters winners gather for dinner. Hogan started the tradition. Scheffler will keep it going. Everybody sits at one long table and Bernhard Langer, Zach Johnson and Larry Mize sit together in the praise-the-Lord, pass-the-biscuits section of the table. Scheffler will be right at home with them."

Late in his life, King David, the psalmist, wrote, "The steps of a good man are ordered by the Lord, and he delights in his way" (Psalm 37:23). I believe this verse aptly befits a very good man, Scottie Scheffler. One might read this verse and think, *As long as I am good enough and honor the Lord, I won't have troubles.* But failures are steppingstones to success, I once heard. Scottie's steps around Augusta National in 2022, particularly his steps immediately following the two errant shots, will be remembered as long as the Masters is played. May Scottie continue to receive opportunities on golf's biggest stages and bring more glory to God.

80

On the Road Again

On the road again, Just can't wait to get on the road again...

On the Road Again, Willie Nelson

Jesus's final walk before his death began on the Via Dolorosa and ended at Golgotha. But he had told his disciples on three separate occasions that he would rise on the third day. But they didn't understand.

Have you ever thought, *Friday and Sunday are only two days apart. Why did Jesus refer to his resurrection on the third day?* Jesus's lifeless body was removed from the Cross before sundown Friday per Jewish tradition. According to first-century Jews, any part of any day could be counted as a full day. Jesus was in the tomb during part or all of three different days.

The following account occurred on Resurrection Sunday. *...very early in the morning, the women took the spices they had prepared and went to the tomb. They found the stone rolled away from the tomb, but when they entered, they did not find the body of the Lord Jesus. While they were wondering about this, suddenly two men in clothes that gleamed like lightning stood beside them.*

In their fright the women bowed down with their faces to the ground, but the men said to them, "Why do you look for the living among the dead? He is not here; he has risen! Remember how he told you, while he was still with you in Galilee: The Son of Man must be delivered over to the hands of sinners, be crucified and on the third day be raised again.' Then they remembered his words (Luke 24:1-8).

Later that same day Jesus would walk with two downcast followers on the road to Emmaus.

Now that same day two of them were going to a village called Emmaus, about seven miles from Jerusalem. They were talking with each other about everything that had happened. As they talked and discussed these things with each other, Jesus himself came up and walked along with them; but they were kept from recognizing him.

He asked them, "What are you discussing together as you walk along?"

They stood still, their faces downcast. One of them, named Cleopas, asked him, "Are you the only one visiting Jerusalem who does not know the things that have happened there in these days?"

"What things?" he asked.

"About Jesus of Nazareth," they replied. "He was a prophet, powerful in word and deed before God and all the people. The chief priests and our rulers handed him over to be sentenced to death, and they crucified him; but we had hoped that he was the one who was going to redeem Israel. And what is more, it is the third day since all this took place. In addition, some of our women amazed us. They went to the tomb early this morning but didn't find his body. They came and told us that they had seen a vision of angels, who said he was alive. Then some of our companions went to the tomb and found it just as the women had said, but they did not see Jesus."

He said to them, "How foolish you are, and how slow to believe all that the prophets have spoken! Did not the Messiah have to suffer these things and then enter his glory?" And beginning with Moses and all the Prophets, he explained to them what was said in all the Scriptures concerning himself.

As they approached the village to which they were going, Jesus continued on as if he were going farther. But they urged him strongly, "Stay with us, for it is nearly evening; the day is almost over." So he went in to stay with them.

When he was at the table with them, he took bread, gave thanks, broke it and began to give it to them. Then their eyes were opened and they recognized him, and he disappeared from their sight. They asked each other, "Were not our hearts burning within us while he talked with us on the road and opened the Scriptures to us?"

They got up and returned at once to Jerusalem. There they found the Eleven and those with them, assembled together and saying, "It is true! The Lord has risen and has appeared to Simon." Then the two told what had happened on the way, and how Jesus was recognized by them when he broke the bread" (Luke 24:11-35).

Happy Easter! Jesus is alive! He loves you perfectly no matter what you've done in the past, and he died for your sins and rose on the third day so that he can accompany you on your daily journey. Jesus can't wait to walk with you on your road. Again. And again. And again.

81

Please Come In

Whatever you do, work at it with all your heart,
as working for the Lord...

Colossians 3:23

He Is Risen...So What? The Tuesday after Easter, the Crosspointe Community Church marquee on Crossville Road displayed the following phrase: He Is Risen...So What? How should followers of Jesus answer "So What?" How do we walk with Jesus on this side of Easter?

One way is by involving Jesus in all aspects of our lives. Here is an illustration of shutting Jesus out of an area. I picked up my four-year-old grandson Will from preschool. After we arrived home and he had a snack, he scurried to his bedroom to put on his play clothes, which are comfortable pajamas that he likes to pick out by himself. I followed Will to help him, but he got there first. He flipped on the light and shut his bedroom door before I could enter! Then he said, "Don't come in here."

A couple of minutes later he appeared in fresh PJ's, and not the PJ's he wore the night before. Sometimes he wears a dinosaur top and a lion bottom, but that's ok. He's four!

Several years after I came to a personal relationship with Jesus, I was still not allowing him to come into my workspace. I thought, I've been successful doing it my way. Why do I need to change anything? But following a merger, I found myself in a precarious situation. I realized that I needed Jesus in my workspace after all. In fact, I needed him desperately.

Take a few moments to reflect on your relationship with Jesus. Have you consciously or unconsciously excluded him from engaging in your daily activities as a coach, teacher, child, spouse, or parent?

When a team has a glaring weakness in its defensive scheme, the opposing offense can do a lot of damage. So can the devil when you go it alone by saying, "Don't come in here, Jesus."

Instead, include Jesus in whatever you are doing and say, "Jesus, please come in." "Whatever you do, work at it with all your heart, as working for the Lord" (Colossians 3:23). Discover the positive difference that it will make for you and for others!

What are some other ways to walk more closely with Jesus?

1) Learn all that you can about Jesus. Facts about his crucifixion, death and resurrection and the associated prophecies increase your level of understanding and your faith.

2) Keep convincing yourself as Lee Strobel did when he wrote *The Case for Christ*.

3) Place your trust in Jesus. Show no concern for the uncertainties that lie ahead.

4) RPO's (Read, Pray, Obey and Serve) are daily investments in staying strong and minimizing "turnovers" (bad decisions with undesirable consequences).

5) Demonstrate the love of Christ by treating others with respect and acceptance.

82
Jesus's Draft

You did not choose me, but I chose you and appointed you so that you
might go and bear fruit—fruit that will last...

John 15:16

April 28-30 is the weekend of the 2022 NFL Draft in Las Vegas.
It has been estimated that up to a million NFL fans will come to Vegas; that estimate is 65% higher than the 600,000 fans who accessed
the NFL Draft app in Nashville in 2019.

Thousands of fans from every NFL team will be there for the
draft, which follows the NFL Combine, dozens of Pro Days on college
campuses, thousands of private workouts, and endless mock drafts
provided by NFL draft analysts such as Kiper, McShay, Reid, and Miller. These four analysts selected their top forty players in a mock draft.

Here are their first twelve players. Willis, Walker, Hamilton, and
Johnson have ties to the state of Georgia.

1. Kiper: Aidan Hutchinson, DE, Michigan
2. McShay: Ikem Ekwonu, OT, NC State
3. Reid: Malik Willis, QB, Liberty
4. Miller: Evan Neal, OT, Alabama
5. Miller: Travon Walker, DE, Georgia
6. Reid: Kayvon Thibodeaux, DE, Oregon
7. McShay: Ahmad Gardner, CB, Cincinnati
8. Kiper: Kenny Pickett, QB, Pittsburgh
9. Kiper: Derek Stingley Jr., CB, LSU
10. McShay: Kyle Hamilton, S, Notre Dame
11. Reid: Charles Cross, OT, Mississippi State

12. Miller: Jermaine Johnson II, DE, Florida State

As talented as these young men are, and as much as they would like to have a say in the matter, the teams they play for will be determined by the NFL owners and general managers. The player does not choose his team; the team chooses the player. The team appoints that player to get in the best possible mental and physical condition so that he might bear fruit (make plays), fruit that will last (championship rings). Only time will tell what impact these men will make on their respective franchises.

Consider Jesus's draft selections, who were the members of the most important team ever selected. These were Jesus's twelve disciples, also known as the primary disciples or the apostles of Jesus. Have you ever considered the order in which they were selected?

The gospels of Matthew, Mark, Luke and John offer different versions of how Jesus selected his disciples; these gospels are different viewpoints of the authors and thus are not contradictory. Here is a combined view of the order of Jesus's selections from a "draft" standpoint.

Andrew and Simon Peter – First round (Mark 1:16-18)
James and John – Second round (Matthew 4:21-22)
Philip and Nathanael – Third round (John 1:43-51)
Matthew – Fourth round (Matthew 9:9-13)
Thomas, James of Alphaeus, Simon the Zealot, Judas and Judas Iscariot – Latter rounds

Jesus chose these twelve men for his "expansion" franchise. As with any new team, it took time for them to develop and mature. After three years of following Jesus, they were still together until Judas Iscariot betrayed Jesus, which left eleven. The Eleven were given the Great Commission to expand the kingdom of God following Jesus's ascension.

There were times when they didn't get it right. James and John, members of Jesus's inner circle, asked Jesus for special seats at his left hand and right hand, and this caused friction within the team. Peter, the third member of the inner circle, was prone to emotional outbursts. Sometimes Peter's mouth wrote checks that he couldn't cover. He denied Jesus three times before the cock crowed during Jesus's time of despair. The three men couldn't stay awake when Jesus needed them to pray in the Garden. Thomas had doubts about the resurrection.

On the evening of Resurrection Day, Jesus breathed the Holy Spirit upon the Eleven in the Upper Room. Yet they began their fourth year fishing for tilapia when Jesus needed them to be fishing for men!

But Jesus's team clicked in that fourth season after Jesus ascended to heaven and the Holy Spirit came down on his disciples at Pentecost. These ordinary men became extraordinary as they tapped the power of the Holy Spirit. Peter and James performed numerous miracles and led thousands of people to Christ, including Gentiles. According to Christianity.com, ten of the eleven died prematurely for their faith. The groundwork laid by Jesus's eleven selections formed the foundation for the universal church, which has grown to over two billion people.

How does all of this relate to us as members of God's universal church? Perhaps we've been slow to start bearing fruit. Perhaps we started well but have cooled off. The good news is that just like there was hope for the Eleven, there is hope for us. God still has important things in store!

The apostle John wrote, "You did not choose me, but I chose you and appointed you so that you might go and bear fruit—fruit that will last..." (John 15:16). God chose us. He appointed us. God created us in his image and equipped us with "first-round" spiritual gifts to build up and edify the body of Christ on earth.

The Eleven trained for three years to meet the challenges that Jesus gave them before they bore substantial fruit. We can reach our potential as first-rounders by knowing Jesus personally through his Word, prayer, and obedience, loving others as Jesus would love them, and diligently doing the specific work that God gives us.

Each person's opportunities to impact God's kingdom are unique. Therefore, we need not feel pressure to do what other people are doing. Let's try to execute according to his will on our daily opportunities.

Know Jesus, love others, do God's work. Do these three things consistently, and you will bear kingdom fruit that lasts.

83
Student-Athlete Profile: Craig Long

Commit your work to the Lord, and your plans will be established.

Proverbs 16:3

It has been my pleasure to serve as a spiritual mentor for my brother in Christ, Craig Long. Craig is a junior at Milton High School and is a member of the golf team. He led his team to the state title in 2021 by winning the individual medalist and was the GHSA Class 7-A High School Player of the Year. Craig also played in the 2021 Georgia State Amateur.

Craig and I met in August of 2021 via Zoom shortly after Craig returned from an AJGA event. We hit it off immediately through our mutual love for Jesus and golf, and we have continued to meet weekly for Bible study and encouragement.

In September Craig and another Milton athlete initiated the restart of the Milton FCA campus huddle for athletes from multiple sports after a hiatus due to COVID restrictions. They found a faculty sponsor, and Craig put his heart and soul into the new huddle.

Craig's energy and passion make him the perfect "hype man" to kick off the huddle each Friday at 7:15 am. He also booked the guest speakers and shared his testimony with the huddle this winter.

It is always a pleasure to interact with Craig and share our love for golf and our faith. Craig reflects Christ through his positive interactions on and off the golf course. He has an engaging smile and personality and cherishes his relationships with other golfers of faith. Craig is an extremely hard worker and seeks to maintain balance with his schoolwork, his golf practice, FCA, personal worship with God, and his relationships in life. He maintains a positive outlook and excellent attitude, and optimistic outlook. Thank you for living out your faith during high school through smart decisions and consistently making good choices!

Craig and I collaborated on the following Q&As.

Q. How did your feel when you found out that your team won the state championship and that you won the individual title?

A. To be truthful I was just in disbelief. I had been struggling with covid only 3 weeks before. I had lost fifteen pounds and was really struggling getting healthy. But I worked my butt off to get back and felt that I was ready to hoist that trophy high.

Q. How valuable have our meetings over the past eight months been for you, and how have our weekly one-hour Zoom meetings helped you?

A: They have kept me afloat in many cases. I have learned how great my God is and how I should give him the Glory because he paid the ultimate price. I have called Dan out of the blue multiple times, and he always answers when I need him. He is a true brother in Christ and every week I look forward to being guided towards Christ through his mentorship.

Q: How important was it to have that FCA huddle and leadership team in your life at that particular time in the fall?

A: It was crucial. I was truly struggling with my game in the fall and God blessed me with an amazing community of Jesus loving high schoolers. Many of mornings I have woken up at 4 am to make sure that we are giving people the best representation of what Jesus did for us. It has given me community but also an opportunity for me to share my story.

Q: It is evident that you are driven to play for a top-tier college program. Those desires and expectations can bring a lot of pressure. How difficult is it to find balance in your life with such demands on your time that require you to travel to AJGA events across the country?

A: It is very hard for sure. I pray about it all the time. I think it starts with the fact that I believe that God has given me a gift, thus I want to do anything I can to use it for his Glory. That drives me through the pain and the confusion of having to find that balance.

Q: You and I talked about winning the day for Jesus much like you would seek to win a match hole by hole. Talk about your approach to get your day started in Christ and maintain that momentum.

A: This is something that I will continue to work on, but I love starting the day off by reading a passage from the Bible. Any passage, it doesn't matter. Then I love to pray, I love to communicate with our God. Then my final step would be to grab a verse and remember it throughout the day.

Q. Tell me about the gratitude that you have for your mom and dad and your inner circle of family members and friends who support you as you pursue your dream. How grateful are you for their support?

A: I am extremely grateful. There have been so many points where they could've given up on me, but they keep encouraging me. I love those people because they don't care how I play, they care about who I become.

Q. How do you see yourself using golf as a platform to reach others for Christ?

A: I want to play golf professionally. I want to play on the PGA Tour and use my platform to inspire kids to pursue their dreams through a Jesus-loving heart.

Q. Share one of your favorite Bible verses, and how does that verse inspire you?

A. My favorite verse at the moment is Proverbs 16:3, "Commit your work to the Lord, and your plans will be established." This verse is important to me because it is helping me most directly in my life right now. This verse inspires me to give my dream every I have while giving God the glory.

Update: In the summer of 2022 Craig accepted a golf scholarship from Northern Illinois University!

84
Student-Athlete Profile: Rob Ferris

And whatever you do, whether in word or deed, do it all in the name of the Lord Jesus, giving thanks to God the Father through Him.

Colossians 3:17

Rob Ferris is a member of the Roswell HS Class of 2022 and will attend the United States Military Academy at West Point on a golf scholarship. What an outstanding achievement!

It has been my pleasure to be Rob's friend and brother in Christ for the past five years. We met at Crabapple MS FCA where Rob played guitar for the FCA leadership team. It has been a joy watching him progress and develop into an outstanding student-athlete at Roswell High!

It has always been a pleasure to interact with Rob and share our love of golf and our faith. He reflects Christ through his positive interactions, engaging personality, excellent attitude, and optimistic outlook. Rob has lived out his faith during high school through smart decisions that have led to consistently good choices. Rob's strong work ethic, leadership skills, teamwork, perseverance, and discipline make him an outstanding investment for West Point!

Rob and I collaborated on these Q&As.

Q. You've served the Lord playing guitar for FCA campus huddles since seventh grade. How did you learn to play guitar, and what do you enjoy about music? How does music serve as a relaxing outlet from the pressures of school life and competing in golf tournaments?

A. I asked for a guitar for Christmas in the second grade. I took lessons from second to sixth grade and have played ever since. Playing for FCA has always been a great way to connect with God during the week and escape from the pressures of daily life.

Q. How do you maintain your relationship with Christ amidst the pressures, distractions and temptations that student-athletes face?

A. As an athlete, it's not always easy to go to church on Sunday mornings, but the little things help me stay close to God. FCA, bible studies, or reading a devotional book are great ways to maintain a strong relationship with God.

Q. Tell us how your interest in West Point evolved. What do you hope to achieve during your four years there?

A. I started talking to the West Point golf coach last summer and saw it as a great way to play D1 golf, get a great education, and serve our great country. I'd love to have success on the golf course and become a great Army officer.

Q. How do you feel about the personal demands of such a prestigious yet demanding school?

A. It will definitely be intense at West Point, but I know I will be surrounded by a great group of leaders, mentors, peers, and God to help me through the struggles. Your golf career spanned all four years at Roswell HS. You had statewide success as a freshman when you qualified individually for the GHSA 7-A State Tournament.

Q. What was the feeling when you found out you would be moving on from Area and other memories from your freshman year in 2019?

A. It was a great feeling. I knew that I played well, but our team wasn't going to make it. As a freshman, I didn't know individuals went to state. My mom told me walking off the 18th green that I was going to make it, and I was overjoyed!

Q. Your team qualified for state when you were a junior. How would you compare the feeling of being there with your teammates to representing the team by yourself as a freshman?

A. It was infinitely better to compete for a state title as a team! I've always been a team-oriented person, and it made it a lot more fun for me.

Q. This year at Area as a senior you came so close, firing an outstanding even-par round on a windy day, yet missing qualifying for state by one stroke. How did you feel knowing that you played well but would not be going back to state, any regrets?

A. It was definitely a bit crushing, knowing that I wouldn't get to play in state for my senior year. I was comforted by the fact that I had played well, but also knew that I missed a lot of short putts that day that would've helped me qualify.

Q. Tell me about the support for your golf career that you have received from your parents since you were in elementary school. How has your relationship evolved, and why has it been so special?

A. The support I have received from my parents has been second to none. I can't thank them enough for their continued support both financially and with their time. It means the world to me.

Update: Rob completed his first semester as a member of the golf team at the U.S. Military Academy!

85

Continually Serving God

Now when Daniel learned that the decree had been published, he went home to his upstairs room where the windows opened toward Jerusalem. Three times a day he got down on his knees and prayed, giving thanks to his God, just as he had done before. Then these men went as a group and found Daniel praying and asking God for help. So they went to the king and spoke to him about his royal decree: "Did you not publish a decree that during the next thirty days anyone who prays to any god or human being except to you, Your Majesty, would be thrown into the lions' den?" The king answered, "The decree stands—in accordance with the law of the Medes and Persians, which cannot be repealed." Then they said to the king, "Daniel, who is one of the exiles from Judah, pays no attention to you, Your Majesty, or to the decree you put in writing. He still prays three times a day." When the king heard this, he was greatly distressed; he was determined to rescue Daniel and made every effort until sundown to save him. Then the men went as a group to King Darius and said to him, "Remember, Your Majesty, that according to the law of the Medes and Persians no decree or edict that the king issues can be changed." So the king gave the order, and they brought Daniel and threw him into the lions' den. The king said to Daniel, "May your God, whom you serve continually, rescue you!"

Daniel 6:10-16

Daniel's peers in the king's courts were jealous of him, so they pressured King Darius into issuing an edict that anyone who prayed to any god but King Darius over the next thirty days would be cast into the lions' den. But Daniel kept praying three times a day facing Jerusalem. The Enduring Word Commentary points out that most people would consider praying to be dangerous, but Daniel felt praying to his God was the safest thing he could do. King Darius recognized that Daniel served his God continually based on Daniel's high integrity.

I mentor Craig, a high school golfer, and followed him during the state tournament. Before his second round I told him, "You play hard. I'll pray hard!" It would have been easy to just watch golf, but I decided to pray intentionally for Craig. A golfer's nerves are edgiest before hitting the first tee shot, attempting short putts, and executing risky shots. I prayed short phrases. Keep your emotions in check. Stay in the moment. Be where your feet are, which means to concentrate on the shot before you. Don't get ahead of yourself or dwell on a bad shot.

I wished that I had prayed for the young man in Craig's threesome who had a really tough second round. His composure on the course was admirable. After the round I noticed him crying behind the eighteenth green. I motioned for Craig to come over and share some words of encouragement. After Craig spoke with him, his mom hugged Craig's mom in gratitude!

Prayer is a terrific way to serve God continually during the day. The evangelist Charles Spurgeon suggested that Daniel may have prayed three hundred times a day, not just three. What a difference that praying for others makes! When we pray for others, the Holy Spirit prompts us to reach out in Christian love. What a difference that talking to God throughout your day can make! Frequent prayer keeps us connected with God through the Holy Spirit, which helps us "when we don't know how to pray or know what to pray for" (see Romans 8:26 TLB).

Studies have shown that the average person has thousands of thoughts daily. How many of those thoughts are in the Spirit, and how many thoughts are in the flesh? Second Corinthians 10:5 encourages us to "take captive every thought and make it obedient to Christ." How many of our worried and anxious thoughts do we convert to prayer?

Prayer comes in various forms. A brother in Christ talked about the acronym ACTS. The "A" represents offering adoration and praise to God. The "C" is confessing our sins, which restores us in right relationship with God. The "T" represents giving thanks to God for specific blessings. The "S" is for supplication, which is earnestly lifting up prayers for our needs and especially for the needs of others, which is intercessory prayer.

When we praise God for his goodness and faithfulness, thank him for our blessings, pray for many who need healing, hope, and restoration, confess our sins and ask for forgiveness, and worship our Creator who made eternal life with him possible through the death and resurrection of His Son, Jesus Christ, that's a day spent continually serving God!

86
Crack the Code!

"Lord, listen! Lord, forgive! Lord, hear and act!
For your sake, my God, do not delay, because your city and your people bear your Name."

Daniel 9:19

Olympic athletes begin training several years in advance for their next Olympic events. The prophet Daniel prayed several years in advance for Jerusalem's desolation to end after seventy years, according to Jeremiah's prophecy. Daniel prayed with fervor and strong belief in the goodness and righteousness of God. He prayed a prayer of repentance, much like King David's prayer in Psalm 51 and the prayer of confession at many churches that begins, "Merciful God, we have not been an obedient church. We have not done your will..."

Daniel included himself with the people of Israel as he asked for repentance for the sins of Israel that had led to the siege by Babylon. "Lord,...we have sinned and done wrong. We have been wicked and have rebelled; we have turned away from your commands and laws. We have not listened to your servants the prophets, who spoke in your name to our kings, our princes and our ancestors, and to all the people of the land...We and our kings, our princes and our ancestors are covered with shame, Lord, because we have sinned against you. We have not obeyed the Lord our God or kept the laws he gave us through his servants the prophets..." (Daniel 9:4-6, 8, 10).

Daniel pled passionately with God for forgiveness, mercy, and action. "Now, our God, hear the prayers and petitions of your servant. For your sake, Lord, look with favor on your desolate sanctuary. Give ear, our God, and hear; open your eyes and see the desolation of the city that bears your Name. We do not make requests of you because we are righteous, but because of your great mercy. Lord, listen! Lord, forgive! Lord, hear and act! For your sake, my God, do not delay, because your city and your people bear your Name" (Daniel 9:17-19).

Daniel's fervent prayer was rooted in God's goodness and righteousness and expressed great trust in God and dependence on him. Sports teach us to play with intensity, and we should pray with the same intensity that Daniel did.

While Daniel was praying, God sent the angel Gabriel to relay an unparalleled prophetic word to Daniel. God answered Daniel's prayers for Jerusalem, and Daniel received much more than he could have ever imagined because he prayed with conviction and faith. "He instructed me and said to me, "Daniel, I have now come to give you insight and understanding. As soon as you began to pray, a word went out, which I have come to tell you, for you are highly esteemed. Therefore, consider the word and understand the vision:" (Daniel 9:22-23).

God revealed the Seventy Weeks Prophecy to Daniel as a reward for his intentionality. First, God gave Daniel the prophecy of the First Coming of Christ. Jesus rode into Jerusalem on Palm Sunday on April 10, 32 A.D., the exact date according to Scripture and Biblical prophecy. That date was calculated and verified by Sir Robert Anderson, a Scotland Yard investigator at the turn of the 20th century. In the 17th century the great Sir Isaac Newton failed to explain the date. Imagine the sense of accomplishment that Anderson felt after "cracking the code" that went undiscovered for centuries!

Anderson's discovery of the exact date of Jesus's arrival was so powerful that some Jewish scholars admitted that their ancestors crucified Jesus the Messiah, according to the Enduring Word Commentary.

Gabriel said to Daniel, "Here is what you must understand: From the time the word goes out to rebuild Jerusalem until the coming of the Anointed Leader, there will be seven sevens. The rebuilding will take sixty-two sevens, including building streets and digging a moat. Those will be rough times. After the sixty-two sevens, the Anointed Leader will be killed—the end of him…" (Daniel 9:25-26 MSG).

Here is how it played out. In 445 B. C. the prophet Nehemiah received permission from the king to rebuild the gates and walls of Jerusalem, granting a destroyed Jerusalem political sovereignty and making Jerusalem a sovereign city/state. This edict set the clock ticking for the Seventy Weeks of Daniel prophecy. According to Bible scholars, the Seventy Weeks represents seventy periods that are each seven years in length.

Anderson calculated the first sixty-nine weeks. He determined from his study of Genesis that a Biblical month is 30 days, and a Biblical year is 30 days per month x 12 months = 360 days. He calculated that the Sixty-Nine weeks is equivalent to 69 x 7 = 483 biblical years x 360 days per year = 173,880 days, which equals 476 calendar years plus 25 days (based on 365.2242 days per year).

Amazingly, Gabriel then gave Daniel the prophecy of the Second Coming of Christ. "'Then for one seven, he will forge many and strong alliances, but halfway through the seven he will banish worship and prayers. At the place of worship, a desecrating obscenity will be set up and remain until finally the desecrator himself is decisively destroyed'" (Daniel 9:27 MSG). Note: We are currently in the gap of almost two thousand years between Week 69 and Week 70, which has yet to come.

Daniel was blessed with so much more than he prayed for, because he intentionally and passionately put in the time and effort to pray each day for many decades. We can receive much more than we ask for when we intentionally put in the time and effort to pray each day during our lifetimes. We can "crack the code" on deeper understanding of God's truth that he desires for us.

What are you praying for in advance? How does Daniel's prayer life motivate you to strengthen yours?

Here are four ways to enrich your prayer life. I encourage you to select one and put it into action.

1. Create a prayer list, then update it daily.
2. Double your prayer time.
3. Pray with more emphasis on God's goodness and righteousness.
4. Combine Scripture reading with your prayer time.

87

And One!

The Holy Spirit helps us with our daily problems and in our praying. For we don't even know what to pray for, nor how to pray as we should; but the Holy Spirit prays for us with such feeling that it cannot be expressed in words. And he who searches our hearts knows the mind of the Spirit, because the Spirit intercedes for God's people in accordance with the will of God.

Romans 8:26-27 (TLB)

The phrase "And one!" is extremely popular among basketball fans. Every fan thrills to see the old-fashioned three-point play when Stephen Curry or Jaylen Brown takes the ball to the basket, gets fouled as he goes up, and twists his body to spin the ball off the glass into the basket. Fans leap to their feet, fist bump and high-five each other, and scream, "AND ONE!!"

"And one" means that the basket counts, and the player receives a free throw to convert the three-point play. In addition to the two-point basket, the player receives a bonus as a reward for the excellent play.

Immediately when you place your trust in Jesus as your Savior, you receive God's gift of grace and eternal life in heaven. You also receive a huge bonus because the Holy Spirit that descended upon Jesus like a dove, and the Holy Spirit that Jesus promised his disciples as a Comforter and Helper, now lives in you as a Person. God, the Father, and Jesus, the Son of God, are the two most well-known members of the Holy Trinity, but the Holy Spirit, the "And One," can help us in so many ways.

It's difficult to understand how the Spirit lives within you and me, but don't try to figure it out. Just trust it. The Holy Spirit helps you with your daily problems. Concerned because sometimes you don't know how to pray or what to pray for? The Holy Spirit completes our prayers with such passion that it can't be described. Take full advantage each day of all that the Holy Spirit, our "And One," has to offer.

88
The Green Dot

The Holy Spirit helps us with our daily problems.

Romans 8:26 (TLB)

An increase in the number of NFL domed stadiums, which hold much more noise than open-air stadiums, placed a greater burden on quarterbacks.

In 2006, the NFL placed a tiny receiver in the helmet of the quarterback to help him receive plays from the offensive coordinator. A green dot marks any helmet with the special communications device. The device allows one-way communication to the quarterback from the offensive coordinator during the first twenty-five seconds on the play clock.

Two years later, the league installed the same device in the helmet of a defensive player. Usually, an inside linebacker, who is the quarterback of the defense, wears a green-dot helmet. These devices allow teams to execute the correct calls more frequently with fewer mistakes.

Sometimes, we don't execute the play that God wants because we aren't listening closely. Through the Holy Spirit, we have access to his inner voice that tells us what to do if we pause long enough to listen.

Some might say that it's an audible voice, but most would say that it is inaudible. It takes being connected with God through the Holy Spirit to sense that little voice that comes in the form of a thought.

The next time God speaks to you through your "receiver in a helmet" and gives you sound guidance through the Spirit of God, thank him and act on his advice!

89
Daily Workouts

You must work out your own salvation in fear and trembling. For it is God who works in you, inspiring both the will and the deed, for his chosen purpose.

Philippians 2:12–13

Daily workouts are an important regimen for any professional athlete. A top-flight athlete will hire a personal trainer who tailors a program that enables the athlete to achieve peak physical condition. Because each athlete's body is unique and different physical attributes need to be developed for a particular sport, the workout regimen will vary from athlete to athlete.

Gaining maximum efficiency comes down to how much effort an athlete is willing to put into his daily workout. How much of a price is an athlete willing to pay to achieve his or her goals? I recall the late NFL Hall of Fame running back Walter Payton inviting his pro football friends to join him for an off-season workout. They were about to find out why Walter Payton became the all-time leading rusher in NFL history while never suffering a major injury. He took them to the sandy levees of his native Mississippi delta. On a sizzling summer afternoon, Walter challenged them to complete his daily routine of running up the steep slopes. Their feet bogged down in the sand, creating huge footprints. It was a major exertion to walk these steep slopes, much less to run wind sprints! All of them dropped out, and some lost their lunches in the process. Meanwhile, Walter churned out sprints in the scorching heat.

It's important that we put in daily workouts to grow in our faith and draw closer to God. We're all different, so one size will not fit all.

Some may gravitate to reading the Bible, and some will enjoy reading devotions with Bible verses. Still others are naturally drawn to prayer and meditation, and others may be drawn to spiritual music. All of our efforts should honor and worship God. What is important is that you find your daily regimen that will allow you to withstand the enemy by putting on the armor of God.

You must determine the time and effort that you put into your daily spiritual workout. Your time will vary day to day, depending on your schedule. It doesn't always have to be the same daily Bible reading and prayer routine. Athletes will vary their daily workouts. They will run one day and lift the next day to give specific muscles a chance to rest.

I realize that pro athletes are paid to work out several hours a day and have tons of free time that you may not have with a busy work or school schedule and family commitments. But God will honor the time that we can carve out of our days, even if it's fifteen minutes in the morning or evening. God will bless us when we intentionally connect with him daily. You may surprise yourself by reaching spiritual discipline goals that you didn't believe were possible. Be faithful to the daily spiritual tasks, and give God the glory, honor, and praise for the people and situations that he brings you as a result of your dedication to worship.

90
A Helping Hand

When you refused to help the least of these my brothers and sisters, you were refusing to help me.

Matthew 25:45

My friend Taylor invited me to speak at a summer girls basketball camp in Athens about the legacy of "Pistol Pete" Maravich. After my talk, he and I were eating our lunches as we sat against the gym wall. He paused and said, "Look at that girl sitting by herself down there." Sure enough, there were about thirty-five girls chatting animatedly, but one girl sat by herself, obviously downcast and staring across the gym.

I said, "That was really good of you to notice her. I didn't even see her sitting down there. Why did you notice, and I didn't?" Taylor said, "I've been there [like that kid]." To his credit, he called over to the coach, who sent two girls to talk to her. Within a few minutes, she sat in the middle of the girls, doing fine.

The episode reminded me of a story that was shared at a lay speaking class. Sherri, a children's education leader at a local church, participated in a training class about caring and compassion with many lay people and church leaders. There were four tables at lunch. One table had a great spread of food with silverware. Two other tables had box lunches. The people at the fourth table had no food, and they sat uncomfortably while the others enjoyed their food.

Someone finally spoke up and asked why the fourth table didn't have any food. That revelation was the purpose of the training. It had been twenty-two minutes before a believer spoke up. Sherri shared that when the same experiment was attempted with a roomful of kids, it was only three minutes before one of the kids spoke up.

What can we learn from our kids? We are to have our eyes open for those who are hurting and take the initiative to remove the hurt. Perhaps we need to see with the eyes of a child. Jesus made it clear that he hurts when we don't help others in need.

Who can we reach out to today? A text, call or visit can turn someone's day around!

91
Come Out and Play with Me

Behold, I stand at the door and knock …

Revelation 3:20

One of the joys of my childhood was when one of my two best friends would knock on my front door and say, "Come out and play with me!" My best friends were Darryl and Joel. When Darryl came over, sometimes we threw the baseball, rode our bicycles, or went to the community pool. When Joel came over, we would most always play baseball against the side of my house. We would pretend that we played for professional baseball teams. I would pick the Braves, and Joel would pick the Reds and load his lineup with right-handed batters because his right eye was not strong.

He would pitch to the strike zone that we drew on the chimney, and I would hit, and vice versa. The pitcher would announce the game, and we would play a regulation nine-inning game in about two hours. We made up many ground rules. A ball hit over the pear tree was a home run, and a ball hit between two stones that were about three feet apart was a double. We played for hours until we went inside for snacks and cold lemonade. Obviously, it wouldn't have been nearly as much fun to stay inside the house and play Monopoly. The real fun was outside.

One of the joys and responsibilities of being a Christian was described by Kennon Callahan in his book *Twelve Keys to an Effective Church*. Dr. Callahan pointed out that the Revelation 3:20 verse is most often described as the verse where Jesus comes into your heart. "Behold, I stand at the door and knock. If anyone hears my voice and opens the door, I will come into Him and dine with Him, and Him with me." Pretend there is a door into your heart. There's no doorknob on the outside door, so you must open the door from the inside to allow Jesus to come in. Jesus will never force his way in.

Dr. Callahan pointed out that as Christians we are also supposed to step outside into the mission field after Jesus comes into our hearts. Just as my friends invited me to come out and play, Jesus invites us to come out and play with him in the mission field. We are called to go out into the mission field, either globally or locally, by the Great Commission (Matthew 28:19–20). You've probably seen this sign when you leave some churches: "You are entering the mission field." Whether we leave church or our house in the morning, let's realize that we are entering the mission field at work, at school, or at play.

Feel ill equipped to come outside to play with Jesus? Remember how you were better at some games than others. You were a rather good hitter right-handed, but you couldn't hit a lick left-handed. When God creates us, he gives us special talents and a passion that are unlike other people's. If you tap into God's plan for your life, you will be fired up to go out into the mission field. But he doesn't want you out there as a left-hander if you are right-handed. I barely know a hammer from a chisel, so God doesn't expect me to project manage Habitat for Humanity builds. I would be miserable.

My passion is helping young people enjoy sports and using those opportunities to teach them about Jesus Christ. As Paul taught us, he tried to meet people where they were so they would let him tell them about Christ and allow God to reach them. God wants to meet you where your passion lies. That's where the real fun is!

92

Cover One

God will never leave you nor forsake you.

Hebrews 13:5

This explanation of the Cover 1 defense was taken from an installment of the "NFL 101" series. Former NFL defensive back Matt Bowen described the basics of Cover 1, "Cover 1 is a first day install scheme with defenders playing man coverage from an outside leverage position and using the free safety help in the middle of the field...The core idea is to take away outside breaking routes and force receivers inside of the numbers to the free safety."

Bowen added, "A defense that is dependent on solid technique in the secondary, Cover 1 allows teams to create eight-man fronts (strong safety drops into the box) with the protection of the free safety over the top."

When this defense is executed properly, the cornerback should never feel that he is left "on an island" and that covering his receiver depends solely on him. The corner is confident that the free safety is giving him the help that he needs.

Sometimes life's difficulties and challenges come down on us so rapidly that we can feel threatened, overwhelmed, isolated and alone. But we always have help "over the top" whenever we need it. God is our Cover "One," and we can be confident that he is always there for us. We will never be stranded because he promised that he will never leave us nor forsake us.

Need help covering all the things that are coming at you? Our Almighty God has you covered!

93
Faith and Good Deeds
Working Together

But someone will say, "You have faith; I have deeds." Show me your faith without deeds, and I will show you my faith **by** my deeds.

James 2:18

The head football coach delivered the unpleasant news after a scrimmage that his football team was nowhere near where they needed to be. With the season only two weeks away, the entire team was downcast. His assistant coaches withdrew from the team in silent support of the coach's message. Except one coach, the special teams coach, who came into the locker room and spoke to two of the team leaders, the No. 1 and No. 2 QBs. He encouraged them to move forward and to lift up their teammates.

The special teams coach never contradicted the message from his head coach, but he realized that encouragement was needed. A defensive back, who often saw this coach reading his Bible in his office, overheard the conversation and immediately recognized the good work that the coach performed in obedience to the leading of the Holy Spirit. His good work made a powerful impression and validated him as a man of faith.

I found it so interesting that the coach's last name is Doolittle. When you and I "do little" things each day, it can make a dramatic difference! Even doing one little thing can make a dramatic difference!

A host on Sirius XM The Message spoke about "mustard seed moments." This is a moment when a simple act sparks renewed hope that can become a flame. (Jesus) said to them, "…For truly, I say to you, if you have faith like a grain of mustard seed, you will say to this mountain, 'Move from here to there,' and it will move, and nothing will be impossible for you" (Matthew 17:20).

Sadly too many Christians "do little" with the gifts with which they have been blessed. How can you do more with your gifts? Whose hope can you rekindle through a "mustard seed" of love?

94
Keep Hitting the Fade

Therefore everyone who hears these words of mine and puts them into practice is like a wise man who built his house on the rock.

Matthew 7:24

Two high school golfers told me that they were struggling with procrastination, especially spending too much time on their phones when they should be studying. This chart evolved from our discussions.

I encouraged them to list the things that need to accomplish each day in the following five columns: 1) Faith 2) Family 3) School/work 4) Golf/Hobbies 5) Social time. Start your day with scripture and prayer and update the items in the columns from left to right throughout the day and evening until bedtime.

My advice to them was "keep hitting the fade." A fade in golf is a ball flight that moves gently and predictably from left to right. Keep moving left to right throughout the day until you complete all of the items in the first four columns. Then use your remaining time for items in the Social column. Too little time spent in the "God" column and too much time spent in the "Social" column could eventually land you in "deep rough."

It's easy to stay up too late at night watching TV or surfing on your phone as you wind down from a busy day. Consider making a sixth column and schedule sleep. The psalmist spoke of God's desire for us to have ample rest. "In vain you rise up early and stay up late, toiling for food to eat, for he grants sleep to those he loves" (Psalm 127:2).

Interruptions can certainly throw us off schedule. After taking a typical work morning to take care of our sick grandson, I felt good about it because I knew my priorities were in order. I read this quote, "When needs arise, pray less and do more."

Having trouble with procrastination, or do you have students and children who could use some pointers? Keep hitting the fade!

95

How Are Your Threads?

The Lord is my strength and my shield; my heart trusts in him, and he
helps me. My heart leaps for joy,
and with my song I praise him.

Psalm 28:7

In 1934 major league baseball adopted a standard that a baseball
will have 108 double-stitches of waxed red thread. I have a Little
League baseball souvenir that l hasn't been used since July 15, 1968,
the date that I hit my one and only home run in Little League (hey, it
was a grand slam!). The ball is scuffed, but the stitching is still tight,
which shows that the ball was never used for batting practice.

The tensile strength of the waxed thread is still strong. Tensile
strength? It's the amount of force that is needed to break a thread or a
cable. What happens when a thread frays? If a frayed thread breaks,
the cover eventually separates, and the ball unravels.

If Satan spots a broken thread in your life, he will pull on it and
try to unravel you completely. It takes a strong faith and staying in the
daily disciplines to keep from unraveling when pressure and stress
hits. It's particularly difficult when life hits you with a left hook, a
right uppercut, and a gut punch back-to-back-to-back. Oswald Chambers wrote that the sign of a mature believer is managing stress and
strain like a saint. How are your threads?

My pastor preached the difference between white-knuckling
God's promises and standing on them. White-knuckling God's promises means hanging on desperately by our strength. Standing on God's
promises is fully trusting that God will see us through to the other side
and continuing to rely on his strength, not ours.

When you are on a team in sports or business, it is important to perform under pressure without blowing up. Learn to recognize when you or a teammate is reaching a breaking point. Each double-stitch of this baseball can represent a team or family member. If the wrong person comes unraveled, it can affect everyone's psyche, attitude and performance!

Unlike the baseball with the broken thread that ends ups in the Home Depot five-gallon bucket with the other damaged balls, people can be fully restored through healing and forgiveness that was purchased by the blood of Jesus Christ. A new pastor asked that the red door of the church be repainted. The trustee chair told him, "That won't happen. That red door symbolizes walking through the cleansing blood of Jesus Christ."

The strength that keeps us from breaking comes only from God. How we rely on his strength depends on our attitude toward God. Do we really believe that we will take care of us?

Here are nine verses of strength from https://soveryblessed.com. The common theme of these verses is that God is the Source of the strength that we need! Find one of God's promises to stand on!

1. Philippians 4:13 – I can do all things through Christ who strengthens me.

2. Isaiah 40:31 – but those who hope in the Lord will renew their strength. They will soar on wings like eagles; they will run and not grow weary, they will walk and not be faint.

3. Second Corinthians 12:9-10 – But he said to me, "My grace is sufficient for you, for my power is made perfect in weakness." Therefore I will boast all the more gladly about my weaknesses, so that Christ's power may rest on me. That is why, for Christ's sake, I delight in weaknesses, in insults, in hardships, in persecutions, in difficulties. For when I am weak, then I am strong.

4. Psalm 46:1 – God is our refuge and strength, an ever-present help in trouble.

5. Psalm 73:26 – My flesh and my heart may fail, but God is the strength of my heart and my portion forever.

6. Second Timothy 1:7 – For the Spirit God gave us does not make us timid, but gives us power, love, and self-discipline.

7. Psalm 28:7 – The Lord is my strength and my shield; my heart trusts in him, and he helps me. My heart leaps for joy, and with my song I praise him.

8. Mark 12:30 – Love the Lord your God with all your heart and with all your soul and with all your mind and with all your strength.

9. Psalm 121:1-2 (chorus from *Praise You in This Storm* by Casting Crowns) I lift my eyes unto the hills, where does my help come from? My help comes from the Lord, maker of heaven and earth.

96
Lord of the Ring

Trust the Lord with all your heart,
and do not rely on your own understanding;
In all your ways acknowledge him, and He shall direct your paths.

Proverbs 3:5-6

I spent time at a region track meet with Zach, a senior thrower who had improved remarkably since his junior year when we first met. Zach closely followed his coach's training regimen that is especially designed for throwers and participated in numerous meets on the indoor circuit. He transformed his body and became a star in the hammer throw, finishing sixth in the Hershey's Indoor Nationals.

But back to that Wednesday night, we were having our usual chat about throwing and school when Zach said, "I see that FCA on your cap. Let me ask you a question." That question led to a ninety-minute conversation about faith. We delved into different topics about denominations, scripture, pride, and surrender. I became aware that Zach is a deep thinker when he shared that he was reading *Mere Christianity*, the classic work by C. S. Lewis. He asked if I could recommend other books. On Thursday night I stuffed *Knowing God* by J. I. Packer and *Resurrection* by Hank Hanegraaff in my bag to give him after the Friday competition.

I drove to the meet on Friday afternoon to watch him compete in the discus. Zach's personal record (PR) was one hundred forty-fix feet, and I thought, *Maybe he can throw one-hundred fifty today.* It was a sunny but very windy day, and the flags were flapping loudly due to a stiff crosswind which made throwing a disc more difficult. During warmups Zach threw one good safety throw, but his others fell short and a long one was out of the sector by sixty feet. This was not the rhythm that he wanted as he stepped into the circle for his first of three preliminary attempts.

Zach scratched on the first throw, which nose-dived and landed less than one hundred feet out. Another thrower had already posted one hundred thirty-five feet. If the second throw failed, it would really put pressure on his third throw to reach the finals. On his second throw Zach shortened his wind-up and let it go perfectly. It had the perfect arc with no wobble and pierced the wind right down the center of the sector. Zach thought that he had thrown over one hundred forty feet, and the official announced, "One hundred fifty-one feet, three and a half inches." With a huge grin Zach thrust both arms high in the air, a la Tiger after his winning putt on eighteen at Augusta! That throw beat his PR by five feet and won the competition by fourteen feet!

After the competition, his coach and I were standing with him as he packed his belongings. I asked Zach, "What was different about that second throw from the first one?" Zach shared, "As I sat in that chair (waiting for his second attempt), I started talking to God. I said, 'I don't understand what it means to give my throwing up to you. I don't know what that entails. But I'd like to give up my throwing to you, Lord.'" He asked God to help him and bam, the winning throw! The next day he set a PR in the shot put. Glory to God!

Zach and I had discussed pride on Wednesday night and how pride can express itself. Zach recalled from our conversation that pride can be not giving up your sport to God or defining yourself by your sport, and that nothing is achieved but by the grace of God. He shared, "I hadn't thought about pride much before (that conversation), but I started to think about it." On Friday he sat in a blue chair by the discus ring and gave his throwing over to God.

It's very satisfying when something you said helps someone else. I was most thrilled because Zach will always remember when he swallowed his pride and allowed God to help him in a sport that he already excelled in, and God took him to a new level in his throwing and his faith.

Let me ask you. Has there been a moment in your life when you decided that you couldn't do everything on your own? Is it time to learn from Zach and give it to God? God wants us to acknowledge him in all aspects of our lives, and he will guide us and direct our paths. It could be as simple as him helping you relax and getting out of your own way. Surrender and dependence upon God are exactly what he wants from us. Let's use his power that is "exceedingly abundantly more than we can ask or think" (Ephesians 3:20).

97

Bad Banana

"Do not judge and criticize and condemn [with an attitude of self-righteous superiority as though you are a judge], so that you will not be judged (unfairly). For just as you [hypocritically] judge others [when you are sinful and unrepentant], so will you be judged; and in accordance with your standard of measure [that you use to pass out judgment], judgment will be measured to you. Why do you look at the [insignificant] speck that is in your brother's eye, but do not notice and acknowledge the [egregious] log that is in your own eye? Or how can you say to your brother, 'Let me get the speck out of your eye,' when there is a log in your own eye? You hypocrite (play-actor, pretender), first get the log out of your own eye, and then you will see clearly to take the speck out of your brother's eye.
Matthew 7:1-5 (Amplified Bible)

Our grandson picked up the phrase "Bad Banana" at preschool, as in, "You're a bad banana!" I do not know the context of his phrase, but he liked repeating. "Bad Banana! Bad Banana!"

I showed a group of high school students these two photos of bananas and asked them which banana they preferred. Then I held up an actual banana with a dark, spotted peeling and asked If they thought it was a good banana or a bad banana. The response was 50/50.

We agreed that to know if the banana was bad or good, we must peel the banana. A volunteer peeled the spotted banana halfway down, and it was as clean as the banana you see in a Dairy Queen banana split! The volunteer continued to peel the banana, and three fourths of the way down there was an ugly bruise on one side. I compared the good side to our social media self, which represents all of the good stuff in our lives. The ugly bruise represents the hurts and struggles that we don't want people to see.

Just as we were passing judgment based on the banana's outward appearance, too often people are judged by their outward appearances. We must know their experiences and hearts (the inside) to appreciate where they really are. I read that true empathy includes believing a person's personal stories even when it isn't possible to walk in their shoes.

Jesus rebuked thinking the way to make yourself more righteous is to be more judgmental of others. We break Jesus' command for how to judge others when we think the worst of them, speak to their faults, judge an entire life only by its worst moments, judge the hidden motives of others, don't believe their struggles, and are not mindful that we ourselves will be judged.

It is common to judge others by one standard and judge us by another standard, being far more generous to ourselves. Be generous with love, forgiveness, mercy and goodness if you want those things from God.

When you looked at people this week, did you see the bad or the good? Did you attempt to discover if and why a person was behaving in that manner? Jesus challenged us to love one another as he loved us and loves us still. When we truly get to know someone, we are peeling back layers which gives us greater insight and love for that person.

Have you been a bad banana lately? Commit to withholding judgment and understanding people and their experiences better.

98
A Perfect Fit

You did not choose me, but I chose you and appointed you so that you might go and bear fruit—fruit that will last—and so that whatever you ask in my name the Father will give you.

John 15:16

Main Thought: Jesus will ask us to do what we are *perfectly fit* for.

We know coaches with impeccable character. We remember coaches who were characters. It's great when a coach has both! When I considered the phrase perfectly fit, I thought of the unique skill and ability with which Coach Cook Holiday was gifted. He built boys state championship track and field teams at Treutlen County HS (GA) because he was adept at discovering athletes with potential, fitting them perfectly to certain events, and coaching them at a high level.

Coach Holiday saw a young man named Rommel walking down the hall at school. He went up to him and said, "I will make a triple jumper out of you." Rommel triple-jumped forty-two feet that spring and won the state championship.

His mind was always working to find athletes to compete in track. Coach Holiday was umpiring the bases when I played against Treutlen. Standing at second base, I heard his voice behind me. "Farr (He always called me Farr), if you went to Treutlen County, I would make an 880 man out of you." I never ran the 880, which is a half-mile race, but I wonder if I missed an opportunity to accomplish something memorable in track. John, my college roommate who played basketball and ran track for Coach Holiday, texted me, "Coach Holiday would have definitely made you into an 880 champ!"

John remembered that Coach Holiday saw Kenneth on the first day of school, approached him and asked, "Do you want to be a state champion in the high hurdles?" Kenneth became a state champion in the high hurdles…twice!

Coach Holiday was a great encourager. As a hyperventilating, five-foot-one-inch sophomore, I was thrust into action during overtime of a basketball region tournament game. Picture Ollie in Hoosiers, but shorter. I stole a pass that helped us win the game. Afterwards Coach Holiday shouted, "Farr, you're a hero!" His enthusiastic, heartfelt atta-boy still resonates within me!

Thank God for coaches who understand how to perfectly fit athletes. Call or text or visit a coach who impacted you in a special way and thank that coach for the encouragement that you received and for the warm memories that you still cherish.

Oswald Chambers penned in an My Utmost for His Highest lesson, "Our Lord's making of a disciple is supernatural. He does not build on any natural capacity of ours at all. God does not ask us to do the things that are naturally easy for us; He only asks us to do the things that we are perfectly fit to do through His grace, and that is where the cross we must bear will always come."

If your heart is all about your team, you can honestly say, "Play me anywhere, Coach. Use me where it will help the team." Jesus allows stress and strain on his disciples in order to build a personal relationship with him that has been tested, purified and examined until a servant can say, "Jesus, use me where you will! Allow me to help others. Put your nature in me."

Chambers challenged his students to become disciples of Christ. Jesus chose us first and reveals his purpose for our lives. Depending upon our willingness and readiness, he can use us or bench us, but according to Chambers, we can never escape that purpose. We can receive the supernatural nature of Christ, and he becomes our Coach for eternity. For that we should be eternally grateful!

God perfectly fit us when he formed us uniquely in the womb. He designed us with passion for our purpose and perfectly fits us to live out our purpose so that as disciples, we can significantly impact his kingdom! Let's consider the ways that we can respond to the purpose for which God perfectly fit us.

99
Build Wisely on the Rock

"Therefore everyone who hears these words of mine and puts them into practice is like a wise man who built his house on the rock. The rain came down, the streams rose, and the winds blew and beat against that house; yet it did not fall, because it had its foundation on the rock. But everyone who hears these words of mine and does not put them into practice is like a foolish man who built his house on sand. The rain came down, the streams rose, and the winds blew and beat against that house, and it fell with a great crash."

Matthew 7:24-27

The University of Georgia won the National Championship in 1980, and I still tease Becca that I married her for good luck after the 1980 season, because she went to every game with me, and UGA went 12–0. But the 1981 season would kick off at Clemson's Death Valley. There was a tremendous amount of excitement because Clemson had its best team ever, and tickets were exceedingly difficult to find. The newlyweds searched outside the stadium for almost two hours and finally found two in Section GG just before kickoff. On the way to the stadium, I asked a fan where Section GG was. He laughed and said, "Oh, that's green grass. You're on the hill that the Clemson team runs down." Becca and I managed to squeeze our way to the top of the hill with the Clemson team just a few feet from us.

That's when I spied Howard's Rock. Frank Howard, the legendary coach of the Tigers, placed a rock from Death Valley, California, in Clemson's Death Valley to create an intimidating aura for opposing teams. The monument for the rock was concrete and about four feet square. I cleverly told Becca that we could sit with our backs against the monument and watch the game. When the team ran down the hill, I patiently waited until the last player came by me. But nobody else waited. The Clemson students swarmed the hill to get good seats behind the goalpost. A student bumped into me, and I lost my balance.

I realized that Becca was being swept away from me and was in danger of being trampled. Reflexively, I reached and grabbed the rock with my left hand, and I wrapped my right arm around her waist. Becca was really upset, and we never sat against the monument. In fact, we didn't even sit on the hill. We wandered around for a quarter and finally squeezed into the other end zone. The Dawgs turned it over nine times and lost the number one ranking to the eventual national champions, the Clemson Tigers. What a day to forget!

When life sweeps you off your feet and you're about to tumble down the hill, take one step, reach out as far as you can, and cling to God, the Rock of Ages. Psalm 62 proclaims that God alone is our rock, our salvation, and our refuge. Build your faith wisely on the Rock each day through Bible reading, prayer, obedience and serving others, the RPOs. Build wisely on relationships with your family and close friends, who are your extended family. When you consistently build your foundation on the Rock by investing time in eternal things, there is a cascading effect across all areas of your life. You discover that your focus on schoolwork and/or your job improves, your perspective of the sport that you play or coach will be grounded better, and you will use your free time more wisely.

Your legacy will either be based on the solid foundation of Jesus Christ or something else. Selfish living creates a sandy foundation, and you will eventually find yourself in "quicksand," begging God to pull you out of a mess like the workaholic husband and father in the Casting Crowns music video of "American Dream." The man spent virtually spent all of his time building castles in the sand and completely lost sight of what is most important, which is family and faith. Build wisely and create a legacy that will impact God's kingdom for eternity!

100

Don't Let 'Em Steal Your Zeal

Let us not grow weary while doing good, for in due season we shall
reap if we do not lose heart.

Galatians 6:9

Our grandson Will demonstrates zeal for building with Legos. He
is focused and persistent in following the directions, stays patient, and
typically only needs our help to separate or find pieces. Whenever he
is told that he is getting a surprise, he says, "Is it Legos?"

The definition of zeal is great energy or enthusiasm or tireless devotion in pursuit of a cause or a goal. Just before Will turned five, he
tirelessly pursued the completion of a 755-piece tiger!

Zealous is synonymous with fervent, passionate, energetic, force-
ful, and intense. This kind of drive can be beneficial when it is directed
toward a good purpose.

Think about someone that you know who is tirelessly devoted to a
noble cause. It could be a family member, student-athlete or fellow
coach. What is it that separates this person from the pack in terms of
their enthusiasm?

The opposite of zeal is apathy, indifference, dullness, discouragement, and lethargy. Saul, who became the Apostle Paul after his Damascus road experience, demonstrated zeal that was both good and
bad. Saul demonstrated bad zeal that was dangerous. He remarked in
Galatians 1:14, I was advancing in Judaism beyond many of my own
age among my people and was extremely zealous for the traditions of
my fathers. In the Hebrews rating system, Paul would have been a
five-star recruit and number one in his class.

Paul became the enemy of early Christians as he passionately per-secuted members of The Way, which led to numerous deaths, includ-ing Stephen's when Paul held the cloak of those who stoned Stephen to death.

Before Paul was a Christian, the emphasis was on himself. After Paul became a Christian, the emphasis was on God, and he zealously preached Jesus Christ and began a thirty-year "Hall of Fame" career of advancing the gospel. But when God, who set me apart from my mother's womb and called me by his grace, was pleased to reveal his Son in me so that I might preach him among the Gentiles (Galatians 1:15-16).

Galatians 4:18 reads, It is fine to be zealous, providing the pur-pose is good. It is still good to be zealous in a good thing. But zeal in a terrible thing is dangerous. Vladimir Putin, described as a "zealous student of Russian history," seeks to replicate the Russian eras of Len-in and Stalin through countless inhumane and destructive acts of war and terrorism.

A zealous pursuit that is not centered on Christ can be harmful. In the pressure that comes with coaching, you can become zealous about your career and win-loss record while justifying the means which may not be Christlike. Be zealous about developing student-athletes, im-plementing sound practices, and giving God the glory for the results.

The Enduring Word Commentary offered this prayer for good zeal: Father, as opportunities unfold in my job, please keep me from self-seeking motives and actions. I desire to honor you with how I work, how I treat others, what I produce, and depending on you mo-ment by moment.

My father-in-law, Damon Ray, had zeal as a high school principal for helping his students excel. The following verse is inscribed on a church stained-glass window in memory of Ray: Let us not grow wea-ry while doing good, for in due season we shall reap if we do not lose heart (Galatians 6:9). When you sow into teenagers, you may not see visible results for months or years. But those delays should not cause us to lose heart about pouring into them and patiently trusting God to produce the harvest in his opportune timing. Don't grow weary, don't lose heart, and keep sowing and watering!

The devil and his troops, which include his demons and the people that are under his control, attempt to steal your zeal. The thief comes only to steal and kill and destroy (John 10:10 (a)). But Jesus added, "I have come that they may have life, and have it to the full (10:10 (b)). Here are ten suggestions to keep 'em from stealing your zeal!

1. Confront sin quickly. Ask for forgiveness and give it in like measure. Don't hold grudges. Protect and grow your personal relationship with Christ by all possible means.

2. Beware of fatigue. When your schedule is already full, surprises can trip you up. Becca and I kept Will one weekend, and when I found out we were keeping him Monday and Tuesday since his school was closed, I reacted selfishly, partially due to fatigue. My zeal disappeared until I collected my thoughts and adjusted my plans.

3. Don't dwell on downers. Fixating on a negative situation brings you down and sucks the life out of you, stealing your joy and enthusiasm. Replace those negative thoughts with positive thoughts of blessings and gratitude.

4. Replace selfishness with selflessness. Selfishness is a sin of idolatry when we place our interests above God and others. When we are selfish, we are zealous for the wrong things.

5. Focus on God's approval. When you perceive a lack of appreciation from others, it can demotivate you. Remember that you perform for an Audience of One; it's God's approval that we seek.

6. Recharge your batteries ASAP. Take a long weekend or short getaway to restore your energy level. Reserve a catch-up day to get the rest you need. Work out. Simply go to bed earlier. Psalm 127:2 (TLB) says, It is senseless for you to work so hard from early morning until late at night...for God wants his loved ones to get their proper rest.

7. Rediscover God's purpose in your life. When you are fulfilling God's plan and his purpose for your life, you receive supernatural energy and enthusiasm to do the work that he has laid out for you. Operating from a plan that is separate from God's plan can burn you out.

8. Seek encouragement when you are discouraged or feeling defeated. Social media posts can steal your zeal because they lead to comparisons, which is one of Satan's favorite strategies. When your plans are not working out, and you feel like you are behind the 8-ball, you can become discouraged. Find a sounding board and be one for someone else. Encourage each other.

9. Improve your planning. It's difficult when you don't control your schedule and schedule changes are dictated with short notice. Plan as best you can, but sometimes you must bow your neck and rely on God's strength and protection.

10. Work the following priorities left to right on a daily basis: Faith, Family, Job, Hobbies and Free Time.

Here is a final thought concerning zeal and God's love. Will received a bouquet of balloons for his fifth birthday. The air-filled balloons deflated first, and he enjoyed popping them one at a time! Eventually two latex balloons and three helium balloons remained in the bundle, which hovered waist-high because the weight of the latex balloons brought down the helium balloons.

I spotted a fourth helium-filled balloon floating near the ceiling. I retrieved it and tied a string to it. When I attached that balloon to the bundle and released it, the entire bundle of balloons rose to the ceiling! As the balloons rose, I told Will, "When other people are sad, you can lift them up by showing them God's love."

Are you zealous in an effective way, or are you drained and exhausted? If you are out of gas, perhaps implement a suggestion that will lift you so that you can lift up others with the good zeal that comes from the work of the Holy Spirit.

101

Grateful for a Dawg Day Afternoon!

This is the day that the Lord has made, let us rejoice and be glad in it!

Psalm 124:18

On a brilliant, sun-splashed afternoon with a light breeze and temperature in the mid-seventies that God surely designed for football and tailgating, our five-year-old grandson Will attended his first Georgia football game in Athens! His mom and our daughter Allison, our daughter and Will's Aunt Jillian (AJ), Will and I arrived on campus and immediately went to a small grove of magnolia trees on North Campus where Allison and Jillian played and climbed when they were young.

Will repeatedly climbed up the low-hanging trunk of one small magnolia tree (with some help) and hung from its branches. I told Will, "Hey Will, if you come to UGA, you can play in these trees all you want!"

I hoisted him onto the trunk of a large magnolia tree, and he called us to come over. Will loves to pretend, and he had each of us knock on his "house" to let us in. Sitting up in the tree, he said, "Let's all (pretend to) be alligators." Will loves animals of all kinds, but he has decided to be an alligator at Halloween, which caused much discussion and some consternation within our family about his choice of animals during SEC football season. Then he added, "Not from Florida."

I placed Will onto my shoulders for the fifteen-minute walk to the stadium, and he insisted on mussing my hair and wearing my cap!

We listened to the pregame ritual of the soloist in the upper level of the South stands. When the fans pointed to the soloist, Will pointed his shaker and shook it! Will ate a whole bucket of popcorn during the first quarter, but by the middle of the second quarter, his interest was clearly waning.

We returned to North Campus for another round of climbing magnolia trees and a game of chase on the lawn. Our afternoon ended on the patio of a BBQ restaurant on Broad Street where we watched the end of the Georgia game and the Alabama-Tennessee game in Knoxville, where Will's dad Kevin was watching his team from Tuscaloosa.

Recall for a few moments a special day that you spent with one of your grandparents. Those of us who have been blessed with children, grandchildren, nieces and nephews can relate to special days like this one. I poured out my thanksgiving and praise to God through the night for the memories of our incredible day. I thought, I cannot stop praising you for my good fortune! As hard as I tried, I could not adequately express my thanks for what I had experienced, being on the campus with Will where Becca and our daughters and I have so many fond memories over two generations (now three!) and the fourteen combined years that Allison, Jillian and I spent at UGA.

Clearly this was a mountaintop day. But it does not take mountaintop days to praise God and thank him sincerely. Expressing our gratitude to God is giving thanks, which is a form of prayer. Let's thank him frequently in all possible ways for his goodness, which includes always being with us in the "valley" days and the challenges and trials we face during the ordinary days.

The Book of Psalms contains hundreds of verses of the psalmists praising God and how he blesses his people. Here are some Scriptures that remind us how and why we should thank him continually.

1. I will give thanks to you Lord, with all my heart; I will tell of all your wonderful deeds. Psalm 9:1

2. I will extol the Lord at all times; his praise will always be on my lips. Psalm 34:1

3. I cried out to him with my mouth; his praise was on my tongue. Psalm 66:17

4. Every good and perfect gift is from above, coming down from the Father of the heavenly lights, who does not change like shifting shadows. James 1:16-17

5. We should express gratitude to God for specific gifts that he gives us each day. The best way we can thank him is by

spending ample time with him in his Word and in prayer. As we receive gifts from others, we should express our thanks.

    6.   Rejoice always, pray continually, give thanks in all circumstances; for this is God's will for you in Christ Jesus. 1 Thessalonians 5:16-18

The key word is "in." God is with us in all circumstances, which is reason to give him thanks continually for always being there for us, no matter the situation.

Do not be anxious about anything, but in every situation, by prayer and petition, with thanksgiving, present your requests to God. And the peace of God, which transcends all understanding, will guard your hearts and your minds in Christ Jesus. Finally, brothers and sisters, whatever is true, whatever is noble, whatever is right, whatever is pure, whatever is lovely, whatever is admirable (if anything is excellent or praiseworthy), think about such things. Philippians 4:6-8

Presenting our requests with thanksgiving "guards against a whining, complaining spirit before God when we let our requests be made known. We really can be anxious for nothing, pray about everything, and be thankful for anything" (Enduring Word Commentary).

My friend J. Carl Newell wrote *The Gratitude Attitude: A Gift Within Your Grasp*. I highly recommend this book which offers many suggestions for how to give and receive the gift of gratitude.

How can we express our gratitude to God? How can we express our gratitude to others? Who can we need to thank God for today? How can we receive gratitude from others with grace?

This prayer of gratitude comes from biblestudytools.com. *Dear God, Thank you for your amazing power and work in our lives, thank you for your goodness and for your blessings over us. Thank you that your Word teaches us the power of gratitude. Thank you that you are able to bring hope through even the toughest of times, strengthening us for your purposes. Thank you that you are always with us and will never leave us. Forgive us for when we don't thank you enough, for who you are, for all that you do, for all that you've given. Help us to set our eyes and our hearts on you afresh. Renew our spirits, fill us with your peace and joy. We love you and we need you, this day and every day. We give you praise and thanks, for You alone are worthy! In Jesus' Name, Amen.*

102

What Is Your Thorn?

"Therefore, in order to keep me from becoming conceited, I was given a thorn in my flesh, a messenger of Satan, to torment me. Three times I pleaded with the Lord to take it away from me. But he said to me, "My grace is sufficient for you, for my power is made perfect in weakness." Therefore I will boast all the more gladly about my weaknesses, so that Christ's power may rest on me. That is why, for Christ's sake, I delight in weaknesses, in insults, in hardships, in persecutions, in difficulties. For when I am weak, then I am strong.

2 Corinthians 12:7-10

When I was nine, a ten-year-old boy named Mickey limped into the gym where Dad was practicing basketball one evening with his high school team. His name was William Michael, but he was called Mickey after the New York Yankee star Mickey Mantle.

Mickey had a squeaky brace on his lower left leg. I discovered two things about Mickey. First, he could shoot the heck out of a basketball as I watched him (with a touch of jealousy) drain fifteen-footers from the corner! Second, he was born with no left calf muscle, and his left foot was smaller than his right foot. In high school he wore a size seven shoe on his left foot and a size nine shoe on his right foot. So when he bought shoes, he always had to buy two pairs.

When he was a child, Mickey's mother told me about calling for him because they were late leaving for a doctor's appointment regarding his foot. She discovered him praying in his bedroom. Mickey explained, "Mama, I was praying that God would heal my foot." He prayed that God would remove the "thorn in his flesh."

In fifth grade I transferred to his school, and we instantly became good friends because we were both sports nuts. We played baseball as rivals from opposing towns but played together on all-star teams. We were teammates as high school juniors. I played point guard, and Mickey was the shooting guard. He scored eighty-two points in back-to-back games on a Friday and Saturday. Amazing! Then we competed against each other as seniors after Mickey transferred to a rival school.

Mickey was perhaps the most intense competitor I ever competed with and against. God blessed him with a strong right arm, and he had excellent foot speed despite his left leg. His determination, will to win, and athletic skills earned him a Division I baseball scholarship from the University of Georgia.

When you played against Mickey, he never admitted that he had a disadvantage. He just played harder than you. He never let the "thorn in his flesh" stop him from becoming a tremendous athlete who competed at the highest collegiate level. In fact, Mickey stopped the 28-game hitting streak of Condredge Holloway, the legendary Tennessee quarterback.

Mickey demonstrated tremendous perseverance to achieve his athletic goals. He became a strong Christian serving the youth and men in his Athens church. It's great to know that he and I will share a heavenly playing field as brothers in Christ!

The apostle Paul didn't let the "thorn in his flesh" stop him either. God empowered Paul with the Holy Spirit that enabled him to overcome shipwrecks, imprisonment, beatings, the thirty-nine lashes five times, and countless other hardships to spread the gospel like none before him or since.

God answered Paul's prayer to remove the thorn from his flesh. "Three times I pleaded with the Lord to take it away from me" (2 Corinthians 12:8). However, the answer was no, not what Paul was looking for! Paul was desperate for relief, but instead God gave grace to Paul and showed his strength through Paul's weakness.

Paul had to believe that God's grace is sufficient. So do we! Grace expresses God's acceptance and pleasure in us and is available all the time. Grace is the very strength of God, right here, right now. We are never beyond God's grace.

Although Paul was so mature and strong in his faith, God made Paul completely dependent on his grace and on his strength, but it was all for good. God deliberately engineered debilitating circumstances into Paul's life so he would be in constant, total dependence on God.

Many Christians long for the day when life becomes "easy." We hope that our major struggles with sin are behind us. But if the Apostle Paul himself constantly experienced weakness, why are we any different? In the end, Paul did resign himself to his fate; he embraced it! He rejoiced that God forced him to rely on God's grace and strength so he could say, "when I am weak, then I am strong" (2 Corinthians 12:10).

What could the world do to a man so firm in the grip of Jesus? God did not allow this thorn in the flesh to punish Paul; God allowed it to show a divine strength in Paul. You and I are capable of showing the same divine strength when we are sold out to God, dependent on him and committed to his cause.

Despite persecutions, shipwrecks and imprisonment, Paul preached to kings, established strong churches, trained church leaders. Therefore, we conclude that Paul was an extraordinarily strong man, but he was only strong because he knew his weaknesses and looked outside himself for the strength of God's grace.

If we want lives of such strength, we also must understand and admit our weaknesses and look to God alone for the grace that will strengthen us for any task. The grace-filled Paul said, "I can do all things through Christ who strengthens me" (Philippians 4:13). Jesus added, "...Apart from Me you can do nothing" (John 15:5).

The greatest example of the principle Paul communicates here was lived by Jesus Himself. "Could anyone on earth be meeker than the Son of God who hung on the cross...in our place that He might redeem us from our sins? As that point of absolute weakness was met by the mighty power of God as He raised Him from the dead, I wonder if the pressure of the thorn in Paul's life was a reminder of the power of the cross" (Redpath).

Everyone encounters temporary thorns in the flesh, and most inevitably encounter permanent thorns. What thorn are you pleading for God to take away? Anxiety or depression? A physical condition or ailment? An addiction? A sin that keeps raising its ugly head? Your financial condition? An overly demanding job or an insufferable supervisor? Unemployment or underemployment? A crumbling relationship? A tough class this semester? What about the cumulative mental drain from the pandemic?

How will you rely on God to see you victoriously through your thorn? His grace, his strength, and his perfect love is sufficient to see you through the situation that you face today. God is nearby. Lean into him.

103

Be the Storm!

Then he got into the boat and his disciples followed him. Suddenly a furious storm came up on the lake, so that the waves swept over the boat. But Jesus was sleeping. The disciples went and woke him, saying, "Lord, save us! We're going to drown!" He replied, "You of little faith, why are you so afraid?" Then he got up and rebuked the winds and the waves, and it was completely calm.
The men were amazed and asked, "What kind of man is this? Even the winds and the waves obey him!"

Matthew 8:23-27

I mentored Max in the faith ten years ago at Open Gym when he was in high school. He graduated from LSU with a degree in petroleum engineering. Max is happily married and inspects oil rigs in the Gulf of Mexico.

I asked him how he and his wife fared during Hurricane Zeta. He wrote, "...*Hurricane Zeta was very scary. My wife and I hunkered down for a few hours. It was nuts how after the first half of the storm passed, the city of New Orleans was in the eye of the hurricane for about twenty minutes. Everything was so calm and peaceful during that time. Neighbors walked outside to convene momentarily and talk. Then the rough second half came through.*" I pictured the back end of the storm lashing the city with the ferocity of Godzilla's tail.

We never know when we are going to be whipsawed. Just when the coast looks clear, something else unexpectedly comes along. But we are fortunate that through our relationship with God that we can find the eye, where calm and peace reside, standing on the unshakable promise that God will be with us until we get to the other side.

At halftime a football coach told his team that had just weathered a barrage of big plays by the opponent, "Gentlemen, you weathered the storm. Now go out and be the storm!" It was their turn to make big plays in the second half!

How can we make big plays for those who have been lashed by illness, misfortunes, setbacks, and discouragement, even while we are in the midst of a storm? First, remember that Jesus is there with us in the storms of life, just like he was with the disciples in the boat! Second, daily preparation is paramount. Remember RPO. Read the Bible, pray for others, and obey. Third, unleash the power of the Holy Spirit that resides within us in order to demonstrate love, empathy and compassion to those in need.

Ryan Stevenson sings these lyrics from *Eye of the Storm*.

In the eye of the storm, You remain in control,
And in the middle of the war, You guard my soul.
You alone are the anchor, when my sails are torn,
Your love surrounds me in the eye of the storm.

What storm are you going through? Jesus calmly waits to help you.

104
Student-Athlete Profile – Stone Smith

Stone Smith is a senior inside linebacker for the Roswell Hornet football team and a starting defenseman for the Roswell lacrosse team. It has been my distinct honor and pleasure to know Stone since his freshman year as a friend, a student-athlete, and my brother in Christ. It has been very fulfilling to see his physical, emotional, mental, and spiritual maturation.

I have come to know Stone very well while discipling him and another student-athlete, Henry Troutman, on Zoom for 30 to 45 minutes three to four times per month for the past two and a half years. Stone also participates in our FCA football weekly discipleship huddles throughout the calendar year, and it has been a pleasure to interact with him in person on a consistent basis.

Stone became a Christian when he was six and has a strong history of participation in children and youth church groups. He reflects the light of Christ through his personal interactions, his engaging personality, and his everyday life. I have watched him live out his faith by making smart decisions, maintaining a cheerful outlook, developing his leadership skills, and displaying a respectful demeanor.

Stone has a heart for people and is a prayerful young man and is always ready to pray when I call on him at a huddle. He is a very loyal, caring person and has a deep affection for his teammates regardless of their racial or socioeconomic backgrounds. Stone's leadership on the football team has emerged this season, and he has become noticeably more vocal. I attribute part of this leadership growth to Stone earning a starting position at inside linebacker, which gave him more visibility and influence.

Stone is highly respected by his teammates and coaches. He was named a National Merit Scholar, one of seven at his school, and has achieved a weighted GPA of 1.015 despite being a multi-sport varsity athlete in two sports that require a huge time commitment.

Stone shared these thoughts about our in-person and virtual FCA huddles. "FCA has been a great opportunity to grow my faith through periodic devotion. Along with attending the weekly after practice meetings, I also participate in an online devotional with Reverend Dan, which helps to further establish my faith through biblical readings. These weekly meetings created a habit of prayer and community with Rev and other men of faith on my team."

Stone's demeanor is very consistent on and off the field. He is very well-grounded in his faith, has good friends who share his values, and is set on achieving his life goals, one of which is to receive an appointment to the Air Force Academy.

He is a role model and has shown his teammates how to compete successfully and to be a great person while you are doing it. This season Stone and another senior football player spoke to the seventh-grade football team about what it takes to succeed on and off the field.

Stone is selfless and focuses on the team's success rather than personal statistics. His dedication to the team is apparent throughout practice and through his excellent discipline in the classroom. Stone's faith, strong work ethic, leadership skills, teamwork, perseverance, and discipline make him an outstanding student-athlete now and at the next level.

105
Stetson's Sequel

…He makes everything work out according to His plan.

Ephesians 1:11(b)

Stetson Bennett IV dreamed of playing quarterback for UGA since he was three years old. He was a five foot eleven inch two-star rated quarterback from Pierce County HS in Blackshear, Georgia. He received his two stars by competing at numerous Elite 11 quarterback camps as a rising high school senior. Bennett wore a U.S. Postal Service cap at those camps to "have something that people would remember me by." That's when he received his nickname, "The Mailman."

When Bennett reported to UGA as a walk-on, he was assigned locker number 122A, which he shared with another walk-on, who was assigned 122B. That's a really high number for a locker! The equipment manager gave him a number 22 practice jersey. Bennett remarked that he felt better about the scout team when he could wear a jersey with the number of that week's opposing quarterback because it was a real quarterback number. He drew rave reviews from his coaches and teammates in 2017 when he mimicked Oklahoma quarterback Baker Mayfield so well during Rose Bowl practices.

Stetson left UGA to play QB for Jones Community College (MS) because Georgia had five-stars Jake Fromm and Justin Fields even after five-star Jacob Eason transferred to Washington. After Fields announced his transfer to Ohio State, Bennett accepted a scholarship offer from UGA Head Coach Kirby Smart to return to Athens.

Stetson appeared briefly in four games in 2019 and played in eight games in 2020, but he lost his starting position to five-star JT Daniels, the five-star USC transfer and preseason Heisman candidate. In 2021

Daniels was injured, and Bennett started ten games and played in every game.

Despite leading the Dawgs to a 12-0 record, many Georgia fans clamored to replace the former walk-on following the SEC Championship loss to Alabama. But Stetson bounced back with arguably the best game of his career in the College Football Playoff semifinal win over Michigan! Then Bennett led Georgia to the national championship, bouncing back from a fourth-quarter fumble to throw the game-winning TD pass to AD Mitchell.

Bennett led the number one seeded Bulldogs to a 13-0 record in 2022 and faced Ohio State on New Year's Eve in the CFP semifinal game. With his team trailing by fourteen points in the middle of the fourth quarter, he completed two touchdown passes in the final eight minutes and led Georgia to a come-from-behind win.

What a Cinderella story! Former walk-on and underdog Stetson Bennett, aka "Prince Charming," fit the "glass slipper," the winning touchdown pass to AD Mitchell (again!), just before midnight and prevented Georgia from turning into a pumpkin! A split-screen video, which showed the ball dropping in Times Square and Ohio State's kick sailing wide left exactly at midnight, clinching the victory for the Dawgs in this "instant classic," immediately went viral.

The perfect timing of the New Year's ball drop and the game-deciding play is a reminder of God's perfect timing. Do we recognize those moments when God saves us from the brink of defeat? Do we recognize those moments when he gives strength just when we really need it?

On the first play of 2023, Stetson Bennett took the snap from center and took a knee. Georgia fans mentally took a knee, thankful for what they had just witnessed! Taking a knee each morning to thank God for his new mercies is a terrific way to start our plan in 2023. Let's commit to a plan to grow our relationship with Christ in 2023 so we see more moments of God at work in our lives in his perfect timing.

Stetson led Georgia to a 65-7 win over TCU in the 2022 national championship game that culminated the most-decorated career of any college football player in the BCS/CFP era!

106
Student-Athlete Profile: Owen Phillips

Owen Phillips is a senior defensive end for the Milton Eagles. I have discipled Owen in his faith walk since he was a freshman in high school. I recall the day in February 2020 that I told Owen and his friends, "We may not be able to meet again soon." Although the pandemic closed down our in-person meetings, he and I continued to meet virtually several times per month for the next thirty months.

Despite the time pressures and demands that football has placed on him, Owen has been an outstanding high school student who has earned a 3.9 GPA while taking numerous advanced courses. He worked tirelessly in the weight room to gain strength and worked himself into the top physical condition that is necessary to become a top lineman in Georgia 7-A football.

On the field he became the epitome of hard work, discipline and desire and always put his team first. During his senior season Owen had 122 tackles, 17.5 tackles for loss, 15.5 sacks, thirty-nine hurries, and 2 forced fumbles as he helped his team to a Final Four playoff appearance. Lucas Pruett, our mutual friend and brother in Christ, commented, "He was all over the field all year long!"

I was watching a state championship game on Georgia Public Broadcasting finals when the GPB All-Star Team was announced. I was thrilled to see Owen's name and picture pop up on the screen and immediately sent him a congratulatory text!

Although his fall schedule was incredibly busy with football and school, Owen co-taught a fourth grade Sunday School class at his church and has frequently participated in the Milton FCA campus huddle since his junior year.

I asked Owen the following questions, and here are his responses.

Q: How did our face-to-face and virtual meetings and discussions in the past three years help you grow in your faith? I know that you especially enjoyed the sports devotions, true?

A: When I showed up for my first FCA meeting I hadn't been to church or anything like FCA in years. The meetings with Coach Farr over the past three years have helped grow my relationship with God in a huge way. Learning to find purpose in Jesus and knowing that he is always with us even in our lowest moments have been the two messages that have stuck with me the most. I especially love Coach Farr's sports devotions are always great as they tie in a sports story to the Lord's teachings.

Q: How has the campus FCA huddle at Milton impacted your life?

A: FCA huddle has allowed me to come closer to Christ in ways I thought I never would. I am able to put my trust in Him which is a great feeling. Through the FCA huddle, I was inspired to join the FCA club at my school and I have met so many great people through this club that have helped me expand God into my life even more. Deciding to come to the FCA huddle was easily one of the best decisions I have ever made.

Q: If you have one piece of advice for teenage athletes to grow their relationship with Jesus, what would it be?

A: Play the game in the name of Jesus. Glorify Him in your actions and work to where you want to be with relentless effort within your sport and relationship with Christ.

Owen has received offers from Mercer University and Presbyterian College, and others may be forthcoming. He is weighing his options about playing college football. If he does not continue his playing career, he would like to make it to Athens and earn his college degree at UGA. Whatever Owen decides, I am confident that God will guide the steps of this fantastic young man!

Verses by Devotion Number

1 Chronicles 4:9-10	76
1 Chronicles 4:10	76
1 Chronicles 16:11	46
1 Corinthians 3:10-15	10
1 Corinthians 9:24-25	75
1 Corinthians 9:25	75
1 Corinthians 10:13	18
1 Corinthians 10:31	63
1 Corinthians 13:4-8	24
1 Corinthians 13:13	24
1 Corinthians 16:1	15
1 John 2:1	9
1 John 4:8	48
1 John 4:19	34
1 Kings 3:8-12	44
1 Kings 3:10	44
1 Peter 2:24	53, 62
1 Peter 3:15	2
1 Peter 5:7	43, 46
1 Peter 5:8	18
1 Samuel 15:22	78
1 Samuel 17:45-47	51
1 Samuel 17:49-50	51
1 Samuel 18:1	52
1 Samuel 20:1-4	52
1 Samuel 20:41-42	52
1 Samuel 24:6	53
1 Samuel 24:10	53
1 Samuel 24:12	53

Ephesians 6:10	46
Ephesians 6:10-13	18
Ephesians 6:10-18	18
Exodus 4:13	40
Exodus 20:3	4
Exodus 28:12	18
Ezekiel 28:15	18
Exekiel 28:35	48
Ezekiel 36:26	60
Galatians 1:14-16	100
Galatians 2:20	15
Galatians 4:4	39
Galatians 4:18	100
Galatians 6:2	66
Galatians 6:7-10	27
Galatians 6:9	73, 100
Genesis 1:27	26, 58
Genesis 41:38	37
Hebrews 10:24	16
Hebrews 11:1	73
Hebrews 12:1-3	22, 61
Hebrews 13:5	92
Hebrews 13:5-6	68
Hebrews 13:8	15
Hebrews 13:38	21
Hosea 10:12	11
Isaiah 9:6	9, 65
Isaiah 26:3-4	68
Isaiah 40:31	46, 95
Isaiah 41:10	43, 46
Isaiah 45:5	48
Isaiah 55:8-9	5, 68
James 1:12	10
James 1:16-17	101
James 1:17	65
James 2:18	9, 14, 42, 47, 78,

Luke 13:18-19	12
Luke 14:27	66
Luke 22:42	71
Luke 22:43-44	71
Luke 23:24	28
Luke 24:1-8	80
Luke 24:11-35	80
Luke 24:18-21	29
Luke 24:32	29
Luke 24:34	71
Mark 4:30-32	12
Mark 8:34	66
Mark 12:30	95
Mark 15:21-32	28
Mark 15:33-39	28
Matthew 5:3-10	57
Matthew 5:5	56
Matthew 5:9	8
Matthew 5:9-12	76
Matthew 5:16	23, 57
Matthew 5:23-24	58
Matthew 5:43-44	58
Matthew 5:44	60
Matthew 6:14-15	58
Matthew 6:20	10
Matthew 6:33	4, 15
Matthew 7:1-5	97
Matthew 7:12	74
Matthew 7:24-27	78, 94, 99
Matthew 8:23-27	103
Matthew 12:34	45
Matthew 13:8	11
Matthew 13:30-32	30
Matthew 17:20	12, 13, 93
Matthew 20:20-24	25
Matthew 20:28	78
Matthew 22:37-39	58

Matthew 25:21	78
Matthew 25:45	90
Matthew 28:19	17
Matthew 28:19-20	24, 91
Micah 6:8	73
Nehemiah 8:10	46
Numbers 13:28	30, 77
Numbers 13:30-32	30, 77
Numbers 14:6-9	30, 77
Philippians 2:12-13	89
Philippians 2:12-16	15
Philippians 4:6	78
Philippians 4:6-7	1, 46
Philippians 4:7	48
Philippians 4:13	15, 68, 95, 102
Philippians 4:19	9, 46, 55, 71
Proverbs 3:5-6	13, 41, 68, 96
Proverbs 3:26	43
Proverbs 4:9-10	44
Proverbs 4:23	45, 47
Proverbs 16:3	83
Proverbs 27:17	57
Proverbs 29:23	49
Psalm 9:1	101
Psalm 16:11	64
Psalm 19:12	45
Psalm 28:7	15, 95
Psalm 34:1	101
Psalm 37:7	71
Psalm 37:23	38, 54, 79
Psalm 46:1	46, 95
Psalm 57:2-3	53
Psalm 66:17	101
Psalm 73:26	95
Psalm 104:34	39
Psalm 118:24	64

Psalm 121:1-2	4, 95
Psalm 121:5-8	46
Psalm 124:18	101
Psalm 127:2	94, 100
Psalm 136:1	46
Psalm 139:13-14	13
Psalm 139:17-18	43
Revelation 3:5	2
Revelation 3:20	91
Revelation 20:12	2
Revelation 22:15	48
Romans 2:11	74
Romans 5:3-4	22, 61, 73
Romans 5:3-5	7
Romans 5:4	22
Romans 8:26	2, 9, 85, 88
Romans 8:26-27	87
Romans 8:28	5, 13, 46
Romans 12:2	15, 18
Romans 13:1	73, 77
Romans 15:1-6	11
Romans 15:5	16

Topics by Devotion Number

References by Devotion Number

1 https://fivestarheart.org/story, Bobby McLarin, 2013

2 https://www.goodreads.org/quotes

5 https://www.ajc.com/sports/high-school-sports-blog/roswell-46-north-cobb-43/FQUUMZEPZBG6ZC52WI2M5GHYOM/, Chip Saye, November 20, 2021

5 https://www.cbs46.com/news/roswell-high-football-star-robbie-roper-dies-after-complications-from-medical-procedure/article_b7298a12-6340-11ec-a57e-6b32abf7b461.html?block_id=1107653, Mariya Murrow, December 25, 2021

5 For the Good, Riley Clemmons, 2021

5 Amazing Grace, John Newton, 1772

7 https://fcaresources.com/devotional/confident-hope, Roger Lipe, April 22, 2021

8 John Roland, Source

9 https://www.equip.org/video/are-there-greater-rewards-in-heaven-based-on-what-is-done-in-this-life/ Hank Hanegraaff, The Bible Answer Man

10 https://www.theplayerstribune.com/en-us/articles/matthew-stafford-detroit-lions-nfl-racial-injustice Matthew Stafford, September 18, 2020

11 https://www.gardeningknowhow.com/garden-how-to/soil-fertilizers/what-is-fallow-ground.htm, Darcy Larum

12 https://www.youtube.com/watch?v=8alu-dJyUQI, Amy-Jill Levine, 2018

13 https://www.bible.com/reading-plans/28946-every, FCA EVERY Reading Plan, 2022

14 https://www.youtube.com/watch?v=7BCScklTfs0&list=PLXAptcMQLoM6jeadgiA4YZZbgW4BDovTB&index=8, Emmanuel Acho and Carl Lentz, 2019

15 ESPN Broadcast on August 11, 2020, Kirk Herbstreit

17 Video, https://www.facebook.com/trey.stevenson.986, Trey Stevenson

18 War Games, Director John Badham, 1983

18 Surrounded, Michael W. Smith, 2018

19 This Way with the Master, The Sacrifice of a Son, April 4, Rev. Dennis Kinlaw

19 Hosanna, Hillsong United, 2007

20 https://www.youtube.com/watch?v=SHKzH6zR8xE, Jim Valvano, 1993

20 A League of Their Own, Director Penny Marshall, 1992

23 https://www.cnn.com/2012/04/24/sport/olympics-norman-black-power/index.html.
The Third Man: The forgotten Black Power Hero, James Montague, CNN, April 25, 2012

27 https://www.fca.org/fca-in-action/2021/01/25/pursue-love, Manny Maldonado, January 25, 2021

28 Lent, The Seedbed Daily Text, J. D. Walt, 2021

33 Apollo 13 The Movie, Director Ron Howard, 1995

33 The Holy Spirit, Fellowship Bible Church Leadership Institute, Dr. Crawford Lorritz, 2019

37 http://www.bradlomenick.com/brad-lomenick-8/8-key-leadership-qualities-of-joseph, Eight Key Leadership Qualities of Joseph, Brad Lomenick, 2012

38 Atlanta Hawks Broadcast, Atlanta Hawks Announcer Bob Rathbun, May 11, 2021

42 https://www.nbcnews.com/news/world/euro-2020-denmark-soccer-player-christian-eriksen-stable-after-collapsing-n1270602, Rhea Mogul, June 13, 2021

43 God Only Knows, For King and Country, 2018

43 Surrounded, Michael W. Smith, 2018

45 This Way With the Master, Sloshing Sins, Rev. Dennis Kinlaw, September 18

49 Remember the Titans, Director Boaz Yakin, 2000

50 https://www.stabroeknews.com/2019/08/30/sports/warholm-runs-stunning-race-to-win-400-metres-hurdles/, Reuters, August 30, 2019

51 Assemblies of God (USA) Official Web Site | David and Goliath – Setting the Stage, Amy Flattery and Jeremy Stein, July 21, 2020

52 https://www.youtube.com/watch?v=hTE5ep2ddco, Somebody's Baby, Jackson Browne, May 2, 2015

53 Coach John Wooden One on One, John Wooden and Jay Carty, 2003
54 https://www.mlb.com/news/braves-fall-yankees-freddie-freeman-out-replay, Braves dealt tough loss in finale, Mark Bowman, August 25, 2021
55 https://mobile.twitter.com/ndfootball/status/1436828876949295114?s=10, Game Ball, September 11, 2021
55 The Problem of Discipleship, Mark Clark, 2021
56 https://www.biblestudytools.com/commentaries/matthew-henry-complete/matthew/5.html
56 https://enduringword.com/bible-commentary/matthew-5/
58 https://goodfaithmedia.org/can-we-love-people-without-liking-them-cms-18231
56 https://enduringword.com/bible-commentary/matthew-5/
58 https://goodfaithmedia.org/can-we-love-people-without-liking-them-cms-18231
59 Power of prayer: High school football rivals pray for mom's ...https://tylerpaper.com › news › local › power-of-prayer-h..., John Anderson, November 6, 2019
59 https://ugive.app.utah.edu/designation/4424, University of Utah, 2021
59 https://kslsports.com/470241/espns-college-gameday-airs-special-tribute-story-for-ty-jordan-aaron-lowe/, Trevor Allen, October 16, 2021
59 ESPN Broadcast, December 25, 2020
59 Uncommon Life, Tony Dungy and Nathan Whitaker
60 https://www.youtube.com/watch?v=fkYL1b7MCEw, Less Like Me, Zach Williams, 2019
61 https://www.mlb.com/news/hank-aaron-phil-niekro-don-sutton-remembered-at-world-series, Braves Legends Remembered Fondly at WS, Mark Bowman, October 28, 2021
65 https://www.bible.com/en/reading-plans Advent, The Journey to Christmas Reading Plan, Day 7
66 Fever Pitch, Directors Bobby Farrelly and Peter Farrelly, 2005
67 https://www.bing.com/videos/search?q=youtube+immaculate+ reception&view=detail&mid= 992C757D83A1447BDB92992C757D83A1447BDB92&FORM=VIRE, NBC Broadcast, Curt Gowdy, December 23, 1972
68 This Way with the Master, The Dungeon, July 2, Rev. Dennis Kinlaw
69 https://www.bible.com/reading-plans/28946-every, FCA EVERY Reading Plan, 2022
74 https://www.npr.org/2022/02/03/1077927110/brian-flores-nfl-lawsuit, The Limits, NPR, Jay Williams, February 3, 2022

74 https://dfw.cbslocal.com/2022/02/01/african-american-6a-football-coaches-reflect-back-history/, Keith Russell, 21 DFW CBS, February 1, 2022

76 https://africa.espn.com/tennis/story/_/id/33369327/russian-tennis-star-andrey-rublev-writes-no-war-please-dubai-semifinal-win, Africa ESPN, February 26, 2022

78 Last Supper on the Moon, Levi Lusko, 2022

79 https://golf.com/news/scottie-scheffler-wins-masters-uncluttered-approach, Michael Bamberger, April 10, 2022

85 https://enduringwordcommentary, Enduring Word Commentary, David Guzik

86 https://enduringwordcommentary, Enduring Word Commentary, David Guzik

91 Twelve Keys to an Effective Church, Dr. Kennon Callahan

92 NFL 101 Series, Matt Bowen Commentary

94 Sermon by Rev. Rob Lanford, Sacred Tapestry UMC, Marietta, Georgia

95 https://soveryblessed.com

95 My Utmost for His Highest, Oswald Chambers

96 https://enduringwordcommentary, Dr. Enduring Word Commentary, David Guzik

98 My Utmost for His Highest, Oswald Chambers

99 https://m.youtube.com/watch?v=DumlIIHSrsQ, Casting Crowns, "American Dream," 2004

100 https://m.youtube.com/watch?v=RpR9P14BAfo&feature= youtu.be, HBO series "Hard Knocks," 2022

100 https://enduringwordcommentary, Enduring Word Commentary, David Guzik

101 https://enduringwordcommentary, Enduring Word Commentary, David Guzik

101 https://biblestudytools.com

101 The Gratitude Attitude: A Gift Within Our Grasp, J. Carl Newell, 2003

103 Eye of the Storm, Ryan Stevenson, 2016

CPSIA information can be obtained
at www.ICGtesting.com
Printed in the USA
JSHW010039030623
42616JS00001B/5